Blue Water Women

Making the Leap from Landlubber to a Life at Sea

Gina de Vere

BLUE RIVER PRESS

Indianapolis, Indiana

Blue Water Women:
Making the Leap from Landlubber to a Life at Sea
Copyright © 2018 by Gina de Vere

Published by Blue River Press
Indianapolis, Indiana
www.brpressbooks.com

Distributed by Cardinal Publishers Group
A Tom Doherty Company, Inc.
www.cardinalpub.com

All rights reserved under International
and Pan-American Copyright Conventions.

No part of this book may be reproduced, stored in a database or other retrieval system, or transmitted in any form, by any means, including mechanical, photocopy, recording or otherwise, without the prior written permission of the publisher.

ISBN: 978-1-68157-148-5

Cover Design: Glen Edelstein
Book Design: Dave Reed
Cover Photo: Christian Selaries
Interior photos courtesy of Ann Valmadre, Cathy Gray, Christian Selaries, Wendy Bjarne, and interviewees
Editors: Dani McCormick, Sara Johnson

Printed in the United States of America

10 9 8 7 6 5 4 3 2 1 18 19 20 21 22 23 24 25 26 27

Contents

Dedication v
Preface vii
Introduction xi

The Dream and You

1. Why Do We Go? 3
2. Is It Truly Your Dream Too? 9
3. Your Role on Board 11
4. Becoming Your Own Captain 16
5. Interpersonal Communication 18
6. Ways of Having a Life at Sea 22
7. Sailing with Limited Budgets 26
8. No Boat at All 31
9. Getting Started 34
10. The Sailing Lifestyle 39
11. A Normal Day 42
12. How We Learn 45
13. Learning about Maintenance and Repairs 52
14. Practice Is an Important Part of Learning 55
15. Learning the Basics 57
16. Are You Ready to Set Sail? 59
17. Some of the Things We Fear 65
18. To Carry or Not to Carry? 87

You and Your Boat

19. Making Comparisons 95
20. Our Boat Buying Experience 98
21. Main Construction Types 103
22. Changing Needs 106
23. Interiors 110
24. Exterior of Your Boat 121

Before You Set Sail

25. Arranging Your Watch—Keeping Schedule 135
26. Arrangements for Communication and Email 138
27. Arranging Skeds 141
28. Safety Items on Your Boat 144
29. Desk Work 147
30. Health Matters; Which Medicines to Take? 156
31. Sailing Etiquette 167

Life at Sea

32. Long Passages 173
33. Provisioning for the Voyage 175
34. Fun on Board 184
35. You and Kids at Sea 188
36. Women's Matters 205
37. The End of the Dream—Swallowing the Anchor 232

You and a Career at Sea

38. Careers at Sea 241

Acknowledgements 261
Resources 263
Shutdown Checklist for *Stardancer* 289
Stardancer Maintenance List 291
Contributors 299
About the Author 323

Dedication

This book is dedicated to my sister Prunella who died before she could become a fully-fledged Blue Water Woman. Her favourite poem, by John Masefield:

Sea Fever

I MUST down to the seas again,
To the lonely sea and the sky,
and all I ask is a tall ship and a star to steer her by
and the wheel's kick and the wind's song and the white sail's shaking
and a grey mist on the sea's face and a grey dawn breaking.
I must down to the seas again, for the call of the running tide
is a wild call and a clear call that may not be denied;
and all I ask is a windy day with the white clouds flying,
and the flung spray and the blown spume, and the sea-gulls crying.
I must down to the seas again to the vagrant gypsy life.
To the gull's way and the whale's way where the wind's like a whetted knife;
and all I ask is a merry yarn from a laughing fellow -rover,
and a quiet sleep and a sweet dream when the long trick's over.

Any profits I may make from this book will enable me to make a donation to the UK Cancer Society.

Preface

- "Been looking at a new mainsail, know a good local sailmaker?"
- "Not sure if I want extra crew along for the big haul. Any thoughts on the pros and cons?"
- "I like to get out on some different boats, gain some more experience, know anyone who is looking for crew?"

The conversation ebbed and flowed, sailors sharing drinks, discussing engine problems, crew problems, sailing plans. It could have been a gathering at any sailing club almost anywhere I've been. However, there were two big differences; this was a virtual boating club, a Facebook group who were meeting face to face for the very first time at the Annapolis Sailboat show, and all of the attendees were women. Their sailing skills and aspirations ranged from professional tall ship captains to charter skippers to vastly experienced world cruisers to first time boat owners, plus a fair smattering of women who were timidly testing the idea of blue water sailing at the invitation of a male partner. I happened to arrive late at the outdoor bar where the WWS (Women Who Sail) event was taking place. To reach the 100 or so women, I had to negotiate my way past some of their husbands. Several of these men stopped me to introduce themselves, and in most instances, ask directly or indirectly, why these women needed or even wanted to exclude men from their Facebook discussions. "Because there are times when women are uncomfortable discussing intimate aspects of sailing with the men in their lives. Some don't want their partners to think they are doubting them when they question some seamanship ideas, others feel their concerns will be scoffed at or dismissed by male sailors. It's not about exclusion, it's about having a non-judgmental sounding board women can use to build their confidence."

As I read through the pages of *Blue Water Women*, I realize some people (both male and female) will ask a similar question, "Do we really need a book just for women who are interested in life or careers on the sea?" Yes, is the simple answer. The rapid rise of Women Who Sail Facebook groups around the world, the ever-increasing number of women who contact me for encouragement, prove this book is important and timely. Though women in ever-increasing numbers are discovering the joys of being out on the water, with their partners or on their own, sailing is still a male dominated sport (or if you prefer, pastime). As willing as men are to encourage women afloat, they have different concerns, different ways of handling stress, different strengths and weaknesses, different ways of teaching, and most had father- and mentor-instilled mechanical skills to draw on as they learned to handle and maintain a boat. As a simple example—I was sitting in on discussion of maintenance issues during a sailing course for women. The speaker was a well-known female racing sailor. "Okay girls, here is the most important thing I am going to teach you today," she said. "Write this down. Righty tighty, lefty loosy." Her simple words removed the mystery of using a wrench or screwdriver from my life. When I mentioned this to Larry, he laughed then said, "Guess I just naturally know which way to turn a screw. Thought you did too."

I have known Gina for many years. We spent many hours talking about Christian's dream of going back to cruising once again. Larry and I watched as it became Gina's dream too. Hopefully I encouraged Gina as they searched for the right cruising boat, sold their home, and began the transition to life afloat. I remember some of the questions she asked, questions that she was uncomfortable asking Christian lest they appear to doubt his wisdom or make her appear foolish in his eyes. In the beginning, she would sometimes preface her question with, "this probably sounds silly but . . . ." From personal grooming to provisioning and outfitting to facing fear, the discussions that followed ranged far and wide. It is obvious as I read *Blue Water Women* that Gina remembers those discussions. By using her experiences as the basis for this book, then adding the voices of almost four dozen other experienced women who have spent considerable time at sea, she has provided answers that should quash many of the fears that trouble women when they consider life afloat. And for those who have no qualms about jumping in feet first, *Blue Water Women* offers well thought out solutions to making life afloat more rewarding for not only the women who read it, but the men they sail with.

—Lin Pardey

Kawau Island, New Zealand

Introduction

I spent my working life as a professional facilitator. In my late forties, I met my French Kiwi, Christian, who became my second husband. My life turned upside down; Christian wanted to cross oceans as he had many years before. I had little sailing experience, and none of crossing oceans, but when I was fifty-eight, we finally bought our "boat-to-go" and set sail. Before we set sail together though, I felt huge surges of doubt; would I be good enough? Would I let myself or Christian down? Would I know what to do and when? Naturally enough, over the years my abilities and confidence improved considerably. Fifteen years later, we are now sailing happily into our seventies. However, there were things that, had I known sooner, would have greatly enhanced my cruising experiences.

In discussions with other women sailors I found I was not alone in having to overcome doubts and fears. Over the years, I have met many wonderful, inspiring blue water women, i.e. women who sail across oceans, each with their unique stories but sharing many similar experiences also. I wondered, "What makes these women start a life at sea? How do they keep going? Would they do it again and why? What advice could they give to others thinking of setting sail to make the most of their adventures?" I thought if others could read about the motivations and experiences of women who make the sea part of their life or career, it would encourage women to feel more confident about making that leap from landlubber to a life at sea. And so, the idea for this book was born.

This book is for the young and young at heart who yearn for adventure. It is written for those women considering a life-changing direction and those seeking a career at sea. It is not an instruction book, but you will learn from the experiences of other blue water women what you need to know to have your own adventures.

I interviewed forty women sailors from around the world of differing ages, cultures, creeds, sexual persuasions, and abilities, and it is their advice and their experiences that form the basis of this book. Although I have learned a lot from full time cruising for so many years, I am no sailing guru. Being the facilitator that I am, I have tried to give our Blue Water Women their own voices and facilitate their comments for the authenticity and integrity of the book.

For ease of reading, the book is designed in five distinct parts, and, because of this, you may find occasional overlaps of information. However, to access more in-depth information, you will find an extensive guide to resources in the appendices. This, together with the advice from our Blue Water Women, will prepare you to confidently make the leap to a life at sea.

Life at sea is not all plain sailing. There can be hardships and loss. Relationships are thrown into the spotlight from living in confined spaces. Boat repair and maintenance costs are continuous. The weather can be far from obliging. But, despite this, I believe the joys of a sailing life far outweigh the downsides. So, prepare yourself well and join the growing number of women who become blue water women and love it. You can look forward to events, people, and places you have never experienced as a landlubber. Now is the time to be excited by what lies ahead of you, and turn your dream into a practical, glorious reality!

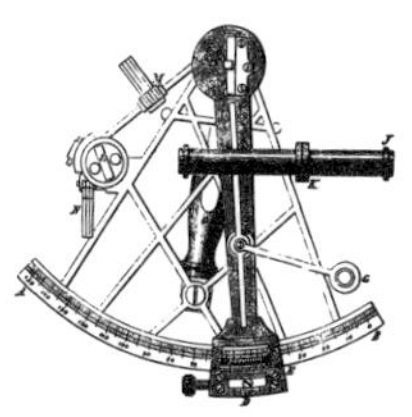

Part 1

The Dream and You

The sea, once it casts its spell,
holds one in its net of wonder forever.

—Jacques Cousteau.

You are dreaming of the voyage. You envision days spent gliding past glorious islands under blue skies, looking for just the right sheltered spot to set anchor for the night. Just you and Nature with sunsets that amaze you, and nights with stars like diamonds shimmering in a black velvet sky. In your dream, you picture waking to gentle dawns and delighting in the abundant sea life and enjoying visits with friendly locals as you sail to different countries every season. Then the time comes when your dream becomes a goal, with plans and actions. And you begin to worry about the downsides—the fact that once you move onto a boat, you will spend most of your time in a space smaller than your living room. You might suffer the misery of seasickness, or, if you encounter bad weather, you could be sitting in wet gear for many hours. Sometimes you will not be able to see anything except sea water crashing over the deck, with the wind making the rigging shriek and howl. You'll hear stories of how, when the boat heels suddenly, things shoot out of cupboards and drawers and hurtle across the cabin because you forgot to secure them well. Then you must cook a nourishing meal on a moving stove top. Just then, you find a few leaks from the hatches you thought were well sealed. Oh, and by the way, the head is bunged up, you can't use the bathroom. ... Scenarios like this could make you want to toss the whole idea out the porthole. Before you do, read onwards because not only do I, but hundreds of other women, believe living at sea is an amazing idea, the best idea of a lifetime.

Beth Cooper on SV *Sarah Jean II*

1

Why Do We Go?

What motivates us to go blue water sailing? It is a glorious way of life, allowing freedoms that are fast disappearing, a life that distances you from the constant demands of our modern craziness, a life where you are more self-reliant, more in control of your time rather than at everyone else's beck and call. It is a life that you constantly create anew as you travel. A life of awe and wonder.

I like being able to choose where I go and, with the weather as ally, when. I love learning and have an insatiable curiosity. I gain satisfaction in achieving things that grow me as a person. As Diana Neggo says, "Sipping champagne as the sun slips to the horizon is the dream, but the self-satisfaction of getting your boat to that sunset scene is the reality, and far more profoundly satisfying."

I have never been so uncomfortable in my life, but neither have I been so profoundly happy and at peace. One tends to forget the bumpy bits and the times when things go wrong or break down because the rewards of being at sea are overwhelmingly incredible. I love traveling, simply going towards the unknown. I love the adventure of it. I love meeting new people, experiencing different cultures, and learning about the history of a new place. I love being close to the water, wind, and nature; seeing pods of dolphins, hundreds of them, surfing the waves; or watching exotic birds I had only previously seen in books. I love the freedom that sailing life gives me. I feel more alive. For me, a day is a really good one when I have had a great sail, set anchor safely in a pretty place, had a swim, and have seen the sun rise and set.

Our Blue Water Women unanimously enjoy a closer connection to nature. As Pat Mundus says, "My love of going to sea is essentially my love of a direct and straightforward connection with the natural world and [using] our latent ability to function off the man-made societal umbilical cord."

She goes on to say, "I hate pettiness, my days filled with email, advertising, telemarketing, and the general politics of corporations monopolizing our whole food and information distribution system. I hate poorly designed and manufactured goods. I hate the temptation to rationalize a reduction of integrity for money." On the other hand, Pat says, "I love being able to be self-reliant. I love forming my own conclusions and observations empirically instead of being 'informed' by outside 'experts,' who are usually making money off the topic. I love catching, growing, combining my own food and resources. I love having unlimited time to read and write on board. I love the knowledge that I'm just a tiny insignificant speck in an awesomely huge universe."

Many of our Blue Water Women agree, having time to use as you wish rather than reacting to others' demands on your time is immeasurably satisfying. You have time to socialise or be on your own, to read, write, follow your hobbies, spend with your partner, do whatever you desire. This, to me, is an addictive luxury.

For Lin Pardey, being offshore gave her time to reflect, slow down and enjoy each moment. She says, "I loved the feeling I could put away shopping lists [and] work lists, that everything I needed was right with us and if I had forgotten to get something or ran out of something, I would figure a way to make do."

Amanda Swan Neal also likes the sense that time stands still, and you get to live each day at a time, without much outside input. She shares her favourite line from Debra Ann Cantrell's book *Changing Course*, "The sea can bring you face-to-face with who you really are and who you have the potential to be." There is plenty of time for soul searching as you master a new technique or way of thinking about or doing things. It is a time to grow. Gradually, the masks we use to get by on land and the things that were once important, simply slip away. We become more in touch with our essential being. We enjoy feeling the power of wind as it fills the sails. We become intensely aware of the colours, the smells, the feelings we have when we are close to nature and living in harmony with it.

Kaci Cronkhite is an author who came to the sailing life from the world of academia. She explains what she gets from being at sea. "Bliss. Truly there is nothing in life that's come close to the joy I've felt on the open ocean, in touch with the moon and held by the wind between the earth and sky." In an excerpt from her book *Finding Pax*, she says, "Life on the blue part of the globe for eight years suited me—the bliss of buoyancy, the volatile, soul-powered wind. Sailing struck a nerve both primal and poetic. On or near the ocean, life made sense."

"You feel the weather and hear the world around you," says Jane Kilburn. "You are aware of every change, and you live in the environment. It gives a sense of freedom, of adventure, and I enjoy being part of the cruising community. I find it more supportive and open than land-based communities."

For Judy Rodenhuis, sailing as a lifestyle gave her and her husband the opportunity to see a lot of the world and to share special times together. She likes "the knowledge that together you have the boat and the skills to choose your life and how you live it." She asks, "How many people can have that freedom?"

"It has been a life-changing adventure for me, for us both," so says Helen Hebblethwaite. She adds "If I'd been asked to write an adventure story about going cruising or how I imagined I would be spending my fifties, I could never have made up such an exciting story about places I would visit, people I would meet, and events I would be involved in. No one would have believed it! The reality has been so much better than the dream, and that was pretty good."

It was the idea of taking four months off work was that initially motivated Anna Fourie to start sailing, but that first trip changed her life. "I met so many fascinating people who shared stories, but never once asked what I did for a living. Sailing is a social leveller. We did however, amongst many things, discuss solar panels, our next trip, best beaches and anchorages, the benefits of monohulls versus the catamaran, world politics, and where to get cheap booze." Conversations were entirely different from those held on land. She continues, "The experience was completely addictive and, today, prevents me from a life on dry land. I love the sailing community and the sharing and support that come with it. When you arrive in a new location you have your friends and family already with you."

Cathy Gray and her husband had the dream from when they were teenagers together. "But," she says, "reality is different from the dream, and you don't really know it until you do it. In many ways, it is better than the dream as the experiences you have cannot be dreamed about. There is potential excitement around every corner. It's like working in an Emergency department; you don't know what's coming next! A squall, catching a big fish, or arriving at an anchorage and seeing fellow cruisers you said goodbye to months or even years ago!"

Others of our Blue Water Women were motivated by reading inspirational sailing books. The motivation for Barbara Sherry was reading about Naomi James's exploits sailing around the world alone. Barbara, like Naomi, comes from a farming background in New Zealand and she says, "The book planted a seed of the remote possibility that maybe one day I too, could learn to sail" (*see* Appendix A for more book suggestions).

For Courtney Jean Hansen, the motivation to make her career at sea was that she knew how strongly she felt about the alternatives available where she lived. For her gap year, she had a dread of having to work at Woolworths and "being like everyone else working at Woolworths and just getting by." This proved the impetus she needed to walk the docks to find her first job at sea at seventeen years old, and now ten years later, she captains vessels for the maritime and tourism industries which take her into the Pacific Ocean and Coral Sea.

We go for the adventure. Adventure is facing the unknown. The unknown can engender excitement, but it can also engender the flip side, fear, and we will be looking at how to overcome this. Often as we start out, we cannot tell where exactly our adventure will lead us, but one thing is for sure, no matter how short or long your voyages, you will grow as a person as you embrace the changes and challenges you face as a blue water sailor.

Sailing at dawn on SV *Stardancer*

2

Is It Truly Your Dream Too?

You may be well into living your dream, which became your lifestyle a long time ago, but if you are thinking of starting out, are you totally clear about what you want out of this new life at sea? If you are sailing with a partner, do you both want the new lifestyle to give you the same pleasures? Or if not, do they dovetail? Do you both want to sail for the same length of time? Have you discussed what roles you will each have on the boat? It is important that you truly share this dream—unless you are sailing solo of course. You should discuss any differences and reach some kind of compromise so that each person is satisfied with the results of the voyage. If you do not bring up your opinions at the start, you may find yourself joining those women who complain, "It's not what I thought it would be."

Several of our Blue Water Women started sailing because of their partner's wishes. When I met my partner-husband in New Zealand, Christian—a French sailing instructor jokingly named a "Friwi" as he is now a French Kiwi—had only one goal: to go sailing again. As we talked, I remembered a long distant dream, to sail in the Mediterranean. I was educated in England and always grabbed the desk by the window and, more often than not, was day dreaming over the fields towards the Thames, wishing I were sailing down the river towards the English Channel and on towards the Mediterranean Sea. But life has a habit of coming between you and your dreams and I lost my dream under a whole pile of duty, work, and family. However, the dream re-emerged. We both wanted the same thing. Or so I thought.

In the beginning, what I wanted most out of our sailboat was as a vehicle to visit different countries, to access places few others can, to enjoy learning about the people and their cultures, to absorb different sights and smells, taste different foods, but most of all to be self-reliant without the demands of our consumerist societies. I wanted a simple life close to nature. My Friwi, on the other hand, enjoyed the thrill of the wind in the sails, getting the maximum performance from the boat, and to keep going, barely stopping *en route*. Although he has visited many exotic places around the world, he had no inclination to stop and explore the land. It took many discussions to instigate a change in a habit that came from doing boat deliveries, where time is all important. We reached an understanding. Now we whistle stop less and linger longer at desired destinations. Before long, though, I became as interested in the art of sailing as he is, and he became much more interested in the places we visit and explore. Having those talks about expectations really pays.

3

Your Role on Board

There can only be one Captain at any one time, and she or he is ultimately responsible for every last thing on the boat. If you want to be Captain, perhaps you can share this duty with your sailing partner like Lisa McVey and Gwen Hamlin. Gwen Hamlin and her husband take alternate days to be captain and this has worked very well for them for many years. Gwen got her captain's license aboard a dive ship in the Virgin Islands, so when she and her husband left twelve years later to go cruising together, she already had a large amount of experience.

However, on our boat, the difference in experience and ability was huge, and it was obviously my Friwi's role to be captain. We own the boat half each, which was enough for each of us to be satisfied with the strength of commitment from the other towards the project. We have an equal partnership on land and at sea. Over the years, we have become a close-knit team that can totally rely on each other. I did not take a role name because I do so many other things, aside from part-time navigator and full-time crewing. And frankly, I do not need a name or status.

My responsibilities are firstly to be good support to the captain. Next I manage the finances, provisioning, land travel, destination research, insurance, cleaning, cooking, washing (though my Friwi tends to wash most of his own clothes), medical supplies, legal documents, doctors' check-ups, communications, weather information, and marina details. We share the navigation and destination planning and timing. Captain Friwi is responsible for the overall maintenance and smooth running of the vessel (with my assistance). This covers areas where he has far more experience than I do: pumps, electrics in general, the engine, plus everything on and above deck.

Gwen Hamlin explains, "He was the mechanic, the one who got the power and kept things working. I was the operator. But adding new systems and equipment became maintaining those systems and equipment, and that began to be stressful." I think there are many who would agree that maintenance of the equipment can become a stressful role. There are few boats these days that do not carry sophisticated equipment, and I know my Friwi laments the demise of times when sailing was more simplistic, without the number of sophisticated items he now spends frustrating hours maintaining.

There are many women who relish fixing mechanical problems, and, although I have good understanding and make good suggestions, I am not one of them. I have learned a huge amount over the past fifteen years about mechanical failures and how to fix them, but I will never be as knowledgeable as my Friwi, so we each play to our strengths. However, my confidence builds each time I fix something, no matter how small.

Sometimes you can have a run of blunders and need to get your confidence back, so knowing I have achieved small things rebuilds my self-confidence. Alexandra Mateer says that at one stage she felt she "could not put a foot right, and I lost my confidence on the boat, and that made it a self-fulfilling prophecy, I became a real klutz." One thing she found helpful was "to start a little book where I wrote everything down, how to do simple repairs, our safety procedures etc. I just went over and over them … until I felt I knew what to do in certain emergency situations. This helped me regain confidence."

Christian Selaries, my Friwi

As captain, my Friwi always has the last word. Or so I think. Although, I must admit, he does not refer to me as the admiral for nothing. We share problems. If I see something I do not agree with, or something that needs fixing and I cannot do it, I will bring it to his attention. If I think we should change our sail trim, I will suggest this, or if I see bad weather coming, I will suggest we reef earlier rather than wait and do it last minute. When anchoring, I have equal say in where we anchor unless he has a very good reason why not. We listen to each other and are willing to change our point of view given good reasons. A good support person or team can really help lessen the load for the captain. If this is your role, be proud of it. It is an important role.

Women vary in how involved they are when it comes time each year to put the boat up for repair and maintenance of those items that are normally below the waterline. Colleen Wilson takes on the project management side of things. “Many countries,” she says, “have lots of issues with strong women roles so men don’t like to deal with me. I try to have a good relationship with the guys in the yard and gradually take over a project. Sometimes it works, other times it does not.” She adds, “Food is always a good way to get the guys to like you!”

When the time comes for us to haul our boat out to clean the hull, I will do what I can to assist with preparation, but I can go no further. In the 1980s, I suffered from severe chemical poisoning (so much for clean, green New Zealand) which has left me with acute sensitivities to chemicals of all sorts, especially any glyphosate-based or associated chemicals, paints, glues, or cleaning agents. So apart from doing what I can in a support role, I have to leave the boat when we are using chemicals. When I feel guilty about leaving my Friwi to do this on his own, or these days with hired help, I think of one sailing woman who said to me, “I simply don’t do haul outs!” Fair enough, that was part of their role agreement. Merinda Kyle, on the other hand, says, “I am the anti-foul queen. I am not allowed any detail work because I am too messy, but sanding, scraping—let me loose!” There is no one right way to divide the roles, but each person must clearly know what they are responsible for.

Most Blue Water Women work equally as hard as their partners, or work on their own, on the paint scraping, timber varnishing, or many cleaning and fixing jobs required when the boat is in the yard. Alexandra Mateer, like the majority of our Blue Water Women, was very involved and hands on in numerous refits, with endless rust chipping and painting in awkward areas, creating a slipway spreadsheet, and generally organising the flow of work. She cautions, "Keeping house in that situation is a nightmare—it gets disgusting—good to avoid living on the boat when you're [in the yard] if you can afford to!"

SV *Stardancer* on the hardstand, Malaysia

4

Becoming Your Own Captain

Diana Neggo started sailing as a twelve-year-old with her father, did some crewing, then managed to persuade the man in her life that he, too, needed sailing in his life. She had never skippered a boat before, but somehow knew what to do. The knowledge seemed to be innate. Rob was a willing student, but they still wondered if they were up to a long trip. After a three-year circumnavigation of Australia, they decided they were ready for anything. Diana says, "Our boat is run fairly democratically, but I am the skipper. When the chips are down, and decisions have to be made quickly, I take the helm, so to speak."

Jenny Gordon-Jones made the transition from first mate to captain when her partner's health started to seriously decline. She says, "Deep down, I had wanted to try my hand at skippering, I knew I had what it took: the enthusiasm, ability, care, and diligence, but I knew nothing of diesel engines, marine electronics, or the workings of electrical and mechanical equipment, which was a real dilemma." So, through networking, she found sailing crew who could provide what she lacked until she learned herself. Also, she was able to Skype her partner for advice when equipment failed. "Dealing with equipment breakdown has been my biggest challenge in sailing." She notes she spends a lot more time worrying about technical issues and relaxes less now, but the satisfaction and knowledge gained are immensely rewarding. She has recently successfully captained her forty-six-foot Bavaria for the fourth season in the Mediterranean.

Anna Fourie's role on board has totally changed from doing "pink jobs" when she was sailing with her ex-husband to now being skipper, engineer, navigator, and helmsman of her own boat. She says, "Having sailed with my ex-husband for several years from Oregon, USA to Australia, I still felt completely incompetent and was not confident to sail on my own, navigate, or steer in and out of a marina, and boat maintenance was a complete mystery. However, when you are extremely motivated, and with the right support, so comes the desire to learn. I wanted to become a female skipper and be able to take my son and my friends out on the boat. At the time the challenge seemed daunting, but I have been supported by the most amazing group of friends, family and fellow sailors who have been there to help me get over my fears and have been with me every step of the way." Now she maintains the engine, services the heads, winches, and other equipment, and really enjoys it. "Occasionally I indulge in cooking!" she says.

Both these women and many others have found it satisfying to change their roles, so don't feel you are stuck with just one set of responsibilities or role for your voyage. Communicate your needs to the captain to learn more and do more on board so you can choose what you wish to do.

5

Interpersonal Communication

How we each communicate is important. One word that our Blue Water Women use a lot in their comments about good communication is Respect. Once the respect goes, relationships founder, so take a moment to think about the subtext of your words, body language and tone of voice and consider the effect they will have. You and your partner are together in a confined space for long periods of time. Jane Kilburn says the key to on board happiness is, "Talk, talk, talk and then talk some more. Have patience for yourself and for others around you."

When you argue you cannot simply jump off the boat and go somewhere else. You either leave the issue or come back to discuss it later at a calmer time. Chances are high that you were not arguing about the exact same thing anyway. When I feel I have been misunderstood, I simply leave my Friwi to go into his cave and think about things. Usually this works and the air clears. If not, I will write a letter using the "sandwich" technique; good things, the problem, suggest an outcome, end with good things. Learning how to argue is something few couples learn to do successfully, but very worthwhile. Because there is a lot of adjustment required to making the transition from land-based living to living in a confined space at sea, arguments are normal. At times you simply have to let off steam.

Cate Storey says on their thirty-two-foot gaff-rigged cutter, "I find it hard when I have no space from David when we have a fight and there's no one to 'vent' to." It is at times such as these that we need to find other diversions. A good meal, perhaps a glass of wine, nice music and a pleasant atmosphere can contribute to sorting problems. After six years sailing and gaining more experience Lilly Service said of her husband Tom, "He seems more ready to take my advice … however, we are both STRONG personalities, and once the danger has passed we often have some pretty good knock down, take no prisoners, types of 'discussions!'"

Colleen Wilson admits to having a fair amount of arguments in their early years. Her mother's advice to hang in there, never go to bed without talking, or at least saying "I love you" did not always happen, but things got gradually better over time. Many arguments are fuelled by disagreements on how to act in situations we are afraid of and rather than put the arguments away unexamined it is better to state your fears. Your communications will improve if you start in an atmosphere of goodwill and with a sincere wish to understand the other party.

Also if you and your captain cannot communicate clearly and concisely what is required in any given situation, it can result in there being grey areas, which could lead to problems. Instructions to "grab that thing over there" are not allowed. There is a correct language for sailing parts and sailing actions, and it is a must to learn these, maybe not all at once, but as you encounter them. When my Friwi and I first got together he did not know the right terminology in English and I did not know them in French, so, for a while, we had a bit of Franglais happening until, as he wished, he learned the correct English words and phrases. Also we agreed; no shouting, no patronising and no recriminations. We all make mistakes. Questions about "Why this?" "Why that?" are not welcome in stressful conditions, whether it is an emergency or trying to fix a broken part. Save the questions for later discussion at a more congenial time when they will be appreciated.

I was not expecting to be stressed at all but there *are* times. We were in Fiji in a glorious almost circular bay with lovely villas climbing the hillsides. It was my duty to pick up the mooring, right in the middle of the bay. I don't know where my mind was that day as I normally excel at this task, but I fluffed it, not just once but three times. As my Friwi was getting understandably frustrated I suddenly burst into gales of laughter. We were the entertainment for the whole bay, and my Friwi was very embarrassed. Our antics of going around and around trying to get this elusive buoy suddenly seemed so ludicrously funny to me that I couldn't move for giggling! Laughter is a great stress diffuser. When I finally did manage to snag it, I took a bow to my audience. I had been simply far too tense about the whole thing. We had, in fact, discussed the procedure beforehand. It was just one of those days.

Things can get pretty tense at times. I was on another boat as crew, along with two other women, when the skipper told us to get ready for berthing, for a bow in, starboard tie up. Easy, but then the skipper shouted, "No, sorry, port-side tie-up" as we continued moving ahead. As we scrambled to untie and re-tie fenders the skipper was shouting abuse at his crew about being slow and no good. This was mainly, I imagine, because this confusion did not reflect well on him personally and he needed someone to blame. After we tied up, we three crew had a quiet word with the skipper to say that instead of proceeding, knowing his boat was not ready to enter, he should have waited and given us the correct instructions well in advance.

I have noticed a marked difference between men and women's style of preferred communication. Women like to discuss plans in advance so they can be well prepared. So, do not hesitate to ask for clarification if you are unsure of *anything.*

Lin Pardey believes this kind of behavior is more about vanity. She says in her book *The Capable Cruiser*, "Women take note: our vanity is more often wrapped up in the actual physical appearance of things, i.e. is the boat clean and organized looking. Men's vanity is more wrapped up in how their actions appear, i.e. did we look like I knew what I was doing when we sailed in. Accepting this difference will help during those times when spectator and the pressures they add, are unavoidable."

6

Ways of Having a Life at Sea

There are countless different ways of having a life at sea. It can be part time or full time, with many combinations. Judy Rodenhuis speaks for a lot of women sailors when she says she and Paul always tried to go back and visit family at Christmas time. Many women enjoy sailing more when they can go back to their home country for a visit. Colleen Wilson is very much a people person who loves her female get-togethers and she is happier now they have a Yin Yang approach to life as she calls it, where she and Tom who have been sailing together for fifteen years can now stay on land part of the time. Colleen says, "One thing that I think we've done right and not everybody can do it. We get off the boat every year. At the end of the sailing season we head home where we have a small cabin, off the grid. We see family and friends. Getting off the boat shifts our perceptions and allows us to do other things."

Often there are family ties on land, perhaps ageing parents to care for. Holly Scott leads adventure sailing trips all over the world but is part time sailing now she is dealing with her father's failing health. For Gwen Hamlin, it was a case of her husband's stresses regarding family that cut short their sailing time, but now they are thinking of returning to sailing but not full time live aboard.

You can tailor your sailing voyages to your personal requirements. Returning to land for a while can be a time for being with family and, sometimes, a bit more comfort too! Others, like myself, have no house, are totally immersed in life at sea, and spend many years living full time on the boat which is home. This gives us more time to explore the countries nearby using the boat as a base plus make local friendships and get a real feel for the country we are in. We prefer not to leave *Stardancer* for more than a couple of months at a time, because in countries with climates of extreme heat or cold, the interior of the boat is affected by the moisture. Mouldy smells have a habit of very quickly permeating clothes, shoes and books in drawers, lockers and enclosed spaces.

In fifteen years, we have been back to New Zealand twice. We sold our home before we left, leaving a container with our worldly possessions in it on two acres of land. I was not sure when we set sail that I would like to keep sailing for the long term, so wanted to keep a bit of land, just in case. Other sailors keep a house in their home country, and many rent these out when they are away. I always imagined we would retire in New Zealand, but we have become so used to tropical weather we have decided to base ourselves in South East Asia. Our three adult sons can fly out to meet us wherever we are in a destination they want to visit. This works for us but those who have ageing parents or grandchildren tend to want more frequent trips back. However, every time you fly out you will most probably also be paying rental for a marina berth to keep your boat safe when you are away.

Laila Kall has recently returned to her home in Sweden after seven years around the world. She and her husband decided to ship their boat from Asia to Turkey rather than sail through the Bay of Aden because of safety concerns as well as the time factor. She was worried about being so far away from ageing family. During their round the world voyage they left the boat during each cyclone season to fly home for several months. Now they sail the Mediterranean where they can be back in Sweden much more quickly if need be.

For other sailing women, their sea time must work in conjunction with their paid work. Kaci Cronkhite and Lin Pardey are both authors. However, working on a book does not stop when the book is written. There are promotional tours, signing sessions and seminars. This means many months on the road travelling from place to place. Kaci travels across the USA to promote her books in the off season, so she can then go sailing when the weather improves. Lin has a full schedule of promotional travels for her latest book, which takes her to several countries worldwide, but she returns home for the summer sailing season. Pat Mundus sails her ketch down to warmer waters to escape the winters in USA, then in summer she charters her boat out, employing crew while she lives in her house where she can work on her other business. Flexibility is a key ingredient to being able to work and enjoy a sailing life.

Instead of a home on land in one country, Lyn Johnstone and her husband have two boats under thirty-five feet; one based in New Zealand which allows them sailing seasons through the Pacific and in Australia, and another boat in Greece, so they can explore the Mediterranean and Atlantic.

Barbara Gladney and husband are in their seventh year of their circumnavigation, leaving their boat in different places around the world in the off-weather season for three to four months and staying with family and friends in USA, then flying back to re-join their boat for the next leg of the adventure. But as Barbara says, "After seven years we are tired of not having a place to hang our hats when we do come home, so we have bought a house in Texas." Comments from our Blue Water Women indicate there comes a time when many of us, as we get older, welcome the idea of our own *pied a terre*, to enjoy in between sailing. This often enables us to continue the sailing life for longer.

7

Sailing with Limited Budgets

Some sailing women have strictly limited budgets which mean they get off the boat and fly to where the work is, and they enjoy the experiences of different ways of living this gives them. Cathy Gray is a nurse and midwife. She flies back to work in hospitals in remote parts of Australia for short nursing contracts to replenish the sailing kitty. This allows her to re-join her husband, who does the boat maintenance while she is away and for them to continue their circumnavigation. Merinda Kyle and her husband top up their sailing kitty by doing short term relief work in trailer parks a few weeks of the year. No matter if your sailing kitty is bottomless or near empty, it is possible to enjoy many years living at sea if you have portable skills or investments and plan accordingly.

Perhaps you simply wish to supplement your sailing kitty every now and again. How to do this was something that concerned me a lot before we set sail. In fact, we organized a lunch meeting with friends with the aim of throwing around ideas as to how we could create an income on board. Even with six good brains working on this we still ended up none the wiser. Except perhaps that it is better for ideas to evolve rather than be forced!

I need not have worried about it because our arrival in Australia decided the subject for us. When we docked we were welcomed with an official letter, from the New Zealand tax department; we had earned too much money that year and owed several thousand dollars. All our sailing kitty savings, gone. I wished I had not slaved away working two jobs with their additional stresses to increase our sailing savings. Being realistic, there was only one way to solve this dilemma; find work, pronto! So, at age sixty we started all over again, which as we had previously been business owners meant we were almost unemployable, plus we had no network to support us. However, digging deep into my store of resiliency and one hundred and forty-six job applications later I got my first contract with the Federal Government in Brisbane which led to further contracts. Reinventing ourselves proved satisfying not only because we earned enough to pay the tax bill on time and create a good sailing kitty for the future, but also because of the new skills we learned along the way. Despite this unwanted hiatus there was a wonderful silver lining. We got to know more of Australia and made many strong friendships. We also managed two fantastic and unforgettable voyages to Papua New Guinea which we would never have had if we had continued sailing straight to Indonesia. Life, it seems, has its own plans for us.

Certain careers are easier to pick up and drop between sailing voyages: for example, women who are professional nannies can get contracts short or long all over the world, but of course you need already to have the training. The same goes for nursing, teaching and most other contract work. You may be fortunate enough to set this up before you leave your home country. Sometimes people work as online consultants to their previous employer, but it doesn't take long before someone else who is on the spot does the job because it is not easy to keep up a strong network of contacts in one country when you are sailing elsewhere, unless of course, you are going back on a regular basis.

Alexandra Mateer, teaching in Papua New Guinea school

Many women turn to writing, either articles for blogs, websites, and magazines, or regularly contributing columns, and we shall be looking at this in the You and a Career at Sea segment of this book. To write you need the internet to do research. Fifteen years ago, opportunities for internet-based businesses were slowly becoming commonplace and the availability of good internet coverage was unreliable. These factors have improved exponentially today making internet-based businesses possible anywhere there is a good internet signal. I had a client who was an architect drawing up plans in New Zealand and sending them back to the company he worked for in Holland to arrive before breakfast there and so beat the competition. But the downside is you have to live your life around good internet coverage which can limit your sailing plans.

Certain skills are more compatible with life at sea than others. Merinda's husband Brian is a hair dresser and has no shortage of clients wherever he sails. Some women excel at sorting computer problems, setting up web sites and dealing with technological glitches and they are in high demand. People who can fix fridges and diesel engines are high on the most-wanted list too. Or you could do sewing, making and repairing covers if you have a heavy duty sewing machine on board. I own some pretty earrings made by fellow cruisers who have workshops for silverwork on board their boats. Some are so good they work on the boat to supply retail outlets when back on land.

My Friwi husband Christian and I thought it would be easy enough with our skills to pick up odd jobs as we sailed. We studied for our Teaching English as a Second Language certificates and felt confident we would find something, but what we had overlooked is that employers want some form of commitment to longevity, not just the month or two which we were going to be in that country. Also, now in many countries it is illegal to take a job that a local can do, so doing odd jobs on marinas or for other cruisers could be problematical.

Frederique and husband Alain are bound to their marina for a few years because they found employment as Sailboat Brokers to help save for the sailing kitty, but it allows them to easily slip the mooring lines and head out to sea to enjoy weekends and holidays on their boat. An added benefit is that there is stability for their son who was taking Baccalaureate exams. You too may be lucky to find something along the way, but generally it is best to build on existing skills. An ideal situation of course would be to have a passive income. Many sailors achieve this by renting out their house or apartment when they are away. Even so, there are times when one must return because of tenants or maintenance problems which entails leaving your boat in a safe place, usually a marina, and paying berthing fees.

It is not uncommon for people to run into financial problems and find they must return to work to fix them. Helen Hebblethwaite and husband were eighty-five nautical miles west of Sri Lanka when their mast broke bringing an abrupt end to their planned voyage. To pay for a new mast, they went to work in the mining industry in Australia which they really enjoyed. They extended their time there and returned after four years to their boat to resume cruising. As Jane Kilburn reminds us, “Letting go of pre-conceived expectations can allow our experiences to flourish in ways we had not expected.” There is no right way or wrong way to go about living a life at sea. There are as many alternatives as there are people. So much depends on your own individual circumstances and how willing you are to “go with the flow.”

Finances and families seem to affect sailing decisions almost more than any other factors save one: attitude. A can-do positive attitude can change problems into challenges and is probably the most valuable characteristic you can cultivate. This together with a good sense of humor will see you breeze through times when things go wrong. You will also need to be boundlessly flexible and accepting of change. Change and sailing go together like death and taxes, two of the few things in life you can count on.

8

No Boat at All

There are myriads of combinations and opportunities if you wish to experience the cruising lifestyle as crew and to learn about blue water sailing.

For someone who loves to sail and to dive but does not have a boat, Victoria Power manages to crew her way around the world to some of the best diving sites. I met her in Borneo as she hitched a ride with me. From crewing and diving around Malaysia, Indonesia and the Philippines, she has since changed boats and crewed in the Caribbean for a season, and the last I heard she was sailing in Venezuela. Crewing fits in with her land life which is based in Spain and enables her to choose a boat that is going to a good diving area, without the costs attached to running her own boat. Victoria started sailing as a girl with her father on small boats then later joined a sailing club in Spain and raced in local regattas, so she has considerable experience to offer any skipper, plus two huge assets; she is a great cook and has a wonderfully cheerful outlook on life. As Liz Stewart says, "Sometimes the best skills you can bring with you are having a strong constitution that never gets seasick, be a great cook and keen to learn with a love of the water."

If you are not sure if long passages are for you, try crewing before you buy your own boat. Victoria's biggest concern before setting sail is whether or not she has chosen a good skipper. Mostly her experiences have been very positive with one skipper falling in love with her, but he acted (reluctantly) as a gentleman, and once having to move off a boat because she disagreed with the skipper's morals. Victoria cherishes the freedom she has to change her environment at will and see the world her way, which means making friends everywhere she goes.

Barbara Sherry manages to create time to crew around her responsibilities to her daughter who has a disability. Barbara prefers short term crewing, more like brief holidays, around the world. She has no wish, nor time for a boat of her own. She holds numerous sailing credentials and is well experienced as a volunteer on tall ships sailing coastal Australia. Barbara crews for Saturday races at her local sailboat club as well as continuing to crew in South East Asia and the Mediterranean for friends. She says, "Every time I sail I feel like I have just found the sixpence in the Christmas pudding, so very fortunate."

If you wish to join friends as crew for legs of their voyage, it pays to clear up basic expectations before you set sail, or it could be the end of a friendship. I have seen friends who paid a sum to the captain to cover their stay but did not discuss what this sum covered. They assumed they would be treated as guests, and not have to participate in keeping watch, sailing, cleaning, cooking etc. They are no longer close friends with the captain.

Jenny Gordon-Jones points out the pitfalls from the captain's point of view, "One of the hazards of taking on unknown crew is just that, they are unknown. Even friends are unknown in this environment. I have worked hard to preserve friendships whilst on the boat, but some friends will not receive a second invite to re-join me. I have dealt with arguments, defiance, refusal to assist, childishness and princess behaviour, also secret drinking, unstated cigarette addiction and overall unsuitability to crew." You need to know what the expectations of the role are, what duties you will perform, what costs you are expected to contribute towards, e.g. share of marina costs, meals on board, water use and share of running costs for the boat. If you wish to get experience on someone else's boat, you can check out the many websites for crew which advertise positions all around the world. Then, when you become such a very accomplished and experienced crew member, the skipper may pay you!

9

Getting Started

It does seem for the majority of women that, "He was the motivator for going off cruising." As Jane Hiett says, her husband is a "sailing fanatic" but after more than forty-three years full time sailing and being on board a boat around the world and more, we can change. Jane is now taking some time off on land, whereas her husband wishes to continue crossing oceans, so she will fly and join him in certain destinations. She says they were young when they set sail and to make their sailing dream a plan they "lived incredibly frugally" to be able to sail full time, getting by on the proverbial "smell of an oily rag." Now it is her time for something different.

Alexandra Mateer was motivated to start sailing offshore because as she says, "I love sailing and I love my husband" but she found out she gets "hellishly seasick" offshore, which spoils her enjoyment of blue water sailing. For several years their shared dream was owning *Shaolin*, a replica junk, which they used to do coastal chartering eight nautical miles from Port Douglas to the

Low Isles in Queensland. Alexandra adored sailing this trip and life on board, but she learned she is happier on land or coastal cruising than crossing oceans.

Other women simply jump in the deep end, with no experience of sailing, putting their total trust in their partner. For Grit Chiu, who met her partner recently, it was a case of love me, love my boat, which she did. She joined him for an around the world voyage, with the boat ready to go, and learned from him as they sailed. She says, "I was scared to death of anything and everything, so I got life insurance and trusted my captain. Never have I felt unsafe, the captain is very competent." For the captain, it is a big responsibility having someone with little knowledge or ability on board, especially in case of emergency. However, now five years later Grit is becoming more confident and competent, and even more in love with her life at sea, and her captain.

Several of our Blue Water Women started offshore sailing because it was their partner's desire to sail and they had total trust and faith in their partner's knowledge and experience. Some admitted to initially being very fearful, but they subsequently learned to sail and to love the life. However, a couple of our Blue Water Women had nasty shocks to find that when they were at sea with their husbands there were moments when they found out that their spouses did not, in fact know as much as they had been led to believe, and they themselves actually knew more. One says, "It can be really scary when you're out in the middle of the ocean and you realise he doesn't have a clue. I found out that because he is so confident and competent, a great mechanic, everyone thinks he is a super experienced sailor, but I discovered he had actually done less sailing than I had! I realized I had a lot to learn."

"I didn't have any sailing experience," Merinda Kyle says. "I was impatient to go. As we started out it was apparent that my lack of experience as well as that of my partner, was enormous.

I just believed he knew everything without actually asking." Subsequently, they did experience problems but with luck on their side they survived them. It is all too easy to rely on another person and assume this will safeguard you from danger.

Chantal Lebet-Heller says she made the mistake of "Being happy in the boat admiring the captain … who was used to doing everything on the boat alone which is why I didn't find it important to know more, a big error on my part for when we set sail from Port Camargue in France, I was petrified!" The more you can learn before you go plus continual learning as you go will help you face any adversity more confidently.

If you are unsure of the amount of seafaring knowledge your partner has, one suggestion is to practise together with another knowledgeable person on board, perhaps chartering a boat with a skipper, or taking sailing lessons together, thereby ensuring your knowledge base is the same. This way you make a good team knowing each other's strengths and weaknesses. I believe by far the best way for your personal safety and enjoyment, though is not to rely on anyone unless you absolutely have to, but to try and learn as much as you can to be able to handle the boat on your own. Hope for the best, prepare for the worst is my belief. Jane Kilburn maintains "It is so important that everyone on board knows how to manage the boat. You never know what is going to happen. This became even more apparent when I had a child on board as I am no longer responsible for just myself, but for Milly too."

Cate Storey came to sailing as a novice on her new husband's boat. She came straight from a being a very successful career woman in a demanding high-profile position and found initially she quite liked the abdication of responsibility, but then found it hard to find a role on the boat. She says, "Much as I tried, pink jobs did not interest me, cleaning is not my forte." Cate's comments make me smile. I'm not sure many women would express cleaning as a strength, but more often as a necessity. However, things improved for her when she could take on some responsibilities and took charge of health and safety on the boat. She had felt she was less of a person because she was used to being responsible and in charge of something. Cate confides, "To be honest, our greatest liability was my lack of skills. Before we set sail again I will take sailing lessons."

Cate Storey on SV *Snufkin* in the Pacific islands

Although I too had trust in my husband's experience I hated being in the position of relying on someone else and could hardly wait to get out of that position by increasing my knowledge and experience as much as possible. It is all too easy to become consigned to the galley (kitchen) by default. The more knowledge and practice you can manage before you set sail, the more you will enjoy the voyage. Some women have admitted they were too naive to be aware of dangers and luckily for them, most encountered few problems.

It was a case of "ignorance is bliss" for Anna Fourie, who now owns and skippers her own boat out of Singapore. She says, "Being so naive meant I had few concerns. When I set sail with my then husband to cross the Atlantic from UK on our thirty-foot carbon fibre racing catamaran, it was my first overnight passage. This quickly became an extreme learning experience in storm force winds, with the carbon fibre bowsprit cracking and the entire mast dropping to the deck. When we reached France, I had never been so happy to set foot on land!" As she learned more she learned to check the marine weather forecasts prior to setting sail and they chose a more suitable boat for cruising, a thirty-eight-foot Sparkman Stevens, sailing from San Francisco across the Pacific to Australia.

Others of our Blue Water Women came to sailing offshore by gradually extending their sailing horizons, usually when they upgraded their boats, but for Gwen Hamlin, it was via scuba diving. She fell in love with the islands (Caribbean), and she wanted to live in these islands but on a boat. For Amanda Swan Neal, after she completed her apprenticeship as a sailmaker she changed trades to sailboat rigging and joined the all-female crew on *Maiden* in the Whitbread Around the World Race, and she simply continued sailing via sailboat racing until she met her husband John and worked on expanding the expedition sailing business with him.

I envy those women who came to sailing at a young age, through their fathers or brothers. About half of our Blue Water Women took the helm of their family's boat at a very early age. They had a head start with becoming confident around water. Holidays were taken on boats on rivers, lakes and seas. They were immersed at an early age in the timeless language of weather and water. As we age the proportion of our lives lived on land usually gets larger. Naturally we become accustomed to this as being the norm. As the years pass it can become harder to leave what you know and the person you have become, to leap into the unknown and learn what you need to learn. But a wonderful challenge!

10

The Sailing Lifestyle

Will you like it, adapt to it, love it or hate it? All these questions and more arise when we think of changing our lives. For sure, it will be very different from your home on land. There are many sailors who want to have their watermakers, fridges, freezers, juicers, washing machines, hot showers, televisions and microwaves with them, and do. But there are just as many who eschew these appliances because they know that the more you have, the more there is to go wrong. The more you have, the more power you need. I crossed the Pacific without a fridge or freezer. I have a fridge now in the tropics because we can afford to run one.

I do not have a washing machine. I do some hand washing and we save the heavy things like t-shirts, towels and sheets for the laundry when we make land which can often turn out to be a happy adventure. Especially when you get your laundry back and some of it is not yours. My husband had collected the laundry. I took a G-string back to the laundry where two middle-aged Muslim women worked. As is the custom, they were totally covered up from head to toe. I asked jokingly, “My husband wants to know which of you two ladies owns this, because he found it in between his t-shirts.” They giggled so much it was contagious, and we all had a thoroughly good laugh. This little episode ended up with us exchanging first names and promises of sharing a tea.

I have no microwave or TV nor any other appliances and am happy like that. We use our laptop to watch DVDs or movies we have been given by fellow cruisers. I do have a good gas oven with two burner rings, but it is way too hot to bake when in the tropics, so I rarely use the oven. The simpler I can make life the better.

One of the reasons I set sail was to free myself from the chains of consumerism. But that’s just me. Perhaps you need these things. Helen Hebblethwaite remembers setting sail with tennis racquets, a tent and other items that were never used and became lost in the mists of time. Now she has space for her newest best friend, a mini twin tub washing machine that just fits under the V-berth. She says, “Every time I lift it out to do the washing I give thanks to its inventor!” The choices are up to you, governed by the amount of storage space and operating power you have on your boat.

We do have a watermaker but have never used it because we carry 800 liters of water, but for Diana Neggo, the watermaker is the best thing they have. She says, “The best thing we ever put on the boat was the watermaker. We never have to worry about carting water and we can have the luxury of not long showers, but at least quick rinses off after a swim” and I know many women would agree. You certainly do not want sand and salt water inside your boat, so rinsing off after a swim is essential.

Lin Pardey’s advice in one of her books regarding expectations of comfort on a boat is, “Don’t try to take your shore-based home comforts with you, no boat will ever be as comfortable or convenient as even the smallest apartment on shore. But no apartment on shore will ever give you the adventures or introduce you to the people you would meet on a boat."

When Barbara Gladney downsized from her lovely home in Texas to their sailboat, she left behind "the walk-in closets, pantry, hot tub, Jacuzzi bath, dishwasher, and washing machine." She says it took a bit of adjustment initially. "However," she adds, "we have simplified life and now enjoy it so much more without all the trappings." Jane Kilburn shares a favourite saying from Oscar Romero, "Aspire not to *have* more ... but to *be* more."

Gina on SV *Stardancer* setting sail for Indonesia

11

A Normal Day

What I love about the sailing life is that no two days are ever the same. Either you enjoy routine, or you can't wait to get away from it. If you need a predictable life, life on the sea is not for you. After we set sail for Thailand, a day ago as I write, an unexpected tropical depression arrived, and we could not make headway, so we had to turn around and sail all the way back to our former anchorage, where we had started, and then wait. To me this is a special time, an unexpected gift. Time and expectations are suspended for a while. We have found an anchorage in the lee of an island, where it is sheltered and very pretty. As I write this we are anchored in twenty feet of turquoise water near stunning steep limestone cliffs. We catch up on some jobs for the boat. I make muffins, do some minor washing, have long chats with my Friwi, do some writing then reward myself with a swim. Pretty much like life on land. Except there is water all around us, no houses, but I can see another sailboat has anchored close by, also taking shelter. So, if we wish to socialise, we can.

I can hear birds, cicadas and the occasional small fishing boat. No stress. We have no urgent time commitments. Sailors get used to waiting for the weather. It is part of everyday life. That is why all sailing plans are made in sand. Maybe the weather will improve tomorrow.

I used to lead seminars and coaching sessions for executives in businesses all over New Zealand on Planning and Organizational skills. Some of those skills in time management are still valuable, but I had a hard time giving up those fixed longer-term plans. These days I use words like "perhaps" and "maybe" a lot more, and I prefix statements with, "Our latest plan is" or "Weather permitting." Usually, we end up having loose plans A, B, and C when we set sail, taking into account weather patterns, tides, and currents. But if someone says, "It is amazing in the Galapagos or Alaska, do you want to join us?" whatever other plans we had are suddenly out the porthole. We change our minds like the wind.

Crossing from New Zealand to Tonga we struck some foul weather. We had planned to be in Tonga before the King's birthday because everything closes for a week. However, we were sailing close hauled into the wind and being a deep keeled boat with low freeboard we felt very much like a submarine as waves covered the entire boat. At the end of a long day we could see Tongatapu in the distance but found we simply could not make head way. So, we hove-to for two days, and the motion was much easier. I made pickles and chutneys with excess fruits and vegetables because we had been told that Customs confiscated all fresh foods. We later found our oranges for sale in the local market, label and all! Time passed quickly. My Friwi said, "The wind has died down, we might set sail." I disagreed. It seemed the same to me. To prove his point, he undid the keeper on the blades of the wind generator. I heard an enormous explosion. Someone firing at us? No, all the generator blades had blown off! The wind was still too strong. When we finally were able to head towards land, we found we had drifted back 120 nautical miles and had to do them all over again. And of course, it was the King's birthday holiday, and of course Customs was closed too. Patience is another virtue that sailors need, in abundance.

If you were to ask each of our Blue Water Women for a description of a normal day, they would all be different. Each day is so different from the one before, there cannot be a "normal" day, which is another reason I love the voyaging life. Amanda Swan Neal sums it up well, "The best thing of boat life is that it's always different. You're living close to nature and she always has the last say."

12

How We Learn

To prepare yourself mentally means getting to a stage where you feel sufficiently confident in your abilities and in your boat to say, "I'm ready to go." Do not expect to know everything. It takes time and even after fifteen years sailing full time I am constantly learning. You may be a quicker learner! Essentially, learning as much as you can about boats and sailing certainly helps dispel fears of being inadequate or useless when you are at sea. It also allows you to be more in control of your boat and therefore, of your life. So how can you learn?

There are hundreds of books that purport to teach you how to sail. We each have different learning styles, some of us are action learners, some visual, others auditory or a mix of each. I love to read and devoured several how-to books as well as reading sailing magazines. I am a visual learner, so I would make a "mind map" (*see* Appendix A for more information) of the essential points. Using plenty of colours I then committed the shapes and colours to memory. You will have your own best way of learning. You can watch DVDs and videos as a virtual reality experience, the next best thing to actually being at sea. Blogs on the internet are another valuable source of advice. However, do not believe everything you read! Some sailors enjoy sensationalizing events that other sailors would take in their stride and deal with without all the hoopla that makes for a good read. If you ask a dozen sailors, the same question you will get several different answers. Barbara Gladney warns, "We have fallen victim to a lot of misinformation, and have suffered as a result, I've learned that everyone is an expert!" It is up to you to ensure your information comes from reliable sources. For example, sailors are often keen to give you their waypoints to perhaps guide you through a tricky entrance, which is great to have, but not to rely on. You need to think for yourself, because people can, with the best of intentions, steer you wrong.

For those of you who prefer action learning, on the job, Linda Morgenstern says, "I knew absolutely nothing about boats. … I knew the first thing I needed was to learn to sail. As I was living in Seattle on a boat there's lots of local training. I took most practical seminars and chats and attended sailboat shows where there were products being shown and asked lots of questions to understand what was being sold and why someone would need something like that. I took a basic Coast Guard Course and then found the Seattle Women's Sailing Association. I loved this organization. I was eager to learn; members were eager to share." Once each month Linda could sail on a trip organized on a boat owned by a member, and also listen to interesting and knowledgeable speakers and she says, "All for an incredibly affordable thirty-five dollars per year membership." There are many sailing schools around the world based on the idea that women might prefer to learn from other women as Linda says, "in a softer more congenial environment" (*see* Appendix A for contact details).

Amanda Swan Neal now runs Sail Training Expeditions for seven months of the year in various parts of the world with her husband. They present at four major boat shows in North America where you can view free Power Point presentations on cruising and the offshore sailing life. She says, "I'm not your average cruiser … as I grew up cruising around the South Pacific with my parents," but, even so, she adds, "there are always fears and concerns before any offshore passage. I just try to be the best prepared I can." So, make the time to be well prepared.

Bernadine Reis and husband, a capable couple, knew next to nothing about sailing, had no time to learn so bought a cheap steel boat in Malaysia to learn on and set off. They got into all manner of predicaments ending in a mayday call. She says, "I wouldn't say I love [sailing] like my husband does. Four-hours-a-day maintenance was far more than expected and the reality did not live up to the dream." She is now looking forward to having a garden on a property on Vancouver Island. I believe that had they been better prepared their seasons on the boat would have been much more rewarding. You need to be aware of the pitfalls as well as the pleasures of a life at sea, and prepare for their eventuality, even if it never happens.

If we are fortunate we learn at a young age, growing up with the sea in our veins. About half of our Blue Water Women learned to sail early in life, learning from brothers, father or boyfriends, and I envy them those opportunities. The closest I got to the sea was when at the age of two, I was given to my father to be looked after. He was on his fifty-five-foot fishing boat in the port of Bluff in the South Island of New Zealand. He sat me on the gunwale, turned around and back again, by which time I was floating face down in the cold waters of the Foveaux Strait. In spite of this early baptism I messed about in small powerboats of my own until I finally learned to sail at the age of fifty-five in the warmer waters off the North Island of New Zealand, learning from my husband and taking a sailing course with Penny Whiting. It is never too late to learn to sail.

Penny is something of an icon in the sailing world running her sailing school for fifty years and teaching 33,000 adults. I recall going to her training boat on Auckland Harbour when it was blowing thirty-five to forty knots. As a novice I quailed at the thought of going out in that wind, however it was the best thing that could have happened to me. I learned not to be afraid of the weather but to be prepared for it. I learned how to properly reef the sails and how to use the wind to sail safely and comfortably. I also learned I do not get seasick! For ages, I drove my husband crazy with "Penny says this, Penny says that"! I still recall her major piece of advice when things do not go according to plan on deck, "If it is hard to do, you are doing it wrong."

Many of us learn from our partners or friends. This can either be a great bonding experience or a traumatic event! Anna Fourie maintains, "Don't learn from your partner, learn to sail with a professional, not your partner." As Lilly Service says, "We see many couples learning together, and that can be difficult." However, Lilly's husband Tom is an ex-Navy sailor with a lot of experience. She adds "Watching Tom's every move on our boat and being quite an observant student has taught me a whole bunch."

Helen Hebblethwaite learned from her husband and says that the most important thing she learned is that "The leads will line up." You do not need to know everything at once. She adds, "What you need to know will become apparent when you are in the right place for it. Years ago, with just a paper chart and a little handheld GPS we were entering a river, for the first time, at night. It was a busy river with wharves on one side and an airport nearby. The skipper said, 'I'm looking for a red flashing light with a period of four seconds'. There I was scanning the scene and there were lights everywhere. The wharves were ablaze with lights, lights on ships, overhead lights, flashing lights on forklift trucks, and a concrete plant beyond that had lights on its tower, perimeter fence and car park. Over on the other shore the airport had sweeping searchlights, even airplane landing lights. Then there were the lights on the river; fishing boats, other boats, shore lights and car lights.

"'Okay,' he said, 'just keep looking'. So, we eased slowly ahead, scanning for this flashing red light and then, gently pulsing its red beam to me across the water, there it was amidst the wonderland of this busy river mouth. One down, two to go. Up the river we made our way, checking on the chart for the bearing of the next buoy, lining up to see the next one, finding it, and so on. The moral of my story is that the leads will line up, just take one thing at a time."

What at first seems impossible when you start learning will turn out fine if you take it chunk by chunk. Gwen Hamlin was lucky she says, after working two and a half years on dive ships she learned a lot because "My captain was a wonderful mentor," and indeed you are lucky if you find someone like that to help you learn. Others are not so lucky and consider learning from their partners similar to being taught to drive by them; a harrowing experience where tempers frayed. I vividly recall seeing one skipper actually jumping up and down, both feet at once, and shouting at his poor partner when she did something wrong. Quite a spectacle. But this is not conducive to learning or to happy relationships!

Learning from your partner can have plusses as long as you know what you want to learn. It is widely acknowledged that men and women have different ways of communicating as well as different expectations from their communications. Chantal Lebet-Haller went out on Lake Lausanne every weekend where she says, "I had to fight to learn some things. It was difficult because the captain gave me lots of explanations with why here, why there, and it was too long. I wanted an answer in two words, and that is it." Later on, she realized it would have been useful to have had more knowledge but at that time she could only absorb her two words.

I find if I write things down I become clearer in my own mind of what I need to know, so, for me, writing a list of my questions or subjects I want to learn about, serves two purposes. I can present it to my captain at an appropriate time, not in snatches at a busy time, but when we can discuss one or two of these items until such time as my brain is satisfied but not overloaded. This way I am in control of what I learn. I know if I get too much information dumped on me at once I learn little and I go into a state of numbness.

It is not essential to get a piece of paper to say you can sail! But it may give your confidence levels a boost. If you prefer to learn sailing in a more one-on-one situation, another option is to have a skipper on board to teach you or if you don't yet have your own boat, charter one complete with skipper and learn from them.

Major boat shows are a wonderful resource for learning about boats; there are seminars, talks and power point presentations which are great ways to learn about specifics. Lin Pardey's seminars are always great value backed up as they are with many years' experience, books, videos and DVDs.

Linda Morgenstern was determined to learn to sail in as short a time as possible, so she could prepare to skipper her own boat around the world. So, like many other Blue Water Women, she regularly crewed on racing boats in every spare moment, all the time asking questions. On some boats the racing can get pretty serious and intense but on other boats it is more of a social outing. You can choose what suits you.

In her early years of sailing Diana Neggo crewed with an all-female crew racing out of the Royal Perth Sailboat Club, West Australia. From initially being apprehensive she came to love the experience. She says, "We showed the misogynistic stuffy old codgers a thing or two by winning the prestigious Diggers Cup. It was terrifying, exhausting but totally exhilarating!"

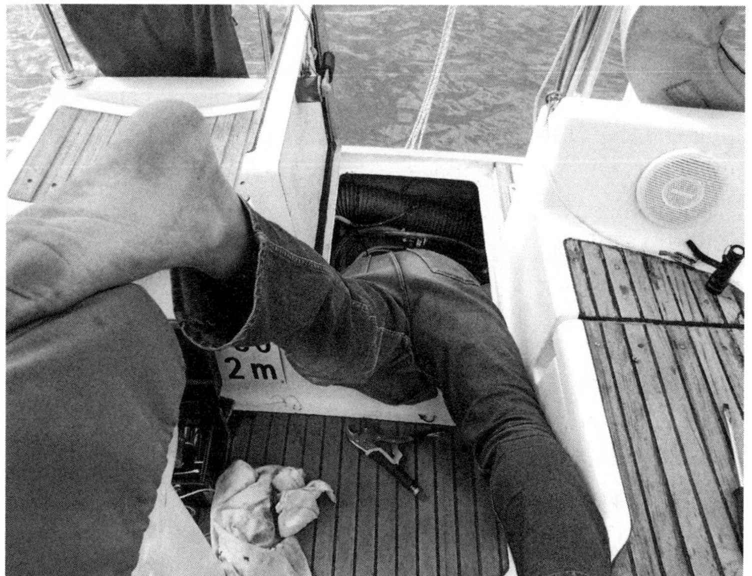

Christian performing maintenance in the lazaret

13

Learning about Maintenance and Repairs

These days although it may be easier to physically sail a boat because of modern technology, this comes at a cost. Do not rely totally on technological aids; technology breaks down. It is essential that someone on the boat is technically minded and able to repair the many working parts on your boat. Jenny Gordon-Jones says, "Men who take their women sailing need to teach their partners rudimentary sailing skills if they have none, from how to turn on the engine, do the daily fluid checks, how to steer, use the radio to call for help, man overboard drill, and to navigate." She says, "It is about sharing the knowledge, not keeping it secret. Encourage initiative. People's confidence levels need a solid practical basis. Involve [partners] in daily activities, after all many women are well out of their comfort zone and are only there because their menfolk want to go sailing." For your own feelings of self-esteem and safety, I urge you to take more than a passing interest in the working systems on your boat and how they interact.

I recall as we were motorsailing to Papua New Guinea from Australia we had a bad leak in the water cooling part of the engine. We could see where the leak was coming from but did not have hose of the correct diameter to replace it. As luck would have it we were sailing in the company of friends on *Erica* who just happened to have a length of the right hose. Again luckily, the sea was fairly flat, and Cathy, intrepid kayaker that she is, set out from *Erica* in the middle of the Coral Sea to cover the half a mile in her kayak, bringing us the spare part. She returned to her boat with the entire contents of our freezer which was quickly thawing to put in her own freezer, a welcome act of friendship while we sat there gently rocking on calm waters quite happily taking the cooling system apart and fixing it. I learned a lot more about our engine that day. However, fixing broken parts when the wind is howling a gale in mountainous seas would not be as pleasant!

It surprises me how many times this bad luck/good luck experience has happened to us. We had just collected *Stardancer* and had been sailing all day and were night-sailing up the coast of Queensland when the weather turned foul with steep short waves and a strong headwind when the autopilot stopped. The previous owner had mentioned it was fickle! I steered, or rather tried to steer her in circles to recalibrate it, but without success. We did laugh later when we looked at our track, nothing like circles at all. So we hand steered all night taking turns of two hours each in the rough weather. We sang every Beatles song we could remember at full voice to keep ourselves awake. As fate would have it, the port of Bundaberg loomed as day dawned and we made safe anchorage. I learned that although what at first seems like an overwhelming problem in actuality most probably is not. Anxiety reduces as logic and action take over. We were tired and hungry, with an unexpected hole in our sailing kitty for a new autopilot, that's all.

In the sailing world there is always someone with a story more dire than your own. Merinda Kyle had no sailing experience and was "thrown in the deep end" when first on her boat she and her partner had to hand steer from around Queensland to Indonesia. In times gone by of course there was only hand steering, but now we rely on the autopilot or self-steering, until it breaks down. Advances in technology over the past twenty or so years make sailing a boat easier and more available to everyone. However, as we have more electronic aids on a boat in the harsh sea environment, you can count on mechanical and electrical breakdowns or engine failure at some stage. The saying about sailing being all about "doing repairs in exotic locations" has a basis in solid fact!

There will always be something that needs attention. Perhaps your partner has the expertise required or perhaps you will find a specialist to fix the problem, but that can be a very frustrating exercise and is not always possible in some remoter parts of the world. It can also be very expensive. So if it is going to be you doing or helping with repairs it is well worth attending courses on various types of maintenance. Your local technical school is a good place to start. Many of them hold diesel engine maintenance courses. Look for seminars at boat shows on rigging, sail repair, what to look for in buying a boat, how to provision, look after crew, handle your boat in rough weather and so on. Linda Morgenstern attended a seminar on rigging with Brion Toss whom she hired to rig her boat over several weeks but when it came time to later re-rig her own boat she could do it herself. So, as she says, "The training paid off."

Today, information on everything and anything is readily available at the press of a button. YouTube can be invaluable when you need instruction on how to fix something, providing you are in range of the internet. Also as a wonderful resource for information, there are several clubs and associations online specifically created for women sailors which provide a wealth of knowledge and experience sharing via blogs and chat rooms, (*see* Appendix A for details).

14

Practice Is an Important Part of Learning

Can you imagine taking your practical driving test when all you have done is learn a few pages from a book and never taken the wheel? Practice and plenty of it is the only way to embed what you have learned. So be bold, don't worry about looking foolish, ask millions of questions, and then take over the helm, the anchoring, setting the sails, adjusting the rigging as often as you can. Share the maintenance jobs so you learn how things function and interact on your boat. Pat Mundus, who holds a 1600-ton captain's license, was motivated to be an independent woman because as she says, "I simply saw the all-dependent position my mother put herself in." If you want to be an autonomous woman sailor, practice is key.

I have two regrets; one is that I wish we could have set sail on our adventures sooner. The other is that I had insufficient time to practise what I had learned before we crossed oceans. When we set sail from New Zealand to cross the Pacific I had been working two jobs to bring in the money for the sailing kitty, plus packing up and selling our house and finishing my master's degree, while my husband remodelled the interior of our boat. When we set sail I was utterly exhausted and only too pleased to not be in charge for a bit and lean on my Friwi who is a very experienced sailor. However, this was a mistake because I got into a habit of leaving the sailing, repairs, and maintenance to him. Later as I revived and did not want to be consigned to the galley forever, this changed. I enjoy being more knowledgeable and deeply involved, and I derive satisfaction from little challenges I set myself.

16

Are You Ready to Set Sail?

Leaving a Career Behind

Coming to terms with the transition from being thoroughly involved in your work to suddenly spending your days sailing can be an emotional time for many women. Mary Anne Unrau felt guilty about not working when she started sailing. She says, "The real difficulty was that at first I felt I should make better use of my talents and time than to have the luxury of constant travel. I wanted to get a job at every place we touched upon. It took me some time to shed any guilt I had about no longer being a contributing member of society." Also when our idea of who we are is tied up in our work the feeling of loss can be painful.

When we set sail in 2005 I lost the sense of who I was. I was so used to being in charge of many things where I did not have

Looking for an anchorage, Thailand

to ask for assistance and was consummately knowledgeable on a wide variety of subjects. I found it quite disturbing to have to ask so many questions, but I knew if I didn't, I would not learn. I was not used to asking for advice but more used to dishing it out! This was my first step in becoming a different person. The expectations I had of myself were unattainable. I had to settle for the fact that I would never have as much experience as my Friwi. I was and am still in awe of his seafaring knowledge. His navigation skills and knowledge of the sea itself amaze me. From him I learned how to read the weather, how to set the sails, how to read the sea, how to enter coral reefs and how to stay safe. But making the transition from landlubber to blue water woman was not without its pains. I was used to using my brain all the time, being busy all the time, being useful all the time. I had to unlearn these things and learn a new way of being. No one was judging me. I did not have to feel guilty sitting gazing for hours at the sea. It took a while for me to slow down to the pace of life. For the first few years, I kept a journal, then slowly I realized I was living so much more in the Now, that I had no inclination to record everything I did and saw.

Cate Storey was working in International Aid in her dream job, but one as she says, "that was eventually going to kill me. I had three phones." She went volunteering for United Nations World Food Program in Bangladesh, worked in Africa, Philippines and the Solomon Islands. But as she says she became "jaded with the aid industry and working so hard that my relationship and sanity were at stake." Leaving that work was tough and she had intense post work blues. She says. "I wondered, who was I? If I was not the high achieving Aid worker who was going to save the world?"

She suffered an identity crisis. Cate says, "I really struggled to find a role on the boat. I feared I would simply become David's wife, who could not sail, and to be honest was not really good at much except being an academic and a workaholic. This fear embodied itself in the depression I fell into for about the first ten months. Mostly it was loss of control that I felt. I did not know much about boats or sailing, so I simply had to trust David but it was a big leap of faith. This was only overcome by experience, by getting to know David's skills and getting to know our boat, and realizing I could trust them both."

However through sailing in the Pacific and increasing her skills day by day, she slowly learned, "I am an alright and at times, interesting person, without my career. Something that will be an asset for life, I know that I am a valuable person even when I'm not being super career woman. I learned to love each moment, to learn from the people I met, to value the places I visited for their uniqueness, strengths, and what they could teach me rather than seeing them as a potential aid project. I learned to be alone and to have time to relax and be ok with that. I learned how to be a cruising sailor though I still lack confidence. My big learning curve was not just to learn to sail but to learn to live."

Cate and David are now land-based for a while before they set sail again, because they are proud parents of a baby boy. But the sailing life beckons, and baby Henry will be brought up on a boat.

If you live with your heart open,
fear becomes an adventure

—Rina Tham

Overcoming Our Fears

Out of all our Blue Water Women, only one has said she would not like to have her voyage of a lifetime again. There are risks associated with sailing but we deal with many more risks in our land-based lives every day. The majority of Blue Water Women have experienced decades of enjoyable sailing without serious mishaps. But there are a few who have experienced what we all fear. One was dismasted in a storm, another had her boat holed on a coral reef, two experienced ripping sails, another two experienced losing steerage, one had her boat boarded in the middle of the night, one experienced a lightning strike that knocked out all her electronics, and another experienced being airborne on the back of a whale.

But they all coped and continued sailing happily. Some of us start out being severely seasick or having to deal with medical problems. But we cope. We are not super woman, not particularly strong or especially brave women, simply all types of women, and we rise to the occasion. These extreme events happen only rarely and none of them may ever happen to you, but the possibilities do exist. These women have said they would willingly have their voyaging experiences all over again because on balance, there were so many more fantastic experiences on the plus side.

Rather than leave niggling fears to fester and grow to become big fears which then diminish the excitement of your dream to go, confront them and prepare yourself by taking action . We need to change F.E.A.R. or "False Expectations Appearing Real" into "Feeling Excited and Raring-to-Go!" There is a very thin line between fear and excitement, and this line is different for each of us.

When I first heard that friends of ours had an encounter with a whale I was sure every day that a whale would find us, and in the past fifteen years we have seen a few whales fairly close to the boat. Once between Fiji and New Caledonia I was on watch and yelled urgently to Christian to come up on deck. We saw this enormous gray shape 200 feet dead ahead with something white about twelve feet long swimming alongside it. Humpback whales! And we were on a collision course! I was afraid we would bang into them; the adrenaline pumped. Christian jumped on the automatic pilot and changed course immediately to give them more room as we continued to watch, awestruck, as mother and calf carried slowly on their way, not the least bit interested in us. I learned that day that baby humpback whales are born white but I also learned that fears need to be kept in perspective. As Elizabeth Gilbert says in her book *Big Magic*, "Fear is a desolate boneyard where dreams go to desiccate in the sun." We cannot give up on our dreams because of our fears. It is certainly no shame to fear the unknown; it is perfectly natural to feel apprehensive about tackling something radically different.

However, being too blasé or having a "she'll be right" attitude on the other hand can be a recipe for disaster. As experienced sailor Amanda Swan Neal admits, "There's not much that fazes me now. Most often it's my blasé approach to some matters that trip me up, or not realizing that our crew don't judge matters as John and I do. I was caught out once when I was on standby down below at the nav station when the crew pointed out that a ship was approaching but all was O.K. I did not take a good look at the ship as I trusted their judgement, but a while later and when I did sight the ship I realized the crew had read the lights wrong and we were on a serious collision course. I should have paid more attention to the crew's first conversation on the vessel." Danger was averted, but this episode goes to show how easy it is to make assumptions.

Constant vigilance is essential and do not be afraid to question the skipper about the situation rather than make assumptions. The more we learn, the more confident we become, which leads to becoming more competent, which in turns helps allay fears and gives us more pleasure, which is what it is all about!

17

Some of the Things We Fear

Leaving Friends and Family

For Judy Rodenhuis, the worst thing about voyaging was "Missing the day to day events in our children's and grand children's lives and those of our friends." Beth Cooper speaks for a majority of our Blue Water Women when she says she found being away from her family was the hardest thing about setting sail.

This was due either to the simple fact of missing being with loved ones or else feeling guilty because they were not there to look after them. Cate Storey felt, "I have abandoned my family when I am not helping my mother with my elderly grandparents." Colleen Wilson's biggest concern was being able to stay within regular touch with her parents because when they left over fifteen years ago internet was not readily available. "We got SailMail and it was a lifesaver for a few years before Wi-Fi really kicked in." Merinda Kyle says, "I had an elderly mother who was getting increasingly frail and she hated me sailing away for periods of time because I was her main support. For two years up the east coast of Australia, it was stop start until my mother passed away."

Saying farewell in Sandspit, New Zealand, 2005

When my Friwi and I left New Zealand we organized a regular sked (scheduled on-air meeting) each night with the weather man in Russell who relayed information on our progress to friends and relatives for us, as well as helping us with weather forecasts. However we had problems with our single-sideband (SSB) radio and after a couple of days we could not transmit. Of course people thought the worst had happened to us, and in many ways we wished we had not agreed to this sked because instead of allaying fears it ended up exacerbating them. It is not always possible to keep skeds or keep to any timetable except the weather's when you are cruising, but technology has improved enormously over the past years providing a variety of on board communication devices (*see* Appendix A for information on Technology and Communication). After the debacle with the SSB we assured friends and relatives that we would write regular newsletters to them, which later became articles for magazines around the world.

If at all possible it is a good idea to invite your family or close friends to stay on board for a time, so they get a better idea of what your life is like for you, which in turn makes it easier to share things with them. Our son was particularly fearful for me, so we invited him and his girlfriend to come on board and cruise the Yasawa Islands for a few days when we were in Fiji. We stopped at Musket Cove so they could get off and explore and have time away from us. This worked well because he then understood more what cruising was all about and was not so worried for us. I have seen guilt about not being there "in case you are needed by families" become so strong an emotion that rightly or wrongly, people have cut their voyage short.

My mother was a challenge. She was dead against me going off to live on a boat and go sailing. She would say things like, "I want you to promise that when I die you do not buy a boat with your inheritance" because she could never understand how I could give up my business when it was doing so well, and she could only see sailing and crossing oceans as uncomfortable and dangerous. I figured she was worried about my safety.

For a year or two after leaving land, I still felt guilty going against her wishes, but there was no way I could change her mind and there was no way I was going to give up our dream for some emotional blackmail either. So I sent her lots of happy photos of the amazing places we have been and shared the wonderful adventures we have had, which I believe helped reduce her fears. I know she loved to share the photographs with her neighbors and friends.

When she became ill and my sister looked after her, I felt guilty all over again. But luckily my sister understood our lifestyle and how happy it made us. Although I flew back to UK a couple of times to help my sister regarding funerals and estate duties, it is still not the same as being there to support family when needed. However life is about making choices, and I had made mine. Happily, my father was all for us setting sail and had cheered us on, only wishing he had been fit enough to join us on board. Families; it is impossible to please everyone. We have each to plot our own course in life, for better and for worse, and live with our decisions.

"If there is something you want to do, just do it" says Lisa McVey, "and don't make excuses why you can't. We took a 'midlife' sabbatical. I was thirty-eight and my husband forty-two when we both quit our jobs to go sailing. When people say they can't do that because of their children or their career or yada yada yada, I think it's bull. Don't think you can do all those things you want to do when you retire. Who knows what shape you'll be in when you get older? We met lots of sailboats with children on board. And we both got jobs within three days of returning to Arizona. Do something you are passionate about. For me that was cruising!"

Leaving My Treasures Behind

Or can I take my treasured things with me? I am glad I did take a sampling of treasured items with me. I have a few silver spoons, a couple of pieces of heirloom jewelry, a china mug my mother gave me, a bone china cup and saucer and an impossibly grand tea pot I have tucked away. I took our wedding album and a handful of photos of our sons at different ages. We have a painting of where we used to live. I took about a dozen favourite books, our music CDs, my paints, my best bed linen and my childhood teddy bear. Plus a much reduced selection of clothes for all weathers and my wet weather gear. Everything else we left in a specially insulated container on our two acres. We left beds, sofas, antique dressers, hundreds of books, several paintings, photo albums, dining table etc. In fact everything you would need to start out all over again in a house. Our insurance would not cover the container because we were not there on the property and no one was checking on a regular basis because our sons lived too far away. After ten years it was clear we were not going to go back to New Zealand to live, so I asked one son to go and empty the container one weekend. He could sell the contents as he thought fit and the container too. It turned out to be a wretched job for him.

The container had a rust hole on the roof and everything inside had been sitting in water for many years. Cardboard boxes had disintegrated and all glassware and chinaware was smashed to pieces. Furniture had rotted past recognition. There was a black mould inches deep on everything, including books, photo albums and paintings. Pots and pans were holed with rust. Just about everything was destined for the dump. A very sad weekend for our sons as many of their childhood memories had disappeared. But did I miss it all? Apart from a few sentimental items, no.

As a dutiful daughter I had mailed my mother copies of photos of us and our sons over the past thirty or so years. She gave them all back to me so I was able to make up a couple of albums and give them to the boys. Hindsight is a marvellous thing, but looking back maybe I should have left a box of really special things with a girlfriend to look after for me and made up albums for the boys as gifts *before* we went, as well as sell the furniture. However, I had had no idea if I would be sailing for three years or fifteen.

So the moral of my story is probably this; go into your adventure boots and all. Put valuables in the bank safety deposit box. Keep a few mementos, but put your books onto disc or go digital (we use e-readers mostly), put music tapes and DVDs onto sticks, photos onto your external hard drives and so on. Paintings need special storage. But fashions change and I bet your tastes will change too, so the furnishings and items you thought so great when you left will not have the same allure when or if you return. Travel light.

My treasures now consist of a bowl that was woven by old Aunty Betty in Tonga, a carved spear made for me in Papua New Guinea, silk I bought in Thailand, hand embroidery from the hill tribes of Vietnam. So yes, I have changed. My value system has changed immensely. I have treasured memories of amazing experiences that I know few can have and I feel truly privileged. The variety of people I have met is probably the best treasure and pleasure of all. I have a bounty of riches because I have time to appreciate our complex and wonderful world.

How Can I Be Contacted in an Emergency?

This may sound brutal, but this is someone else's emergency, not yours. The chances are that whatever the emergency was, someone has already dealt with it before you even get to hear of it. My sister died and I was unaware of the situation as we did not have email on board and only found out when we visited a cafe with Wi-Fi in Indonesia that she had died a few days previously. What could I have done if I had known earlier? Not much, considering we were making an ocean crossing just then. Wherever you are in the world it will take some time before you actually arrive at the site of the emergency but you can put in place an emergency plan.

Emergency Contact Plans

If you wish to make an emergency contact plan you could set one up using satellite phone, cell phone, VHF radio, SSB or ham radio (*see* Appendix A for information on these communications). If you are anxious about friends or family in disaster areas you could purchase a satellite phone. Satellite phones are becoming cheaper and more readily available and many people choose to have them on board for emergencies. The three main companies which provide the service are Iridium, Inmarsat and SPOT/Globalstar. Satphone coverage depends on the architecture of a particular system. Coverage may include the entire earth or only specific regions. You buy minutes, data, and text messages the same as you do with a prepaid mobile and these minutes have an expiry date. If you do not buy more minutes your SIM card becomes inactive. The calls can be quite costly, therefore the system is best used for short conversations. You can configure your satphone to access internet, meaning you can send text-only short emails and receive weather GRIB files. Sailmail.com has detailed information on how to set this up.

Keeping Up with Friends

These days it is so much easier to keep up with family, and friends of long standing as well as with friends just met thanks to Facebook and Messenger. There are now Viber and What's App as well as Skype and similar software coming onto the market all the time that will enable you to keep in touch with your friends and loved ones worldwide, as long as you are within internet and satellite reach.

Because as a sailor you are governed by the weather I try to not make firm promises to contact anyone on a specific date or time. This also applies to folk who are meeting you at a certain destination. You can be held up by bad weather, ill health or any number of reasons so it is best to make only loose plans with back-ups. Rushing to get somewhere on a particular day to meet people can cause problems if the weather is adverse because the tendency is to press on when normally you would wait for a better weather window. Friends of ours have recently blown a sail by doing this.

It is better to have visitors stay in accommodation on shore for a while, allowing you more contingency time to meet with them.

When I went back home for a visit several years after we had set sail, I was worried about fitting back in with my long term friends again, but because I had kept up communication with photos and emails over the years I was up to date with changes in their lives, and vice versa. It was not as hard as I had feared. Availability of the internet in many countries has improved drastically since we set sail in 2005. I find Facebook works well for me, but can become a bit of a time waster if I let it!

Or it can be a life saver. Chantal Lebet-Heller really missed mixing with her friends so she wrote a lot of emails and in fact she says her computer became her best friend. When joining a rally she says she would have liked to have had longer stops to get to know people better, but at least she can keep up with them via the internet and Facebook.

Courtney Jean Hansen who makes her career captaining ships has a few sage words to add about friendships and people. She says, "If you are someone who needs constantly to be surrounded by friends or family, the sea is not the place for you. When I am at sea I am AT sea. I have little contact with the outside world and am focused on the job at hand." Luckily for her, Courtney has friends who accept a part-time friendship and the fact that she flits in and out like the tide.

Missing Girl Time

"But nothing beats a girl's day out," says Colleen Wilson who started early on in her voyage to institute the ritual of having girl-only days. Often these would entail a lunch, massages, shopping or visiting something special.

Girls' days can also take place on boats anywhere. We were in the remote islands of Papua New Guinea with four boats in the bay, when Cathy Gray held a ladies' morning on board her boat. Husband Eric was sent off to have a man morning on board my boat. We four women in the bay did our hair, our nails, gave each other facials and massages, chatted, drank cappuccinos, laughed a lot, and shared problems over lunch and a glass of wine. After a day like that we were happier wives, mates, skippers and sailors in general.

Chantal, Lucy, Gina, and Tiwi enjoying girl time on *Micromegas II*

Fear of Lightning Strikes

I do have a fear. One I cannot do much about. I am afraid of lightning taking out all our electronic gear and then having to interrupt our cruising and spend time and money to replace all the wiring and equipment. Blue Water Woman Jane Hiett and husband John have recently spent an entire season working on their catamaran which got struck by lightning.

A friend Jim, a fellow sailboatie, had been having a depressing time with everything seeming to go wrong at once. To cap it off he had an accident in a hire car which was not insured and he had no idea how he was going to pay for the damage. So to cheer him up, we invited him and his wife on board for a chat and a drink, which turned out to be several drinks to drown his sorrows. At almost midnight they said goodnight and rowed safely back to their boat. However, next morning Jim was back again, with a very long, sad face. He knocked on the hull and told us of his latest misfortune. "Last night" he said, "while we were with you, someone came on board my boat and stole my computer." Naturally enough we commiserated. Then just before lunch Jim was back again, with a smile from ear to ear this time, "I have found the computer. It was in the oven!"

Now, putting your computer in the oven may sound very strange, but we do it too. Whenever there is lightning, and there is plenty of it in South East Asia, if at all possible, I disconnect all electric cables and put our laptops and iPads into the stainless steel oven, which creates a Faraday cage. I often give mental thanks to the English scientist Michael Faraday who invented this back in 1836, however, although this reduces the chance of lightning damage, it cannot block a really strong bolt.

Reassuringly, there are steps you can take to minimise lightning damage. You can create a pathway for the lightning to find its way quickly to the ground by ensuring there is a good ground connection between the bottom of the mast and the keel or earth plate if you have one fitted. At least this way lightning may not blow a hole in your boat. However, it is not something I worry about every day because worrying is not productive.

Fire on a Boat

My Friwi worries about fire on the boat so we are super careful around the propane stove, making sure the burner rings are turned off and the gas is turned off at the bottle when we leave the boat. Propane is denser than air and sinks to the lowest level, so it is not easy to detect, which is why it is so very important to create and stick to a gas-off plan when you leave your boat for a long time. It would also be prudent to have a propane leak detector on board, along with a household fire detector. We have one or two fire extinguishers in every room in key locations plus a fire blanket near the stove. A carbon monoxide detector is a good idea if a heater is being used in a closed boat in cold weather because of course, an excess of carbon monoxide is fatal!

Fear of Night Sailing

We all have niggling fears from time to time. Diana Neggo has a fear around night sailing, every time the sun sinks below the horizon she fears that she will miss seeing something important. I can relate to that because I do not have good night vision either. However each time we have an uneventful night passage the fear becomes a little less. With the use of radar together with the advent of the Automatic Identification System (AIS), night sailing holds fewer surprises. Constant vigilance is still necessary if you are in some parts of the world where there are fishing nets, fish traps and boats with poor or no lights; all of which is another reason I dislike coastal sailing at night. But crossing oceans at night is a different thing altogether. I adore night sailing then. Not a lot of traffic, just you and the stars and the moon and your thoughts. Wonderful.

Fear of Seasickness

Each time Cate Storey goes to sea she has a fear of feeling seasick. It never seems to get any better. She has to psychologically overcome this fear each time she sets sail. She takes her tablets and keeps busy up on deck in the hope that it will improve. Sadly she is one of the few people who constantly have a queasy feeling at sea but she does not let that stop her going sailing. You may have other specific anxieties. Acknowledging them is the first step in overcoming them then perhaps talking to other cruisers or researching on the internet may help you find solutions. My Friwi often feels seasick for the first three days of a rough crossing and knowing this we prepare for it, with him staying above deck for most of the time and me doing anything below deck. This solution works for us. (*See* book section "Before You Set Sail" for more on seasickness as well as the Medical section in the Appendix.)

Fear of Losing the Mast

Helen Hebblethwaite's sailboat lost its mast when they were eighty-five nautical miles from land heading west to the Maldives. "This," she says, "was life changing for us in several positive ways." She tells her story in her own words, recounting how she felt at the time, what actions they took, and the outcome.

"We were happily sailing with a nicely balanced helm in the sort of conditions our seventeen ton steel cutter-rigged cruising boat was built for in twenty-seven knots and a four meter swell. Then the rhythmical surging dramatically changed. Instead, suddenly we were upright, lifting, tossing, rolling and plunging with the waves. The skipper woke me with a shout, 'We've lost the mast!' The decks seemed vast and bare. We took in the elements of damage one by one. Most of the rigging was a tangled mess of steel hanging over the side. Our first feelings were not fear. Sadness and disbelief; then practicality took over.

"Our mast was a deck-stepped, rolled steel mast that took four men to carry it and now its weight was cumbersome and dangerous as it hung beneath the water alongside us. The thought of salvage was brief. We knew everything had to be cut loose for safety's sake. But at least it wasn't raining.

"After the initial shock of the actual dismasting, we quickly made the decisions and actions required to make the boat and ourselves safe. My mouth went dry, but I didn't cry. We just had to get on with what needed to be done. The skipper got out the bolt cutters and we set to work.

"It was a difficult, tiring, jerky, rolly trip in total blackness, hand steering the eighty-five nautical miles over twenty-two hours, twelve of which were in the dark, until we reached Galle, Sri Lanka. The ordeal was over. We were safe, the boat was safe. Next day we had time to be thankful for many things; we were not injured, and the boat had not let us down. She is strong and was fixable. And we had not let her down either. It is interesting how one's priorities change after coming through what many people call a devastating event. We were talking to a couple of men when one of them said, 'Oh, losing the mast is my worst fear.' I replied, 'Oh, it is my second worst fear.' There is nothing like adversity to make you rethink what is really important in your life.

"The lessons I learnt from this misadventure were:

- Know where things are on your boat so you can find things (like the bolt cutters) in a hurry.
- Trust yourself. You will be surprised what you can do when you need to.
- Make sure you can trust your boat.
- Remember, things could be worse. It could have been raining!

"Our boat was not insured so we decided to return to Australia for a couple of years, which turned out to be four, to work to replace the rigging. We also saved enough for a house and although I'm sad we lost the mast, we met many wonderful people and had many more different adventures."

Fear of the Boom

You are right to be afraid of the boom. One unguarded moment and the swing of the boom could knock you or your partner out cold. We were having lunch in The Mermaid Bar in Neiafu, Tonga, and watching a boat leave the harbour. Two hours later we saw it return. The captain had been hit by the boom and it had sliced off his scalp. His wife had sewed it back on and was bringing him back to the only hospital on the islands. We use a preventer to tie down the boom and to stop it from suddenly swinging, but it is all too easy to bend down and then crack your head when you stand up. Try always to think preventatively.

Fear of Someone Falling Overboard

Always, always, always keep one hand for yourself and the other for the boat. It is better to prevent an accident happening by being thoughtful and aware of the possible consequences of your actions than cope with the results. It is difficult to retrieve someone from the sea. In rough weather insist you and your sailing partner wear a life-vest harness which is tethered by a clip to the boat via jack lines. These lines are made of webbing and run along the deck fore to aft, on both port and starboard decks. You can get harnesses that clip on to these lines with two lengths of tethering. The shorter one should stop you before you actually hit the water. Once the person is in the water it can be a difficult exercise to retrieve them. This is especially true of some of the newer boats today which have a much higher freeboard, so it can be many feet from the water up to the deck; for boats that have scoop sterns with steps it is somewhat easier to hoist a heavy person on board via the transom rather than over the lifelines. However, you can reduce the chances of this happening if you take the correct safety precautions.

Our harnesses are part of our inflatable life jackets and the tether is about 5.5 feet (1.65 meters) and because I have adjusted it to my size, it fits well. Make time to adjust yours so it fits you properly. I have written my name in large letters on mine so we each take the correct harness. Comments from our Blue Water Women indicate that many of them have a difficult time getting their sailing partners to put on the harnesses. It is worth insisting because you will be the one doing the rescuing.

In the very unlikely event that someone falls overboard without wearing a harness the first thing I would do is press the Man Overboard (MOB) icon on the navigation screen to give the correct position for the search if necessary. Slow the boat to a stop. Quickly throw as many flotation devices as possible towards the person in the water; on the stern we have two yellow lifebuoys and a dan buoy which is a tall yellow pole with a yellow flag on it, plus several fenders. Then get to the person in the water a.s.a.p. and implement the MOB actions you have practised.

The more you practise the MOB exercise in different situations the more confident and less fearful you will be about the manoeuvre (*see* Appendix A for websites explaining MOB techniques and equipment).

Fear of Being Caught in a Storm

This is a very valid fear but if you are sailing at the right time of the year extreme conditions are rare. In fifteen years of sailing we have been caught in spells of unexpected bad weather but never in a very severe storm. Some of this may be luck but mostly it is good judgment and preparation. We consult with many different sources; pilot charts which detail the right sailing seasons for each area and several long range marine weather forecasts (*see* Appendix A for sea states and weather information sources). We leave for a crossing with a good weather window of four days to get into the rhythm of passaging and sometimes we keep in communication with other boats to check on the weather ahead or behind.

But even in the right sailing seasons you can experience challenging weather. You can prepare yourself and your boat for this. Knowing that in any circumstances there are techniques to help you cope with the situation will help allay your fears. You will need to have your sails reefed (reduced sail area) ready to use if needed, as well as any equipment to slow your boat, prepared and at the ready. There are some excellent books, videos and DVDs on storm tactics (*see* Appendix A for resources on how to handle your boat in a storm), as well as seminars you can attend at boat shows and elsewhere.

However even the most experienced of us get caught out by unexpected weather changes which can cause consternation. Beth Cooper and husband Norm were sailing from New Zealand to the Cook Islands in 2013, on their way home to Vancouver, taking the recommended Jimmy Cornell route, approximately west along latitude thirty-five, when a weather system they had been watching came their way and finally arrived. Although their weather router, Bob McDavitt, had also been watching this system, sometimes you just do not know what course a weather system will take. As Beth says, "When you are out crossing oceans for two weeks or more at a time it is almost impossible to accurately forecast that far ahead. So you just have to try to deal with the systems that cross your path. In this particular situation the winds increased to over forty knots. We had reduced sail and were prepared for it but I found I was still anxious when it arrived. I was pretty good at handling the boat on my own in most situations but when the rain battered us with squalls, it still scared me."

I think we women tend to have very high expectations of ourselves which at times are impossible to achieve. Seeing waves whipped into a frenzy by the wind and witnessing the power of Nature is awe inspiring and scary. Your strength is in knowing your boat is strong, well built and well prepared, and like most things, bad weather will pass.

There are times however, when we need to regain our equilibrium and take a rest, and for Beth it was one of those times, as she handed over the watch to Norm who was keen to take over. As she says, "Maybe that is the answer, not to beat myself up for missing one watch in three years! For the most part, she says, I did very well crossing oceans and racking up 25,000 nautical miles." So often we do not give ourselves credit for doing well, Beth did not panic, but was justifiably anxious and did the best thing in the circumstances. After her rest Beth was refreshed enough to then take over watch from Norm. Personally, I find the hardest things to endure in bad weather are not only discomfort and tiredness, but the effects of the loud noises of the wind and sea, which can be unnerving. I have found wearing earplugs helps reduce the sounds which thereby reduces my anxiety.

My Friwi and I encountered such strong winds south of Tonga that we simply could not make headway so we decided to heave-to, or fix the boat's sails and secure the helm in order to slow the boat's forward motion. When you decide to heave-to, you will notice a comparative reduction in noise as well as a calmer motion. I found this pleasantly surprising, more of a gentle up up up followed by a long down with the odd slap from a breaking wave. We kept twenty-four-hour watch and were quite comfortable for two days (*see* Appendix A for information on heaving-to).

Some people are afraid when they cannot see land and find this very stressful, however, in almost all instances in heavy weather or storm conditions the safest place when sailing is out at sea, as far away from land as possible. The real danger can be the land!

Going Up on a Coral Reef

Meridian of Sydney on a reef in Papua New Guinea

Judy Rodenhuis and husband Paul were motoring towards the lagoon at Panasia Island when suddenly the weather changed. Judy explains what happened and how they coped. "It was as if a gray curtain had come down and totally obscured the entrance. I was doing lookout on the bow and suddenly could not see a thing. Then we struck a coral head. I shall never forget that noise. Paul immediately full throttled in reverse, but we did not move.

We knew this was serious. Although there were other sailboats in the anchorage this was a very remote part of the Louisiade islands, Papua New Guinea, and Meridian of Sydney weighs over twenty tons. As the squall hit we heeled more to starboard, then we heeled right over as the coral beneath dislodged. Waves picked us up and washed us across the channel onto the reef. We lay at an angle of forty-five degrees with waves smashing onto the port hull. The noise was deafening but we were not holed.

She is a strong steel boat. We were not injured. We were not going to die. We were insured. We saw dinghies coming towards us and quickly collected our personal papers and clothes and headed ashore. Next day with the help of crews from other sailboats and many islanders who had also come to assist we used anchors to kedge Meridian across the reef, about five meters a day, into the deeper waters of the lagoon.

For the next three days we worked with fellow cruisers and locals to inch her towards deep water of the lagoon. It was celebration time when we finally got her there. This was a remarkable example of team work between cruisers and islanders. Once there we had to make repairs to the steering rudder, autopilot and running rigging so she was sailable. The relief was immense. After drying Meridian out and doing a few further repairs we sailed her back to Cairns. When all repairs were completed she was actually better than ever and we enjoyed sailing on her even more, knowing she could withstand the toughest treatment. It is important to be able to trust your boat."

On thinking back over this event Judy has some advice for other sailors, "When things go wrong on a boat they usually go wrong quickly. Sheer terror can overwhelm you but we have found it best to assess the problem before trying to fix it. This usually helps calm you, and talking through what needs to be done is a positive that puts the situation into perspective."

Fears Overcome

We have heard from some of our Blue Water Women about how they coped with calamities that we all fear. These women have enjoyed many years of happy sailing both before and since these misfortunes. These incidences are rare. Chances are they may never happen to you, but like them, if you do encounter problems of this magnitude, you too will cope.

Don't worry, be happy. "Nothing good or bad lasts for ever," as my Friwi said to me when I first started sailing. Learn as much as you can about methods of coping with your fears because this will put them in perspective; prepare your boat well, talk to people whose advice you trust, gather as much information as you can on the weather and your chosen route. Then relax, knowing you have done all you can to ensure a safe voyage and enjoy your wonderful new experiences. The time has come to change **F**alse **E**xpectations **A**ppearing **R**eal to start **F**eeling **E**xcited **A**nd **R**aring-to-Go!

Remember, when you sail through bad weather or are overcoming other obstacles and are feeling tired and maybe a bit scared, there is also a sense of elation and achievement when you come through it and find the sun still shines and the world sparkles anew!

Piracy or Not?

We were admiring the shape of the colourful large fishing boats when sailing in Indonesia near the Komodo Islands. They look like something out of a story book about pirate galleons with their extreme sheer giving them an extraordinarily high bow, looking way out of proportion with the rest of the boat.

We were well offshore when one of these boats was chasing us. We didn't like the look of her or her crew and so we pushed *Stardancer* to the max, in the opposite direction. Then we both looked at each other with the same thought, perhaps they wanted to give us fish? So we did a 180 degree turn and chased after them across the ocean. I filled a bag with cans and packets of western food which we held out to them on the boat hook when we finally came alongside. Lots of smiles and waves later we were the proud owners of a bucket full of fresh fish and tiger prawns. Often we can make the mistake of pre judging intentions. We can tend to be so worried about our security that we assume the worst which makes us afraid, totally unnecessarily. There are movies and books which exaggerate the idea of piracy to titillate the public. They are fear mongering. I make a point of not seeing movies that dramatize either airplane or boating disasters.

I have always felt safe on our boat, even in waters known to have high incidence of piracy. In the vicinity of the Singapore Strait we heard on maritime radio about what we may term "pirates" being referred to as "robbers." On the day we sailed down and past the waiting cargo ships in Singapore Harbour on our way across to the South China Sea, we heard on the radio reports of the boarding of three cargo ships. We saw cargo ships with rolls of barbed wire around the decks plus dummies dressed in uniform and holding big guns to deter would-be robbers. The robbers know exactly which cargo ships to target, when pay day is, and how much crude oil or other cargo they are carrying. It is big business for them. They are not interested in sailboats, so far.

However there is real danger in the North West Indian Ocean region for maritime traffic, for both cargo and sailboats where people and boats are hijacked. In the last few years, European and American navies have been patrolling in an effort to reduce the scale of the piracy problem. In East Asia, the Philippines pose problems for cruisers. There are two reasons for this. Some Muslims claim territory in the very north of Borneo and say it belongs not to Malaysia but historically to the Philippines. They kidnap people mainly in Borneo for ransom money. The second type is Muslim extremists who raise funds by kidnapping people, sometimes from the marina, mainly in the southern half of the Philippines. These are potentially very dangerous areas. There is a rally which passes north of Borneo every year and it is protected by the Malaysian Maritime Authorities. It pays to check websites for piracy activity prior to planning your route. Noonsite has regular updates on hotspots around the world. Face your fear, find out all you can then focus on enjoying your voyage.

Opportunistic thievery usually happens when you are anchored. The rule for not attracting this is to be prudent about what you leave on the deck, to lock your dinghy securely and lock your boat up when leaving it unattended. Once we thought someone had stolen our dinghy only to have it returned to us by two young local men who had found it about half a mile away. I am embarrassed to admit I had not tied the painter securely to the stern. We used not to have to lock up and could leave our boats open but it has become a sad necessity now because our sailboats carry more "toys." However the incidences of theft are probably far less that you would experience on land. Rather than flaunt your wealth with jewelry and clothing it is wise to dress down according to local customs. You may not consider yourself rich but to many third world countries, anyone who has a boat is wealthy. No matter if you do not own a house or a car and are just scraping by, in relative terms, you are rich. As a further precaution, in some areas we try not to be the only boat anchored in a harbour for more than three or four days.

18

To Carry or Not to Carry?

We are strongly against carrying firearms on our boat. It is not part of our culture. My Friwi was a cop in Paris for many years and had to carry a gun. He also had to know how to use one. Whether at sea or on land it takes regular practice to be able to use a weapon effectively in different situations and assess those situations correctly. There are countless examples of people showing their weapon and being gunned down. This is because they do not have sufficient experience in a wide variety of situations. If you do decide to carry a gun you will find there are screeds of paperwork to be filled out when importing firearms into a country, and you could get a spell in jail if you decide not to fill out the required documents.

Alcohol on Board

Although we do carry alcohol on board, we never let on to customs officials or to locals that we do. We have seen sailors who have invited locals, including officials, on board to have a beer and when the locals get intoxicated and behave badly it can result in a falling out of good relations. Lilly Service says that, "The lack of alcohol in our lives is a major quality factor. We get a great deal of satisfaction in helping others in this area. It is a problem seldom addressed by cruisers but almost every major anchorage we have been in has shown that a not insignificant proportion of the cruising population experiences problems with alcohol and drugs."

For Kaci Cronkhite, "Alcohol, fear, and anger were either the cause or result of every problem encountered aboard." She regrets the time she spent "Slipping into the anchorage-based alcohol culture where drinks before lunch and over-indulging at happy hours became the norm. I want all those wasted hours and squandered memories back."

On the other hand Beverley Evans speaks for many sailors when she says her five pm sundowners are an integral part of her enjoyment on board, a point in the day to look forward to. Sometimes a romantic time too. Mostly sundowner-time is for socialising with other cruisers and making new friends. Many of our happy memories are of socialising on boats and around campfires on shore.

I have noticed that some cultures are more into their alcohol than others. In Tonga we visited each other's boats for afternoon tea, sampling the various ways of cooking with bananas which became something of a fun competition, but no alcohol. It was not until we reached Australia that I became aware of the beer at five pm culture. Whatever happens on land can happen at sea as well, cultural habits do not change much. When being invited onto a French boat for an aperitif we took along some wine and snacks; the hosts were mortified. On their boat, in their country, when you are invited the host provides everything. It makes life interesting when not only do you need to learn about the local customs of the country you are in, but international habits as well!

So far here in Part One we have looked at some of the different ways you can have a life at sea, as well as discussing some of the most common anxieties and have addressed questions commonly asked by would-be Blue Water Women. We have heard what other women have done to make their dream come true, now it is your turn to create your own totally unique dream. It is time to find the right boat for you, in Part Two.

Playing petanque with islanders in Papua New Guinea

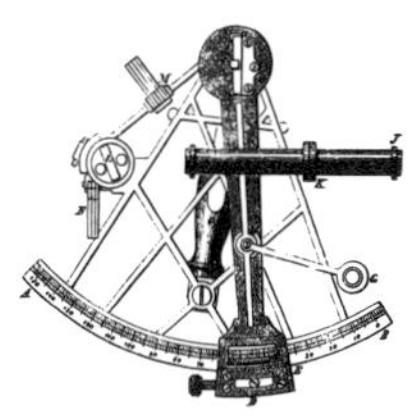

Part 2

You and Your Boat

The goal is not to sail the boat,
but rather to help the boat sail herself.

—John Rousmaniere

You may already have your boat-to-go and simply need some ideas about gear and space allocation, or you may still be thinking about what you would like to buy. This is an all-important decision and it will play a big part in your happiness with your voyage. If you choose the wrong boat, chances are you will end up disappointed in the whole idea of cruising. The focus is on choosing a boat for couples because that covers the majority of cruisers; solo sailors or families sailing will have different space requirements. When you search for your boat you will have to make decisions on the design, a sailboat or a powerboat, the size, the construction, where you will keep her, maintenance requirements, the price and what is included in that price. Perhaps you wish to buy a boat through a chartering company hoping to offset some of the ownership costs? If buying a second-hand boat, you will need to assess if you will be better off with the electronics already on board or buying new? What sail wardrobe do you want? Do you intend to sail mainly in tropical climates or colder ones? There are a hundred and one questions you need to ask yourself because the more clarity you have regarding your needs the more likely you are to have an approximation of what you want. I doubt if anyone ever has everything they want and with boats in particular most things end up being a compromise of sorts. You will be weighing up your wants against performance, space, energy requirements, maintenance and of course finances.

Some of our Blue Water Women saved for many years to buy the right boat for extended cruising. Lisa McVey and her husband initially bought a San Juan twenty-two-foot monohull and began sailing around Lake Mead, the second largest manmade lake in the USA, before deciding they wanted to go cruising for an undetermined length of time. They worked out that if they saved a certain amount each year for ten years, they could sail for three years with all costs covered. There is no rule of thumb to say how much your living costs will be. Some people live frugally others do not. Some use marinas, others do not. Being at sea has had an influence on what foods we buy but generally our lifestyle ends up pretty much the same as it was on land. I have had to be more creative at times when there was no meat available, or no fresh vegetables, but that is part of the fun. We had a large jar for coins by the front door of our house for a few years, with a label that read, “For our forty-foot steely.” A joke really, but it served as a reminder to us to be conservative in our spending and keep the vision of saving for the boat at the forefront of our minds.

Bernadine Reis and her husband had no sailing experience other than reading some sailing books when they decided to go sailing and as Bernadine says, "By fluke I found a 1984 Bruce Roberts steel thirty-six-foot monohull, made in Canada, on the buy and sell internet in Vancouver BC, showed the ad to my husband and next thing we knew we met the owners at a coffee shop and gave a non-refundable $5000 check." It had been sailed by the previous owners to Langkawi where they had to sell her due to ill health. "We flew to Langkawi, saw the boat on the hardstand and after starting the engine we wired the remaining $10,000. It was that easy."

They figured that "If the worst came to the worst we would have a holiday and learn to sail as we knew nothing about offshore sailing." The only mechanical problem they encountered was with the engine in Singapore which meant they could not continue with the rally they were on. Plus learning on the job meant "we tangled a foresail in a squall, lost anchor in the middle of the night in bad weather close to a rocky shore, had an encounter with an unlit barge and strayed into the middle of a shipping lane at night." Normally one would hope to prevent such adventures by learning about navigation symbols and lights, and practising anchoring in safe areas before undertaking such a demanding trip through one of the world's busiest shipping areas. You will likely focus your research efforts on boats that match your budget, but it is worth also looking in the next bracket up because there are often people desperate to sell who will take offers.

19

Making Comparisons

Regarding size, big is not necessarily better. Swiss friends of ours built their thirty-two-foot double ended cutter *Sostene* to sail on a lake and ended up bringing up two children and crossing oceans on her for more than twenty years. They loved their boat, they knew her very well and felt comfortable on her, so no need for change. Lin Pardey has sailed for over fifty years and her boats were all under thirty-foot. Over the decades boats have become bigger and contain more features, mostly technologically driven. You will make the choice of either a monohull or a multihull. Both have their pros and cons. We dreamed of owning a forty-foot steel monohull boat-to-go for several years until we found the right one for us. Then in the tropics we sold our original boat and bought a forty-seven-foot boat which seemed enormous compared to our previous one but the other day in a marina I pointed out to my Friwi that we were easily the smallest boat there. Personally I would not want a bigger boat because I need to be able to manage her on my own if need be. Plus the bigger the boat the more equipment and maintenance she requires, plus more haul out costs and more marina fees. Possibly more power needs and equipment replacement costs also.

We have noticed a spectacular increase in catamaran numbers over the last decade as people become more affluent. There is a common perception that sailing flatter is more comfortable than sailing in a monohull. The lighter you keep your boat the faster she will sail. Often we see catamarans with their bridge too close to the water because they are overloaded, and waves then bang under the boat. This can cause stress related construction problems because catamarans are designed to carry only up to a certain weight limit. Catamarans can sail faster than a monohull as well as having more living area, however newer monohull designs with wider beams are providing more comfortable living space than previously. We have also noticed an increase in power boats, both monohull and twin hull, in this part of the world because during the sailing season there is usually either too much wind, or not enough, and it is usually the latter. Talking to many sailors it seems that an average of around seventy to eighty percent of time is spent at anchor, so the boat has to work well as a living space and also sail well. If you have limited time, your percentage of time at anchor will be less than that and may affect your boat choice. Factors of cost, design, size, age, equipment and most importantly, the quality of prior maintenance and future upkeep, must all be weighed against each other before making your final choice.

There are thousands of boats to choose from so how do you make an educated choice? Where in the world do you buy? There are boats everywhere. First, it makes sense to look close to home. At the same time, do research globally to make comparisons of price. There are destinations in the world which are at the end of cruising routes where sailors have arrived and decided not to sail farther. Perhaps they do not want to sail home against the wind, or perhaps there are disputes on board, or else they simply decided crossing oceans is not for them and they have had enough. Among many others the major areas for boat sales would be Phuket in Thailand, Langkawi in Malaysia, Mexico and the Caribbean as well as destinations for second hand charter boats around the world. To a certain extent in times of economic recession most places in the world offer opportunities to make good boat purchases.

Now that most boats are available for sale on line, you can buy a boat anywhere in the world. Along with which destinations you wish to sail to, currency exchange rates could be another factor that influences where you buy your boat. It is worth taking the time to thoroughly research the market, look at differently designed boats, go on board as many different boats as you are able and then make the choice of a boat that best suits the majority of your needs (*see* Appendix A for some of the larger on line boat sales sites).

Is Your Boat Fit for Purpose?

The perfect boat does not exist; it will always be a compromise. We have to find the best compromise possible, bearing in mind the buying cost, the preparation for your project and ongoing maintenance costs.

You need to ask yourself questions to ensure your boat choice is fit for purpose. Will you be sailing in mainly cooler climates or in warmer ones? This will very much determine what sort of boat you buy. Will your boat be just for you, for two of you, your kids too, or guests from time to time? Will you use her for chartering? Is your boat for short term cruising or for several years? What proportion of your sailing funds are you willing to put into her? You need to be crystal clear about your requirements for your project.

20

Our Boat Buying Experience

Initially we preferred to buy a cheaper boat and keep a higher percentage of investments on shore. We had been planning for three or four years to go blue water sailing, not necessarily around the world, but to make it our lifestyle. We looked for our boat-to-go for three years, during which time we did the necessary preparations. For me this meant learning as much as I could from books, sailing school courses, taking radio and navigation courses, crewing on friend's boats, practising on our own twenty-one-foot Tucker sloop, plus window shopping in marinas most weekends and learning about different boat designs suitable for cruising. We visited boat shows, sailboat brokers, sailboat sales websites and answered ads in newspapers. We looked on line and studied boats across the world then went on board as many different boats as we could when kind sailors at our sailboat club offered us the opportunity. We sailed on as many diverse boats as possible. We looked at hundreds of boats of all shapes and sizes and I learned, bit by bit, what we needed for our own boat.

We were looking for a second-hand boat within our low budget price range, one which had been well maintained and hopefully had any major problems ironed out. All boats need to be sailed for a while to ascertain their weak spots. It may be better to buy a second-hand boat that has been tried and tested and well maintained over the years than buy a new one whose construction faults, if any, show up in the first few years of use. Buying a preowned boat is no guarantee that everything works, but neither does buying a new boat mean there will be no problems.

As we walked along marina pontoons I would see a boat I liked the look of and would discuss it with my Friwi. Our conversations went something like this, "Oh I do like the look of that one," pointing to a sixty-foot monohull. I knew enough that we could not afford a catamaran! To which my Friwi would reply, "Out of the question, firstly too big, costs too much, and look at all that woodwork. Imagine the maintenance!" There was always a negative response from him until I learned to see things through his eyes. No teak on the deck was preferable, because in the tropics teak is very hot to stand on, it wears quickly and is expensive to replace. I still like teak decks! No, he did not like the rigging on that one, for reasons he explained to me. Yes, that was a great hull shape. No, the sail area on that one is not enough for the design of the boat, etc.

And so it continued for three years until we found *Caesura*. A 'caesura' is a pause in a line of poetry which is an integral part of the overall rhythm. She was a boat simple enough that I could sail her on my own if there were an emergency, and my Friwi were incapacitated. This is a very important factor and something to keep in the forefront of your mind when making your choice. However, good as she was, she was still a compromise in some ways; I was disappointed she had such a tiny cockpit but delighted she had good rigging and a roomy master cabin, but then all boats are something of a compromise.

Before we signed on the dotted line we employed an independent marine surveyor, not one associated with the brokers, to extensively check the boat inside and out for problems, including the hull and keel. As we went around with him I learned a lot about the boat and her structure. Luckily there were no nasty surprises. However, friends of ours bought a fiberglass (known as glass-reinforced plastic, or GRP) boat and had it checked without taking it out of the water. When they did haul her out after a year, they found a lot of osmosis and blisters in their GRP hull (*see* Appendix A for info on GRP blisters) which will take considerable time and money to treat. It is essential that you take the boat out for a test sail, not just a spin around the bay, but for several hours on a windy day so you can test the sail wardrobe and rigging and not just the engine. Or you could get to know your boat over time; you may consider buying a new boat to be managed by a charter company which may bring you in a small income, and after a few years the boat can be fully yours. Note, by then these will be much used boats that may possibly have had heavy wear (*see* Appendix A for details).

Our steel forty-foot sloop was a Bob Stewart design, a functional, fairly narrow boat, built in 1982. She had a round bilge design, full length keel and a deep hull, which gave her a good steady motion in rough seas, but she did not like to go to windward very much. She was a heavy girl, so needed a fair amount of sail to push her along but luckily her mast was tall enough to give a large sail area.

Caesura was divided into several compartments; V-berth, head, saloon (sitting room, lounge), galley, pilothouse, a very small cockpit, and a separate, large queen size master cabin which meant we could keep each part of the boat warm. We even had a beautiful Scandinavian diesel heater in the saloon because *Caesura* was built for colder climates. However, as much as we loved her, no boat is going to be perfect. Be prepared to spend time and money on fixing a few things on your boat and customizing it to make it your home. We lived on *Caesura* for a year before we set sail to learn what changes we needed to make. We enlarged the saloon because we wanted to seat six people around the table comfortably. This was at the expense of the head (toilet) and shower area. You will find the saloon is the socializing hub of a boat unless you are in the tropics when your cockpit becomes the entertaining center. We took space out of the V-berth to make a decent head and shower area so my Friwi did not bang his elbows when showering and then remodelled the V-berth area which became our storage area. These improvements created more comfort and gave us more pleasure, which enabled us to really enjoy living on this boat for ten years. Your boat will be your sanctuary so it is important you create a comfortable living space to enjoy being on her.

Caesura also had several dorades which are necessary for fresh air flow when your boat is closed up against bad weather or left unattended. Navigating across oceans was great because the pilothouse had almost 360 degree visibility and a large comfortable leather chair for watches (More on watch keeping in book section Before You Set Sail). We rarely had to go outside but stayed inside, snug and dry. She was just right for the two of us at that time. She was a sturdy girl, strongly built and well designed so I never felt afraid in rough weather. I trusted my boat. It is essential that you feel the same kind of trust with your choice.

My Musts for Caesura

There are fixed determinants for making your choice of boat in purely pragmatic terms, but then there are also emotions associated with your choice which need to be taken into consideration. However, do not be sucked in by fancy trappings and veneers. The boat is not the furnishings, nor the amenities. You can add those later if you wish. You are looking for a pleasing but serviceable design that suits your needs. Pragmatically, here is an overview of the things I looked for, my musts, and for me the most important must, the design must meet the majority of my requirements for the purpose of our project. She must sail well. She must have a logical interior design, i.e. I do not want to traipse through the saloon and galley to get to the head in my wet weather trousers. The head needs to be close to the companionway. This does not seem to bother men as much! I need plenty of accessible space for stowage. And she must be well constructed.

21

Main Construction Types

The construction can be of wood, ferrocement, steel, aluminum, fiberglass or part sandwich balsa or sandwich foam with fiberglass. Each of these has strengths and weaknesses. A timber boat is often more pleasing to the eye and fits with the traditional image of sailboats of olden times, but they can require a lot of maintenance.

Ferrocement boats were popular in the 1960s and 1970s when people thought it was a cheap way to go sailing, however the hull and deck were the only cheaper parts which are the smallest part of the overall costs anyway, so they were not saving much. Some were excellently built and fared, but most were built by amateurs in their backyards and many were not particularly well built at all.

I do not want to find water anywhere in the boat where it should not be. She *must* be dry. *Caesura* was of steel construction, strongly built with the steel well protected and maintained. A well-built steel boat, very well insulated should be a very dry boat. Keeping on top of any rust spots takes vigilance and regular maintenance. Not as many steel boats are being made these days due to the advances in aluminum design and construction.

Aluminum boats are expensive. Aluminum is lighter than steel, but still strong, therefore more performant. Boat grade aluminum is expensive to begin with, more expensive than steel, and building costs are more than for steel because of the particular welding process required for aluminum. These boats do not need to be painted because the aluminum creates its own oxide layer to protect its surface, however owners often like to paint them which requires special preparation and dedicated paints. Similar to steel boats, aluminum boats need special attention when creating their electrical circuit installations to eliminate the possibility of stray current problems and electrolysis.

The attractions of fiberglass in boat construction are many. Hundreds of identical boats can be made from a single mold, thus reducing costs. These are often called "Production" boats. Fiberglass boats can be constructed from plain fiberglass or made of fiberglassed foam or balsa sandwich construction. Compared to steel construction for example, fiberglass can be a lot lighter but still strong. Fiberglass does not take a lot of maintenance. The majority of boats these days are made of fiberglass, built by small to large production boat building companies.

My boat *must* sail well, meaning that she can sail reasonably well upwind and averages a good speed for her water length on all points of sail. On *Caesura* our sail wardrobe consisted of two mainsails with three reefs each, trysail, genoa, storm jib, an asymmetrical spinnaker, and one inner stay jib, which allowed us to sail in any type of weather.

When necessary I want to be able to move around the deck easily with strong lifelines and strategically placed grab rails to stay safe when heeling. The same goes for below deck. She must be safe and perform well when sailing, but agreeable to live aboard when anchored.

And she *must* be aesthetically pleasing to the eye. I want to be proud of her. That's my emotional *must*.

22

Changing Needs

However, when we decided to spend more time in hot climates we found *Caesura* no longer answered our changing needs. Two things conspired to make us decide to sell her. There was little through flow of air because of the very thing we admired in her initially, i.e. the compartmentalization. She lacked sufficient cross wind ventilation, so she became a very hot boat to be on at times. I was going through menopause and would have preferred to be sitting in a fridge all day! Also we wanted to be able to have friends and family come to visit which meant we needed more accommodation. Because we did fewer long passages and could spend more time outside I came to resent the pilot house taking up so much unused space as well as having such a small cockpit. So, the hunt for another boat was on.

But first we had to sell *Caesura*. I learned another lesson. There are some boats, like cars, that hold their price, are always popular and easier to sell than a "characterful" steel boat when all around you are moving into fiberglass. So when you buy, think about how well she may sell in the future if the market is still in the same over supply position as it is currently. We sold *Caesura* fairly quickly as she was well presented and reasonably priced. We did not want her to become one of those sad vessels one sees in boat yards or marinas, rusting away, canvas work fading and varnish peeling because the owners were unrealistic in their asking price. I particularly recall one couple coming on board when we were selling her. The guy was in raptures over her, she had everything and more in good condition that you could want in a first-time cruising boat; safe, efficient and speedy, but his partner did not even want to come on board. The guy came again the next day, check book in hand and this time they both came on board. The partner walked through once and then she abruptly left. It seems she wanted a "white boat like in the advertisements." I hope his wallet could match her expectations. We still feel sentimental when we talk about *Caesura* because we put so much of ourselves into her, so it was a very sad farewell.

We knew what we wanted in our boat for tropical waters. In fact we had met *Stardancer* several years before in Papua New Guinea, but she was based in Australia, which meant flying over there to check her out first and then sailing her back through Indonesia to Langkawi, about 5000 nautical miles. *Stardancer*, is a 1994 forty-seven-foot Gib'Sea monohull built of fiberglass, designed by Joubert/Nivelet, now owned by Dufour, France, and is very different from *Caesura*. She has a large cockpit and because she is beamy there is more room below deck. As a lighter displacement boat she handles very differently too, the slightest breeze sends her skittering across the water. She has a fin keel with bulbs on either side at the base for additional stability. So, no more going up on sandbanks! She has many hatches therefore great air flow. The saloon and galley are large and airy and very enjoyable, which is especially appreciated at anchor in bad weather. Sometimes a large interior space can be dangerous in rough seas because of insufficient places to hold onto, but we have very good grab rails everywhere, which is an important safety feature.

SV *Stardancer* under sail

We have a cabin each which I just adore; I can sleep or read when I want without disturbing anyone. I can decorate it in a feminine way. It is a favorite place to be. Also it is easier to make up the bunk now I have a fitted inner sprung mattress. Under the bed is a large storage area. Things get lost in there for years! Mostly because the mattress is heavy to take off and on, so only long-term storage items go there. We can have guests visit and cruise with us for a while, now we have four cabins. In the meantime though the guest cabins seem to have acquired the status of overflow storage!

On *Caesura* our mainsail lowered into lazy jacks and for reefing we had to go on deck which was no hardship except for the occasional getting soaked. *Stardancer* is lighter and easier for me to handle and she sails beautifully. In following winds we tend to use only the large genoa or genoa and mainsail. All the halyards and sheets come back to under our hard dodger. We do everything from the cockpit; furling the jibs and mainsail (which furls into the mast) on four self-tailing winches and many clam cleats. When using the winches I stand on the top companionway step so I can bend over the winch, which because I am not tall, gives me more power to the elbow. The only things we go forward for are to hoist the asymmetrical spinnaker and use the anchor winch.

Our hard dodger is not the most aesthetically pleasing design but it is very practical. There is plenty of space to hang wet weather gear to dry. In wet weather we have had "clears" made (high grade plastic windows zipped onto the canvas of the cockpit covers) to enclose the cockpit. As Judy Rodenhuis advises, "Have a good safe cockpit dodger with secure clears. It's an extra room on board, protects from wind, rain, cold and sun and makes night watches more comfortable." Gwen Hamlin describes the dodger on her boat, "Our dodger and side windows all rolled up in sections for ventilation and down for protection. Then we had sectional side awnings that rolled up outside the enclosure and rolled down to snap to our lifelines. It made our cockpit a great living space, where we could see in all directions, but be cool or protected as the situation called for. It was a huge asset! One of the best things we did." I endorse Gwen's sentiments; our cockpit space on *Stardancer* is now my most favorite spot in all weathers.

Stardancer ticks most of the boxes for me, so I am happy to cruise longer now. Naturally there are drawbacks in any twenty-plus years old boat. Trying to understand the electrical wiring added by previous owners still has us scratching our heads!

23

Interiors

Berths

When under way you will likely need a convenient pilot berth. Pilot berths are a single bunk designed to keep you secure when you are passagemaking. In some boats there already is a dedicated pilot berth with deep sides close to the companion way, but our boat did not have one. We have made ours using the seating squabs on the hull side of the dining table in the center of the boat, where there is less motion. The idea is to wedge you in so you will not fall out in rough weather, so the lee cloth must be deep to hold you in like a sling but wide enough for you to turn over. It is surprisingly comfortable. You will only need one because your partner will be on watch, then you will swap places. Check that the bunks on board are comfortable and will suit you in width and length, also not so close to the deck above that you bang your head when you sit up.

Boats these days are built with large queen size beds in the master cabin that you can walk around for ease of making. These may be fine at anchor, but are not so safe in rolly seas when you need to block yourself in. A popular design is to have quarter berths with the master cabin in either the V-berth up forward or in center cockpit boats, at the stern.

Sufficient Stowage or, Where to Put the Piano?

When you are looking over various boats think about where you are going to put your things. You may need to provision for several weeks or months; where will you stow it all? Where do you place your wet weather gear? Are there hooks in a handy spot near the engine for drying them? Will the kayak fit on deck? Where do you put the guitar, the fold up bikes? Or if you are Mary Anne Unrau, it is a case of where to put her piano. She and her husband designed their custom made Waterline steel cutter *Traversay III* in 2000 where she enjoys a full size piano in its own piano room.

On *Caesura* my Friwi screwed his guitar case onto the hull lining and kept his guitar safely there in all weathers, but we cannot just screw things onto the hull on *Stardancer* and I have noticed the guitar case gets moved around a lot, usually ending up in a spare cabin. We seem to have more tools and spares than ever before on *Stardancer*. They are in tool boxes and bags but they take up a lot of space. Where will you put your tools? Do the lockers open easily, are they readily accessible? With a little ingenuity you can find ways of considerably increasing stowage space. Screwed onto the wall in my head, I have a large good quality plastic shoe holder, about five feet high by fourteen inches wide with five layers of pockets. Our everyday medicines are kept here with labels clearly stating what is in each pocket. On *Caesura* we set sail with the hold (under the sole or floor of the boat) full of books. I have heard some people keep their wine there for ballast. However now that we carry more water there is less stowage space under the sole, and we have given most of our books away and now read digitally. By now you will be getting the idea that if you put more of one thing somewhere you will have less space somewhere else. It is a matter of priorities and compromises, and always, the functioning of the boat comes first.

On most boats there are many little spots where you can secrete things or add your own storage. Perhaps you can add a shelf here or there, add hooks or nets for extra space. I have nets in my cabin to keep my everyday clothes handy and well aired. Many sailors use nets or hanging baskets to store vegetables and fruit. Knives must be kept in a secure spot so they cannot slide out. I have very large magnets to hold the knife we use most often. We keep an emergency knife by the companionway, accessible to both the cockpit and below deck, in case a rope or line needs to be cut in a hurry.

Grit Chiu has good advice regarding securing items on board, "Your actions on board can affect the safety of you, your crew and the boat. Things like winch handles and window covers have been lost overboard because our crew did not put them down in a secure place. Putting equipment away promptly is essential. One day a big wave hit our boat which threw the captain into the galley, practically onto the big knife being used to make lunch. That was a close one!"

Another thing to remember when stowing is to keep the boat balanced with the heaviest things low and in the center of the boat.

Galley Talk

I love my galley, except for one thing. I would prefer to have drawers rather than cupboards because it is sod's law that says the things you want are right at the back where it is very dark. I have three flashlights stationed at the ready in strategic points around the galley, so I can see in the bottom of the fridge and to the back of my cupboards. Diana Neggo says, "As I dislike cooking and want to make it as painless as possible, during our last refit I got our carpenters to convert all the galley cupboards into big drawers. So instead of going down on your knees and scrabbling around in the back of the cupboards everything is readily available." A small reminder, make sure the drawers are designed so they will not slide out when the boat is heeling. One husband I know is a gem, and I am so envious; he has installed lights that come on automatically any time a cupboard door is opened. These seemingly trivial details can grow into mountainous irritations but it can also be a fun challenge to find and implement improvements.

Galleys usually come in two designs. The U-shape surrounds you and may make you feel safer in rough weather. The U-shape galley is normally placed to either port or starboard of the companionway. The other design goes along the hull for the length of the saloon, either port or starboard. My galley is on the starboard side. I get really ratty if people walk up and down behind me when I am cooking, so the galley is off limits when I cook. On *Caesura* I had a big strong webbing "belt" attached to stainless steel hooks in the galley mast pole to tether me in when the boat was heeling twenty-five degrees plus in rough seas, so I could use two hands when cooking. *Stardancer* has the whole back of the banquette seat of the dining table to lean on. On the side facing the galley the partition is waist height, made of solid timber with shelving, so I can balance myself securely against it. If the boat heels much more than twenty-five degrees I will not be cooking anyway! When looking at various boats check that the work benches in the galley are the right height for your comfort. Mine are about three feet high which I find comfortable and I am five feet, four inches in height. Our dining table on the other hand was designed for tall people; I have to sit on two cushions or else my chin is on my plate!

Keeping Cool

I now have a top loading fridge and freezer which seem to keep food colder than front opening ones which can lose more cold air if the door is left open. Also front opening doors may inadvertently swing open and jettison the contents when you are heeling. The downside to top opening fridges is when the one thing you want is at the very bottom of the fridge and you have to dive for it. To clean the fridge I stand on an upturned bucket so I can reach the bottom, just! Fridges and freezers need considerable power to be effective in hot climates. Because of the availability of fresh food on land I only use the freezer on long passages. For many years we used a cooler, esky, ice box, or chilly bin (depending where you are from), which ran on either propane or twelve-volt power. Note that it is not always easy in foreign countries to find a specialist fridge and freezer repair man who will come onto your boat when they need repairing or to be re-gassed.

Because we are spending more time exploring South East Asia we now have a free standing air conditioner for when we have to be in a marina. It looks a bit like R2D2 from Star Wars, and is about three feet high. Many sailors have units that sit in an overhead hatch. Marinas tend to have less air flow than when you are at anchor because you are next to other boats packed in a sheltered area. I used to think of air conditioning as a luxury but it has become a necessity for me to enjoy my time in marinas. Also it helps dry out the interior of the boat which can suffer from the high humidity in tropical areas. Some cruisers go away and leave their air con on which is fine if someone is checking on your boat regularly but we heard of one sailboat having a fire on board due to an electric fault in the air conditioning unit which had gone unnoticed.

Having a UV ray special backing fabric on the saloon curtains makes a big difference to either keeping the space cool against the sun, or warm, keeping warm air in. Just to add to this efficiency I often place quilted aluminum sheets cut to size, against the portholes and windows, under the curtains. You can buy this by the roll and I also place sheets in the fridge which definitely helps improve the insulation. I am now very pleased with my freezer because we have added extra foam insulation inside, meaning food freezes quicker and therefore lowers power consumption.

The Stove

Modern boats often have a three ring burner but my stove has a simple two ring gas burner built on top of my oven. It works on propane gas. We carry two small ten lb and one twenty lb gas bottles, (approximately 4.5 kilograms and 9.5 kilograms). We are careful with our use of gas because mid ocean is not the place to run out. Different countries often have their own bottles and fittings so we have made a system to transfer gas from the local bottle to our own bottles. I hardly ever use the oven, mainly because of the unwanted heat and the heavy use of gas but also because I have had limited success with baking cakes. They were well cooked on the bottom where the gas flame and heat come from, but not on top. Given my propensity to put on weight this is probably a good thing after all!

When we are passagemaking it is good to use the gimbals or metal pins on either side of the stove to keep the stove level. This means that even when the boat heels the stove swings to ensure it is kept level for you to cook on. To prevent pots and pans from sliding off the stove top I have removable fiddles which I use often when the boat is heeling. These are like long metal skewers, shaped to hold the pot securely and are screwed down onto the stove top. The word fiddle is also applied to the lip, usually timber, which runs around the edges of tables and bench tops to stop things sliding off. Another way to help stop items sliding is to use generous amounts of plastic webbing (which I buy by the roll and cut to size) to place under rugs, placemats, plates, cups and so on.

Many boats have barbecues on the stern which is an especially good idea when it is too hot to cook in the galley because it can take considerable time for the interior of the boat to cool down. In case of emergencies or cooking onshore for picnics, we also have a small portable one element cooker which uses gas canisters that are readily available in most countries. Laila Kall swears by her small portable oven that works on a burner ring, called a Mini Oven Optimus which she uses to bake bread, cakes and gratinees. It is made by Omnia Kola Mar of Sweden (*see* Appendix A for website).

I have favorite pots to cook with; pressure cooker, stove top whistling kettle, a braising pan with a lid and deep sides, a modern small wok and saucepan with steamer. These mostly fit inside each other for storage. Cups, glasses, bowls and plates should have generous solid bottoms so they do not fall over as easily when the bow wave from a passing boat sends everything on the table rocking. We have real glass wine and champagne glasses which go back into their boxes after use to be stowed. Otherwise, crockery is melamine. From the different countries we have sailed to I have collected some wooden platters and woven baskets for presenting food. Pretty paper napkins are not part of the culture of many countries which is when everyday kitchen paper just has to do. For special occasions I have sewed my own napkins because I love to use the indigenous batik fabric designs of countries we visit so as well as being useful they are also a convenient memento.

Warmth and Water

In cold climates many boats have diesel heating stoves. Some designs can double up as cook top too as well as provide hot water. On *Caesura* our hot water was heated by the engine. At times the water was very, very hot, at others barely lukewarm, but if we timed it right it was just wonderful, especially when it was wet and grey outside! And great for filling hot water bottles on night watch.

There is a joke that goes something like this, “The French have their sex; the English have hot water bottles!” Well I was very pleased to have one or two hot water bottles on cold night watches! These days in most boats a hot water tank is a standard fitting. However, there is no hot water on *Stardancer* because she was equipped for hot climates. If I ever need it I boil the water jug on the stove top. For showers we use the stern shower on the transom. If we want a hot shower we have a refillable shower bag, the kind used by campers, which are simple to hang up and don’t take long to warm up with the sun’s heat on the black plastic. But most of all, at the end of a long day I love shower time on clear nights when I can be at one with Nature under a magnificent canopy of stars. To me this is Bliss!

Filling water tanks on SV *Caesura* in Fiji

We carry plenty of water, 800 liters, and can fill up the five tanks when it rains, via the tubing system we have made descending from the canvas roof of the cockpit. This means we do not use the watermaker. Watermakers certainly can be useful with the drawbacks being only that you cannot use them in foul waters and they must be regularly maintained. However, having the habit of being prudent with water use, we have not needed ours so far. We have freshwater pressure taps to all sinks as well as a foot pump for fresh water (which has a filter attached) in the galley. To make our fresh water go further I make good use of the foot pump for sea water at the galley sink when offshore. I wash dishes in sea water when sailing in clean water areas and rinse them in fresh. Note that if you use some sea water in your cooking water, remember that as water evaporates you may be left with more salt than you want!

For your comfort you can never have too many fans; they are great to move the hot air or the cold air around the boat. We have ten fans on *Stardancer.*

Power on Board

There are many pumps on a boat that need maintenance and spares. As well as the foot pumps we have six electric ones which includes two bilge pumps, toilet pumps (one to flush and one to drain), one electric galley water pump and one to empty the shower sump. This is more than enough to look after. Our boat had been a charter boat with four heads, meaning four shower pumps and more head pumps, but thankfully we do not use them all!

The first thing we did when we came on board was to change all the lights to LED lights inside and outside. They use less power to run and you can choose if you want a clear light for close work or softer for ambience. On our boat I am the "power police" and turn off fans and lights wherever possible to reduce power consumption.

Your choice of power supply will depend largely if you are sailing in windy areas or not, in sunny climates or not. We have a mix of power sources. Whatever power source you choose you have to have a system regulating the charge to the batteries; i.e. a smart regulating system. Solar panels come in a variety of sizes either rigid or flexible, monocrystalline or polycrystalline. New technology is now being used to incorporate flexible solar panels into the laminate of your sails and will ultimately become available to the average sailboatie. So, depending on your energy needs and available space you have a wide variety of power sources to choose from (*see* Appendix A for resources describing choosing and maintaining different power sources).

For sources of power on *Stardancer* we have three solar panels, (giving 660 watts), a wind generator, the engine and also a portable generator as back up. We have one battery which is dedicated solely to the starting of the engine and is charged by its own alternator. For domestic use we have three Absorbent Glass Matt (AGM) batteries giving us storage amp capacity of 750 amps in twelve volts (*see* Appendix A for full explanation of AGM batteries). You will need a battery monitor to keep track of the state of your batteries. Our AGMs are charged by their dedicated powerful alternator which is driven by the engine. We can use either the engine to drive alternators to charge the batteries, or the wind generator or solar panels to charge the batteries. We have smart charger systems which are maintained by computerized devices which automatically regulate the charging.

When in a marina we use shore power to charge the batteries and this is a separate system. When on shore power there are two systems for domestic purposes, 120 volts and 240 volts. North America uses 120 volts, South American countries have a mixture of voltage, Canada runs on 120 volts, but most of the rest of the world uses 240 volts. Therefore electrical equipment and appliances on American boats may need devices called inverters to transform 240 volts down to 120 volts otherwise they would burn their 120 volt appliances. Remember to check the grounding if using GFCI plugs when in a marina (*see* Appendix A, re: voltage around the world).

Our high-power output wind generator needs over fifteen knots of wind before it starts to give power, so we can only use it in very windy areas when it can be quite noisy! There are lower power wind generators which require a lot less wind to produce power but the output is not as great. Technology is improving every year and wind generators are much quieter and more efficient than they used to be. There are also transom mounted hydro generators capable of producing large amounts of power with minimal drag. These can be either towed spinner generators or shaft generators which can be lifted out of the water when not in use. Watt & Sea's Cruising Series Hydrogenerators are available in 300W and 600W.

For world cruising you could do like Jimmy Cornell and use a wide range of options; solar, a water turbine as well as a wind generator (*see* Appendix A for contact details for providers Eclectic Energy.com and Semarine.com).

When we have guests on board there is often a queue for charging laptops, iPads, MP3s, cameras and iPhones, all electronic items we used not to have twenty or so years ago. Because of this phenomenon, sailors now spend considerable time and money improving the power capacity of their boats. There is of course a cause and effect because for every electronic item you put on your boat you will need more power. Because everyone's needs are different you will have to work out for yourself how much effort and money you are willing to invest in using electronic items and maintaining their power source.

24

Exterior of Your Boat

On Deck

Sails and Rigging

While you are on your test sail check the state of the sails; have they been stretched out of shape? Check that the fabric is not too thin, also that the sails fit properly. Most boats carry a mainsail, which can be furled either in the mast or in the boom or fully battened or partly battened and dropped into lazy jacks. Cruising sailboats today mostly carry a furling genoa or jib and can also carry an asymmetrical or cruising spinnaker. An inner stay is often used to carry a smaller jib for stronger winds.

Check not only the state of the running rigging (rigging to hoist and control the sails) including their sheaves at the top of the mast for wear, but all the deck fittings. Deck fittings including hatches, portholes and windows sometimes create water leaks inside the boat and can cause damage to the fiberglass, electric wiring, electronics or wood, so these all need to be carefully checked. Leaks can also occur through the bonding between hull and deck. Take your time and look for tell-tale water marks. A teak deck on fiberglass looks lovely but check how worn it is, because replacing a teak deck can be expensive.

Where size can matter is with the winches: oversize winches can make life easier by reducing the effort required. Men tend to have more upper body strength but this can be an issue for women. Another way to reduce effort is to position yourself above the winch so you get more leverage.

Windlass

Today a windlass (capstan or anchor winch) is usually electric rather than manual. When buying an electric anchor winch it is better to buy one which is more powerful than specified because they get heavy use from cruisers who use them a lot more than weekend sailors. Blue water cruisers often carry heavier chain and anchors because they sometimes have no choice but to anchor in deep waters. The grade and diameter of the chain is as important as the state and type of anchor. Cruising boats often have up to four anchors with their rodes (anchor lines) for use in heavy weather. There are innumerable discussions on the best type of ground tackle for different conditions. Asking other sailors about their experiences will help you make up your own mind what is suitable for the places you intend to visit, also bearing in mind the size, design and weight of your own boat.

Life Raft

Your life raft is either secured in its valise in a cradle on deck or in a specially designed niche on the stern or can be stored handily at the stern of the boat. The life raft inflates automatically as the painter cord is tugged when you throw it overboard. Check the age, type and the last time it has been professionally checked because they need to be checked regularly. There should be documentation available from the last check detailing the number of people it should hold plus the emergency contents. A large life raft is not necessarily a good thing if there are just the two of you because unless you have sufficient weight you could be more easily overturned by a big wave.

Life rafts come with varying amounts of rescue and safety gear depending on price and category (either coastal or offshore). Before the life raft is professionally packed you may be able to add items to the basics that come with it. To grab in case of emergencies on ocean crossings we also keep a large round waterproof container that will float with all of the following contents inside: small life raft repair kit, small compass, hand held fully charged VHF radio, small scale copy of chart of our passage in plastic sealed bag, personal EPIRB, energy foods, thermal sheets, fish hooks and line, flares, flashlights, mirror, sunscreen, basic first aid kit, small games, camping cutlery set, pencils and paper in sealed bag, Leatherman knife and a small hand operated watermaker. We also take two ten-liter water containers three quarter filled with fresh water, attached to each other so they float. I also keep a grab bag of extra food supplies in a pillow case handy in case of an emergency. Some sailors take a lot more in their raft and bag, some considerably less (*see* Appendix A for more information on life rafts and grab bags).

Dinghy

On *Caesura* we kept the dinghy, an aluminum Tinnie, well secured on the foredeck. I could just see over the top of it when helming. Some sailors prefer fiberglass dinghies that row well, others have inflatable dinghies or dinghies that split in half with one half fitting snugly into the other to take up less room. Now on *Stardancer* we have davits on the stern from which to hang the dinghy (an inflatable with aluminum hull) and we lower it into the water using block and tackle. This is far more convenient. It is important for your independence that you learn to handle the dinghy because you will be using it a lot to get to shore from your anchorage. You need to learn how to start the outboard motor, fill the fuel tank, steer her and tie her up safely. We still forget to replace the bung at times thereby quickly creating a mini swimming pool but when it is raining heavily and the bung is firmly in we can enjoy the luxury of a bath in fresh rainwater.

We missed opportunities to go snorkelling and diving on distant reefs coming through the Pacific because we only had a three horsepower engine, but now we have a more powerful engine we have more fun exploring. Remember to have oars with you in case the engine stops for any reason, plus an anchor on rope to anchor when necessary. You may need dinghy wheels to make it easier to pull the dinghy up on the beach. Diana Neggo says, "My husband is becoming increasingly incapacitated and I have to take on more of the physical roles. It means thinking things through carefully and devising means of making things easier for us. … He can't help with dragging the dinghy ashore so we bought the best dinghy wheels we could find to make it easier for me."

Steerage

I recall sitting in the open cockpits of three previous boats I sailed many years ago, gripping the tiller with all my strength in sudden squalls, until after several hours my hands were blue from cold and almost frozen onto the tiller. Not fun hour after hour. Now most boats have a wheel and some of the larger ones sport two wheels. Self-steering mechanisms can be electric or hydraulic. The self-steering windvane is pre-set at an angle to the wind so it follows the wind, not a course. The autopilot works electrically or with a combination of electricity and hydraulics to follow a pre-set compass course. We call our trusty autopilot, Terry, after an airline pilot friend of ours. Terry has certainly made life immeasurably easier for us, giving us time to do other things onboard (*see* Appendix A for more info on autopilots and self-steering windvanes).

Handy Technology

Do not worry if your boat to buy does not have a chartplotter, bow thrusters, radar or sailing wind instruments, etc. Nice to have but you do not *need* these things. You can buy these and many more technological aids later. It is easy to be overwhelmed and falsely impressed by the navigational aids on a boat. If you are buying a second-hand boat the chances are the technology on board may be old and out of date and you will have to replace it anyway, so do not get carried away with the inventory of electronic gear. Technology improves so rapidly that devices become out of date very quickly. We still use paper charts in tandem with our electronic software, mainly because I like to do navigation the old way as well, working out our route and position. I find it fun. Also, if anything happened to the electrics it would allow us to continue navigating.

For us on our boats the basic navigation equipment for ocean passages are; the charts of the relevant regions, a good navigation compass, a bearing compass, our old sextant, astronavigation tables, a good pair of binoculars, a depth sounder, an emergency position-indicating radiobeacon (EPIRB), a strong waterproof spotlight, a good VHF radio for short distance communication, a life raft and life vests or harnesses with tethers.

To this basic navigation equipment we add the SSB Radio for long offshore distance communication, and we use a laptop with OpenCPN program and CM93 electronic charts below deck at the navigation station and a smaller notebook computer with Navionics program and charts in the cockpit. It is interesting to note how OpenCPN and Navionics differ at times. In response to recent new legal requirements in some countries we have installed an AIS transponder (which receives the location of other boats and transmits ours). This is interfaced with our navigation computer software. It allows other vessels which also have it, to see our position, speed, name, size and direction, and we can see them and their details on our electronic chart. In fact, people anywhere in the world with internet can follow the progress of a boat if they have the boat's name and AIS identification number. However, in many parts of the world often boats do not have AIS, namely fishing boats of all sizes and tugs that tow enormous barges. There is no substitute for using your eyes (*see* Appendix A for info on AIS systems).

When You Need to Leave Your Boat

There will be times when you either wish to fly back home, or go sightseeing for a few months and need to leave your boat closed up, safe and most probably in a marina. You do not want to be on the other side of the world wondering if you turned off the propane! So to ensure we have not overlooked anything in the closing up the boat process we use a "Shutting up the Boat" checklist on *Stardancer* which you may like to use as a basis for your own, altering to your specific requirements (*see* Appendix B for the "Shutdown Checklist for *Stardancer*").

Keeping Your New Boat Ship Shape

When we bought *Caesura* it was a wonderful surprise to find the previous owner had kept clear records of regular engine maintenance, new electrical wiring, installation of new equipment and haul outs. Although she was ready to set sail having just returned from two years of ocean sailing, we found that we spent a quarter of her cost before we were happy to sail long distance. Be prepared to spend money and time on modifications you may have to make to improve your new acquisition.

Every year or so we haul the boat out, that is, we put the boat up in the boatyard to clean and inspect the hull, change the anodes (sacrificial zinc blocks) and redo the anti-fouling. Hardstand charges normally include hauling the boat out of the water in a cradle and putting her back into the water, plus costs for your hardstand area, power and water consumption. It is recommended to do this annually. This is an example of taking preventative measures to ensure smooth sailing rather than find some unseen issue causing a crisis later on in an awkward situation. However, this part of boat maintenance can be a chaotic time when your home is turned into a workshop and life aboard is disrupted.

Lilly Service's comments on her experiences of being on the hardstand are probably representative of many women's, "Climbing down a steep ladder and walking 100 yards to the community bathroom was certainly different from my spotless convenient bathroom just a few steps from my bed in suburban USA!" For many women, working on the hardstand is their least favorite part of boat work. Several Blue Water Women note that when sailing in countries with cheap labor, they are glad to employ others to do the mucky jobs.

Constant vigilance is needed on a boat. It only takes one small part to wear or come loose to cause a larger and more costly problem. The sea is a very harsh environment. We regularly dive to check if the propeller is clean. It can be covered in marine growths very quickly in warm waters which will negatively affect the performance of your boat. Be gentle when you clean the hull under the waterline so you get the barnacles off but leave the anti-fouling intact. Keeping a good maintenance checklist regarding engine, rigging, electronics, batteries, pumps, seacocks, etc., is very valuable. It allows you to check dates when you last looked at them, and also to think ahead to what may need replacing. For a little bit of extra work it will ensure nothing gets overlooked which is all too easy to do. Keeping a list of spare parts is also a good idea (*see* Appendix C for example of a maintenance checklist).

Keeping things ship shape entails putting things away where they belong, both above deck and below deck, for later quick retrieval and simply keeping surfaces clear of obstacles. So remember the adage "A place for everything, and everything in its place." Polishing surfaces and stainless steel equipment helps protect them against a salty environment. In the galley, wash surfaces with a light chorine solution or with more environmentally friendly vinegar to keep them free of food smells and residue. This will deter ants and even cockroaches that have been known to fly in through the porthole but are usually transmitted as tiny eggs in the folds of cardboard boxes.

Canvas covers can get very dirty from pollution and when it rains long black steaks are visible. It pays to use the best quality canvas you can afford because it will last longer in the sun and be easier to keep clean. I use a dilution of oil of cloves in water to prevent mold from forming and follow Sunbrella's online directions to clean mold in canvas, rinsed with copious amounts of fresh water (*see* Appendix A for details).

We spend a large percentage of our time checking all parts above and below decks and doing small maintenance projects before they become big ones. As Lin Pardey advises, "Inspect every inch of the boat and look for anything that is chafing or fraying and fix it immediately."

Do you remember that old saying, "A stitch in time saves nine?" Although at times I may resent the time and effort involved when I just want to go exploring, I know that maintenance is an essential part of having a strong and safe boat so we can continue to love living on the sea.

Naming Your Boat

Sailors used to believe it was bad luck to change the name of the boat, but these days, people like to put their own stamp on their boat. We had fun searching for a name and coming up with *Caesura*, she was called Adina before and is now Leonora. But we did not feel the same compunction to change *Stardancer's* name, mainly because it is written in huge letters along the first six feet of the port and starboard sides of the hull accompanied by a large starburst design! Beware when choosing a name for your boat that may sound clever in one language but may be misunderstood or even offensive in another. A New Zealand boat we know is named *Morepork*, after a New Zealand native owl, but is not very PC in a Muslim country. Uterus is another name that we have seen, meaning different things in different countries. Mostly though what you are looking for is something that is easy to read with not too much fancy lettering that is hard to decipher, something easy to say and easily understood on the radio by people around the world. And if it can mean something special to you, that is a bonus.

You will have to ask the vendor to deregister the boat before you can register the name and ownership under the flag of your choice. When you buy your boat why not hold a naming ceremony for her? She is going to keep you safe and take you on wonderful adventures. Make her special, she is yours. There are instructions on the internet as to how to purge your boat of its old name from the Ledger of the Deep (*see* Appendix A for websites) before you name your new boat, as well as instructions regarding the ceremony placing your boat with its new name in the care of Poseidon, the god of the sea.

Then make your arrangements for the after-christening party! Celebrate and enjoy the occasion, include your friends and family so they can share some of your own excitement. And don't forget the photos for the album you will make of your adventure.

When you have made that exciting step of choosing your boat and checking she has what you need to carry you safely on the

SV *Caesura* in Hunga, Tonga

voyage of a lifetime, you will then need to think about the practicalities of how your life will function on a boat. You will have to make many decisions regarding communications, banking, mail, health, insurances, visas, and provisioning, as well as your particular ongoing personal needs. All these and more are covered in the next section, Life at Sea.

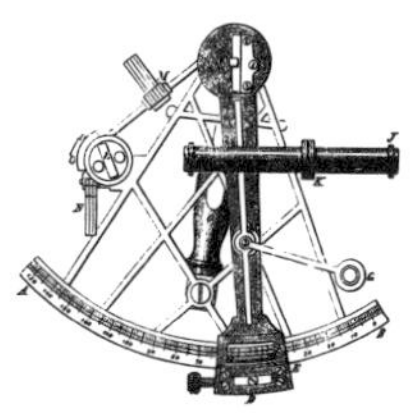

Part 3

Before You Set Sail

Plans are of little importance, but planning is essential

—Sir Winston Churchill

Now you have your boat-to-go and more exciting times ahead. You are planning your voyage and thinking about what you need to do and to take with you. Perhaps there are a few questions lingering; have we got the safety equipment we need, how do I deal with our mail, our banking, what about our health and fitness, our medicines, how do we do watches, how to provision for several weeks? What about the children's schooling? When the day comes to up anchor there will most probably be things you have not managed to do, but we shall look at some of the most important items according to our Blue Water Women.

25

Arranging Your Watch—Keeping Schedule

This can also be called "Standing Watch." This is an anachronism which sounds incorrect because we more often sit, but the words have a long history. For centuries officers in the navy and other shipping have used the ship's bridge to stand and watch to keep look out for designated periods to ensure there was surveillance around the clock. For your safety and that of your boat this is a very important aspect of sailing. I heard of one boat where skipper and crew watched DVDs for the whole four days' crossing, not once going outside to check for traffic. It is very irresponsible to hope that other vessels will see you and avoid you. I was and am shocked. Oceans can be busy, boats can suddenly appear from one moment to the next.

Or you may see hardly any. Sometimes you are crossing a lane which is the quickest route for cargo ships and you will see several ships and then nothing, for miles or days even. Some oceans are busier than others of course which keeps you fully occupied but on some oceans there can be several days without activity. It is essential that you keep a good watch not just for other boats but for obstacles in some parts of the world like unlit disused oil rigs, fishing traps, or possible problems with the sails or a change in the weather. Therefore, you organize your watch system to suit the circumstances. You may go below for a few minutes and set a timer for a thorough 360 degree check above deck. How long you set the timer for will depend on the density of sea traffic, although on *Stardancer* one person is always up on deck.

We are very relaxed about watch times during the day on board *Stardancer*, sharing the watch according to what needs to be done and who needs to sleep. However, at night we keep as close to our agreed time slots as we can, usually four hours about.

My night watch time seems to be between midnight and dawn. Like Penny Whiting, I enjoy the dawn watch the most. I try to hold out for the six hours or so until dawn not only because I want to give my Friwi as long a rest as possible but also because I love this time best. Linda Morgenstern says a good piece of advice she was given when she was double handing offshore for a long passage was to try five- hour watches because REM deep sleep is at four hours plus. This worked fine on her boat for a while, although, she adds, “It can be tough at times to stay awake that long.”

Many sailors work on a two-hour watch system, but it really does not matter how you work out the timings, as long as they are equitable. You need to know when you are off watch that your time is your own. It is not fair for the person doing the cooking to also do full watch duty, but with good communication you can work out a system that suits everyone.

After a long black night to see the rim of the sun warming the world is a wonderful uplifting sight. I love my night watch time: time to enjoy the boat rushing like a bullet through the blackness, to enjoy star gazing or stare at the reflections on the sea on a moonlight night. I like to be on my own and responsible for the sails and tweaking them to see if I can get a quarter of a knot more speed. Invariably though we lose speed on the nights I do watch because I get side-tracked looking at the stars.

We have a pilot berth below for the skipper but if the weather is fine we sleep in the cockpit. This is handy if I need to wake my Friwi when I need a hand or if I need clarification on a possible problem. On my first ever blue water crossing leaving New Zealand, I was like a terrier dog on an adrenaline fuelled high alert, dashing from porthole to porthole every five minutes looking for lights. I mistook stars for lights and watched them seriously until I had worked out they were pretty stationary. I recall I was so keyed up that at breakfast I spilled the whole bag of muesli over the floor. We were picking out sunflower seeds from the carpet for months to come! Subsequently, I got rid of the carpet and will not have a carpet again.

For Mary Anne Unrau standing watch was initially a source of anxiety. She says, "I was afraid I would not be able to carry out my share of the work. It turned out that once we had established the right watch system for us, I had little trouble. I was also afraid that all the lonely times spent outside might make me depressed—that the ocean would seem large and heartless. Instead, I was able to feel a beautiful connection with the ocean, the heavens and multitude of waves, of clouds of stars and of birds." So don't be anxious about it, you will work out what suits you best and I hope, you will enjoy these times of being at one with the world as much as our Blue Water Women do.

26

Arrangements for Communication and Email

If you are offshore for a short time or a long time, the arrangements you make for paying bills, taxes, organizing visas, insurances and paper mail forwarding are different from the arrangements you would make for a coastal trip when you can have regular phone and internet service. Whenever you are more than a few miles offshore you most likely will lose communication with your cell phones and VHF. Most offshore sailing suggests you are going to be in different countries with different customs and regulations and internet providers (We discuss satellite phones and their use further on in this section.). You may opt for using SailMail on board, for which you will need an SSB, a laptop computer and a high frequency modem. Or you may prefer to write your emails and save them to send when you arrive in a port. Most ports of call have cafes or marinas with free Wi-Fi, but this may not happen for a considerable time, perhaps weeks. So how do you cope with your deskwork and keep in touch?

SailMail

Many sailors now use SailMail which is a simple and affordable way to send and receive email worldwide. As well as your laptop and SSB you will need a dedicated SCS Pactor modem. There is an annual fee which covers your membership and network costs. For up to date information *see* www.sailmail.com or if you are a Ham radio user *see* www.winlink.com for a similar service.

Radio Messaging

Amateur radio operators, or Hams as they are called, have access to an excellent network of other operators around the world. You need to have a license which entails classes and examinations to authorise you to operate a dedicated radio. Operators speak to other operators who can pass on messages to your friends or family if arranged with all parties before you set sail. If you need to keep in regular touch with folk and do not mind keeping regular schedules (skeds) with people while you sail, then maybe becoming a ham radio operator would be your best option. Or you can arrange for phone calls via your HF Radio from anywhere in the world but first you need to set up an account with ShipCom.com or your local provider.

You will need to apply for a Maritime Mobile Service Identity (MMSI) number (*see* Appendix A for application information) to wireless.fcc.gov/uls to activate your SSB and VHF for generating an automated mayday transmission that includes your position and MMSI details. When outside of VHF Channel Sixteen range, Channel 2182 kHz on your SSB is the international distress frequency. You will find that there are literally thousands of stations checking this channel ready to act on a distress call. Typically, the SSB is used by sailors for informal information networks (nets) that have regular skeds on an agreed channel where there can be several parties involved, for example participants on a rally. Grab any opportunity you can to be net controller. It may take you out of your comfort zone initially but it is not difficult, listen in to a few first then just follow the logical progression of information. Apart from increasing your confidence, it is a great way to meet other sailors.

We had a critical medical problem with my Friwi in Papua New Guinea, but through radio communication we were able to collect the right antibiotics from other sailors while our nurse friend gave me instructions on how to administer the intravenous injections. Being able to communicate with other sailboats made the difference between life or possible death. Organised skeds are great for sharing information with boats in your vicinity on potential obstacles, weather ahead or coming astern and local scuttlebutt as well as being very helpful when you need advice. However, on board *Stardancer* we prefer not to have any fixed schedules that we may not be able to keep. You may be changing sails, dealing with bad weather or anchoring. Any number of things could come between you and your sked. You cannot risk your boat or safety trying to keep to fixed time frames. As my Friwi frequently reminded me in the first couple of years, the boat isn't a train (*see* Appendix A for information for contacts for radio courses)

27

Arranging Skeds

When we left New Zealand we set up a regular sked with the weather man in Russell so friends and family could phone in to get updates on our progress and allay their fears for our safety. This worked well for the first two days but then we started having problems with transmission, so of course folks back home started worrying when they did not hear from us. The outcome was just the opposite of what we had intended so now we no longer promise to keep contact with friends and family when we are under way. We went sailing to get away from being umbilically tied to the mother country and to simply enjoy the tranquillity and rhythms of a life at sea without the constraints of time keeping, so for us we rely on Skype and Messenger for communication when we have internet availability.

If you are well away from land and are on a collision course with a cargo ship, and wish to communicate that you will take evasive action, your cell phone will be of no use to you. You will use the Very High Frequency (VHF) radio which is good for communicating with other boats and shipping within so called line of sight. Naturally enough the communication distance is affected by obstacles, but also by the height and type of your VHF antenna, and theirs. The higher the antenna, the farther your line of sight.

There is a certain protocol for SSB and VHF communication. You need to know the procedural words and the phonetic alphabet. Something I found handy was to have our boat name written in phonetics (*STARDANCER* = Sierra, Tango, etc.) by the radio with the boat's call sign alongside. This was so I would not stumble or have a memory hole in an emergency.

It is important to follow regulations on keeping certain channels free, for example, not using the VHF Channel Sixteen for chatting. It is the international distress channel and calling channel only. You need to request the party you are calling to go to another channel for chatting. Listen before you speak so you do not talk over another caller. If transmitting on your SSB remember to keep the airways clear on certain channels for three minutes before each hour and half hour. This allows for any emergency traffic to transmit (*see* Appendix A for information on SSB radio).

I highly recommend that in case of emergency, you and your sailing partner *both* take a course in radio communications. You can either call a "panpan" where the situation is not life threatening or a "mayday" if it is. Feeling confident in your radio skills will lessen any fears you may have about what to do in certain emergency situations (*see* the Appendix A for information on courses).

Weather Forecasts

When you are a sailor, changes in the weather and sea state are constantly on your mind. Being aware of the right seasons to sail and updating yourself on the weather ahead are some of the best things you can do for your safety and for your comfort. Compressed digital weather maps (GRIB files) enable you to receive long range marine weather forecasts in detail for up to fifteen days in advance. They have now largely replaced weather faxes. GRIB files can be obtained from several sources now, free once you have paid for and installed the necessary software. A group like Saildocs.com allows you to receive GRIB files daily via HF radio or you can get them daily via internet on a satphone. On *Stardancer* we are not set up for GRIB files. Instead, we use a variety of websites to cross check for marine weather information before we set sail. This is because although local weather conditions can change, generally the overall picture remains similar for each sailing season (*see* Appendix A for weather forecast websites).

Navigation station on SV *Caesura*

28

Safety Items on Your Boat

EPIRB

Your emergency position-indicating radiobeacon (EPIRB) either manually or automatically transmits a coded digital signal via satellites, with information about the vessel in distress. The signal is picked up by the orbiting satellite system giving true global coverage. There can be a delay of up to forty-five minutes depending on where the satellites are making their orbit around the world. This signal will alert your country of registration of the distress situation which dispatches the signal to the organisations in the vicinity of the distress which will assist you. You can also buy individual EPIRBS attached to your life vest as well as hand held options. The automatic life vest version works on contact with water. An EPIRB 406 MHz with built-in GPS may cost a bit more, but it can pinpoint a vessel's position to within 100m. Having an

EPIRB is nowadays considered a safety essential by most sailors and is compulsory in many countries. You will need to register your EPIRB, which you can do online and then need to keep it updated every two years. Remember when selling your boat you need to go back online and list it as SOLD.

Distress Flares

Before you set sail check all your safety gear for currency. Despite the rulings of some countries in not keeping old flares you could be pleased you kept them one day! We hang onto ours, just in case. Keep a pair of strong protective gloves nearby to protect your hands.

In the USA you are required to have a minimum of three standard flares on board. There are different types and all have a use-by date. Regulations vary from country to country. Apart from standard flares there is also the option of a distress flare using bright LED lights with battery life of up to six hours which can be seen up to seven nautical miles away. Read the instructions on the different flares *before* you leave terra firma because in an emergency you would not have the opportunity. Some clubs and organisations such as Coast Guards sometimes have special training days for safely using safety items such as flares, life raft deployment and fire extinguishers.

Life Vests

I believe the quality of our life vests (lifejackets) is important should we ever need them. We each have a high quality easy-to-wear inflatable vest which inflates manually and comes with a whistle and a tether. You can also get life vests that inflate automatically on contact with water with many additional safety features if you prefer (*see* Appendix C for more details).

The length of your tether should be adjusted to suit you and attached to the jack lines that run along the length of the decks. This is to help keep you safe when working on deck in rough weather. Remember to get the jack lines laid out on deck *before* you hit bad weather.

Footwear

I set sail with a new pair of good sea boots but somehow never liked them. I think it was because when the rain or sea water trickled down and found a way inside, my boots stank like a skunk as I was unable to dry them. I wear a pair of strong Keens sandals with the toes covered, so I don't stub them as I move around working on deck. Most countries sell similar shoes under different brand names. As long as your shoes have good grip and soles that do not mark the deck, and you are comfortable in them, you should not need specially bought shoes. My Keens have covered thirteen years of deck work and many, many miles of walking over rough terrain during those years. One sole came off but I glued it back on just fine and I recently had the soles firmly hand stitched on by a cobbler. My Friwi bought his shoes in northern Vietnam for twenty dollars, and I paid almost ten times that amount in Australia! And they seem identical in every respect.

29

Desk Work

Banking

When we left New Zealand and still owned property we organized with our local Council to pay the rates automatically on line. Setting up automatic payments with your bank can save a lot of headaches, but like everything else done through a bank, you need to check your transactions whenever you can, unless you have someone you trust to do this for you. I have a good friend to whom I gave power of attorney over my affairs in case of emergency. As this is a business arrangement, I pay her. This means I feel better about asking her to do many little things that I would hesitate to ask family or friends who would be doing me a favor. For example, one used not to be able to open a deposit account on line, so she did that for me. These days however there is little you cannot do on line with your bank and moving funds overseas.

Most banks have a fraud department that alerts them, and you, to a possible fraudulent action. We use four banks around the world and keeping up with transactions is not easy. It is getting harder to open even simple savings bank accounts in foreign countries now because you need to be domiciled there, but usually your marina will willingly write a letter for you to say that is where you live. It pays to advise your bank where you will be travelling before you set sail so they do not stop your card from working, which happened to us in Papua New Guinea. In fact there was one account I had not checked for a couple of weeks and when we were having breakfast on shore, the fraud department of our bank phoned and asked us if we had made regular withdrawals of so many thousand dollars? They noticed it was not our usual habit! We said no we had not made those withdrawals and after further investigation we lost none of our funds. We were lucky that time.

When we are within internet range I spend considerable time checking exchange rates between countries, checking investments, checking interest rates on bank deposits and checking transactions. There are some debit cards which do not charge as much as other cards at ATMs and it pays to ask your bank about them as these sums can soon add up and give you a horrible shock! Your bank will have reciprocal arrangements with certain other banks in different countries where it will cost you much less to use their ATMs. When leaving a country with strong currency we each take out the maximum allowance to exchange at a money-changer. This is in case there is either a problem with our cards or we lose a credit card. Some countries seem to have more internet hackers than others so having a Pay Pal account can be a good failsafe. There are now several other similar competing organisations which purport to be safe ways of paying bills such as Google Wallet, We Pay, 2 Check Out etc. which are listed on searchenginejournal.com. I have a small book where I write in code the details of our banks and accounts because I trust myself rather than anything on the internet. If you have valuables and important papers and are thinking of taking them on the boat, don't. They are better off in a safety deposit box at the bank. You probably won't need them on the boat anyway.

Tax

I email copies of our financial end-of- year statements to a tax agent we know and trust, for her to put in tax returns on our behalf. If you are not a resident of any country in the world, your tax system will be different, if you have to pay tax at all. Therefore it benefits you to be aware of the rules and regulations which stipulate that if you are out of a country for a certain period of time you are no longer a resident. Note, this can also affect your eligibility for certain pensions.

Snail Mail

These days just about all business, billing, purchases, receipts and so on can be done on line. But there are still countries where the cogs of bureaucracy turn very slowly. France is one of these and all my Friwi's dealings for visas, licenses and pension must be done by formal letter. This poses a problem because by the time it has been forwarded and finally caught up with us it could be months before we get the documents. We have been dealing with a mail forwarding agency which is excellent for this part of the world. We let them know our forward schedule and confirm dates where we stay in a marina for a week or so to receive mail. They know how long mail takes to get to that destination and so forward the mail accordingly. It is quite a costly exercise and now I have managed to get everything we need on line I will be cancelling the arrangement soon, but it has served us well. In many countries Poste Restante and American Express offices work well as a place for you to collect your mail. We had post office boxes in two countries which I have recently cancelled, and now we have one official address care of a friend. The world of bureaucracy was not designed for long term cruisers who continually travel and have no fixed abode. We full time sea gypsies are anomalies.

Insurances

It is not as easy to get travel insurance or health insurance overseas if you are not a national of that country, and even insurances bought in your own country often do not work a certain number of miles off shore. Friends of ours swear by the travel insurance they get with their gold bank card, but on reading the fine print I could see it would not suit our peripatetic sailing lifestyle. It pays to read the fine print! There are global travel insurers which come at a high price, but which some would call, peace of mind. During our travels in South East Asia we have found most hospital services to be surprisingly efficient and of a high standard. We go for full health check-ups each year. We are in and out with all the results the same day. This is our insurance, plus we put aside sufficient savings to pay for a high-quality hospital if we are ever in dire need.

Choosing an insurer for your boat needs careful research. Ask every sailor you come across if they have insurance and who they use and why. We had no insurance for the first five years as we simply could not afford it, but about then marinas started requiring boats to have third party insurance before they could have a berth. Although we prefer not to be in a marina there are times when we are only too pleased to have a respite from bad weather and enjoy marina facilities, so we now have full insurance. This means we need a professional survey every five years. We asked lots of questions of other sailors and did our own research but the clincher for us was hearing about the prompt service of one particular insurer used by friends whose boat went on a reef. Also, some insurers will not insure single handed sailors. Some insurers ask for a minimum of two people to sail the boat, others a minimum of three, which includes the captain. As we never know when an emergency might cause us to sail single handed, it was a big factor in our decision making. Naturally enough coastal cruising can come at a lesser premium than sailing off shore.

We recently did a tour of Thailand on Christian's motorbike and although there is a sort of third party insurance, there are so many disclaimers that it is not worth much. Basically, if you are a foreigner, you must be richer than the other party, therefore you must pay. Simple! Coming from countries where we are choked with care and insurance coverage, it is quite novel to realise that in many countries there really is no accountability held by others (*see* Appendix A for contact information on international insurers).

Driver's License

Before you leave your home country I strongly advise you to get your International Driver's License. One glimpse of this grey card and you are waved on like royalty! We have researched the requirements for having the correct driver's licenses in several countries. They are all different. Also, road rules that look good on paper bear little or no resemblance to what actually happens on the road! A ruling in South East Asia limits the number of people who may ride on a motorbike or scooter at any one time. This law is flagrantly disregarded by all and as many as five people on a bike is a common sight: mother and father, two kids, a baby and sometimes the dog too. My Friwi has just got his motorbike learner's license for a Superbike i.e. unlimited c.c. but he cannot drive internationally for two years. In Vietnam they do not accept this qualification and you have to take their own car and bike license if you are in the country for any length of time. But the International Drivers'

License, car and/or bike, overcomes problems such as this as it is accepted in most countries.

We have not owned a car for fifteen years, and it is a huge relief. I once added up the hours I spent in my car, often frustrated and tired, and it was such a large figure it made me quite depressed! I like to know I do not have the registration fees and fitness check-ups to arrange and pay for. I like to know the car is not sitting in a garage, depreciating and rusting away day by day. Most of all, I like to know I am not adding so much carbon to the atmosphere. When we really need a car, we hire one. Our home country licenses suffice for most countries, but if you stay any length of time it might be necessary for you to sit the license for that country. Although, when hiring a car in some countries we sometimes found it is necessary only to show a passport, without the license even being sighted. If there is an accident it is a simple matter of you paying for damages. If you are the foreigner, you pay. The driving habits of some nationalities are quite scary, with shocking roads that are even scarier which when put together make for stomach churning experiences making sailing look like a walk in the park.

Visas

When making plans to set sail and visit different countries, as well as looking at weather patterns and cyclone seasons you will have to plan how and where to get the required visas and work out how long you will have in that country before you need to renew those visas, if that is possible, or when you have to leave that country and make a visa run. If money is no object you can hire an agent but it is quite a simple operation if you don't mind queuing and sitting and waiting. It is a good idea to write a list of the embassies and contact details you may need in an emergency when overseas, including that of your home country, together with their email and phone contacts (*see* Appendix A for embassy sites).

Jenny Gordon-Jones warns not to take visa requirements lightly. She was sailing in the Black Sea, had just left Romania where visas are available at point of entry but upon entering Ukraine which she had assumed would be the same, she found out they have different regulations. She says, "I found myself without a visa and I was held under armed guard on the sailboat unable to enter. Things became tense so we decided to return to Romania." So do check ahead for visa requirements as they can change rapidly.

In many countries it is a sign of respect to dress conservatively when you are dealing with bureaucracy. We were waiting in a sort of queue at the Thai Consulate for a visa recently when a young man was refused admittance and told to come back the next day wearing neat pants and shirt. Luckily, I was wearing a short-sleeved top together with three quarter length pants and my Friwi had on a shirt and shorts that came to the knee.

Ships Papers

When checking in and out of a country you will need copious copies of boat papers; registration, last port of call, crew list, passports, (remember your passports must have six months use left in them) and insurance for the marinas. It is wise to do a stack of printing before you set sail rather than hoping to find a print shop ashore. Also, if you have a ship's stamp for your boat, use it liberally as this can impress authorities hugely.

Pets on Board

If you have pets on board you will need to follow the rules and regulations of the country you are entering or leaving. Diana Neggo found Motley, her twelve year-old cat, as a kitten in Cairns, Australia. To leave Australia she had to be legally exported and have a battery of shots six months before departure. Anxieties around entering South East Asia were unfounded. Authorities were not interested. If Diana wanted to take Motley back into Australia or New Zealand however, she would have to apply for special permission and Motley would be held in quarantine for a

Motley on board SV *The Doctor*

minimum of ten days, as well as have more immunization shots. So far Diana has been able to find cat sitters on her boat, so Motley has had company but each time it takes a big effort to find someone for the right time frame. For Motley's comfort Diana has made rope scratching posts on the mast and table leg and made a special spot on the boat for Motley's kitty litter. But if your pet is not used to boats or if they need a lot of exercise which is often difficult to obtain, it may be kinder not to take them on board.

Australia and New Zealand have stringent immigration laws for dogs. Anna Fourie crossed the Pacific with their dog, Tommy. She says, "The biggest challenge was getting him into Australia. I had to research extensively the different categories of each country we visited to ensure he didn't go ashore in any countries listed as Category Three and below, as this would result in an extended quarantine period. … This preparation was fairly intense and involved us bringing the Fijian vet and his assistant out to the boat to take blood samples which then had to be sent to AQIS in Australia. The process was lengthy and involved lots of paperwork." Even when they arrived in Australia Anna's dog still had to spend time in quarantine, and be flown to Sydney for this. If your dog is a member of the family you may well wish to take him with you, but months spent in quarantine for your pet together with heaps of paperwork for you plus ongoing costs, are designed to be a strong deterrent.

30

Health Matters; Which Medicines to Take?

Prevention is Better than Cure

If you are sailing to other countries before you set sail you will need to have certain immunization injections. We had booster shots for Hepatitis A, Typhoid, Hepatitis B, Tetanus, Polio, and Diphtheria, plus we bought plenty of mosquito spray containing a high percentage of Deet before we sailed through the Pacific. Deet is a horrible but necessary evil to ward off malaria, especially just on dusk when the risk of mosquito bites is greatest. In many countries, it is advisable to wear long sleeves and long pants if going out in the evening but in certain areas in some countries we prefer to stay on board between sunset and sunrise.

There are tablets to take prior to going into known mosquito infected areas as well as tablets you take when you are in that area and for several days afterwards. We took tablets for a few days before going up a river, deep into the jungle in Borneo to see the orangutans, plus we had mosquito nets over the mattresses in the small wooden *klotok* boat we were on. This journey is one of our most cherished memories. However, tablets taken as a preventative measure cannot be relied upon totally. Our doctor took these tablets more than twenty years ago, caught malaria and still gets relapses.

Dengue fever is escalating rapidly and is now one of the major problems in the tropical world. This is spread through mosquito bites during the day. The zika virus is spreading rapidly too. In countries where packs of dogs are allowed to roam freely it is advisable to have rabies shots. There seems always be some new illness to be aware of, which is why it is important to research internet sites and consult your doctor before you set sail. We keep a couple of comprehensive travel health books plus a simple straight forward first aid manual on board which I have found invaluable (*see* Appendix A for resources).

Before you finally up anchor make sure you have a full health check by your doctor, dentist and optometrist. Take photocopies of your prescriptions, plus as many months' supply as you are allowed. In my home country I can only take three to six months maximum, however so far we have found health professionals in various countries able to write prescriptions for the correct drugs. In some countries we can buy antibiotics and other drugs over the counter, and considerably cheaper. However, one inconvenience, I have found it has not been as easy to get mammograms and pap smears away from large centres. I continue to be part of the colon cancer screening program in Australia, though my contribution has to be mailed a lot farther!

Keeping your health records up to date is as important as keeping the boat documents up to date. A folder with your health history, hospitalization details, blood type, allergies etc. can help you communicate more clearly with your physician. This is an especial boon in countries where English is not the first language whereas medical terms are universal.

Dealing with Seasickness

I am one of the lucky ones; I do not get seasick, but my Friwi gets very seasick at times. It is normal for him to feel squiffy for the first two or three days of an ocean passage. The motion that causes seasickness seems to be better above deck and he tries to stay busy and not go below. If it is likely to be fairly rough weather ahead he will take Stugeron tablets, which most sailors swear by. Cate Storey takes Travel Tum and uses ginger either in candies or in teas. There are several tablets on the market as well as wrist bands and patches, and I suggest having a selection on board until you find what works for you. Be aware that some pills will make you drowsy.

Seasickness can be very debilitating. We were doing a short crossing in the Pacific passing between two groups of islands where the motion of the sea was short, high and choppy due to a depression and a high squeezing the isobars. The sea was a washing machine and my Friwi lay prostrate on the deck for several hours until there was nothing left to vomit. The best I could do for us was to focus on the boat and the navigation. This begs the question, "Are you able to take over in such circumstances?"

Lilly Service and her husband worked together to find solutions for her seasickness. She says, "At sea I usually get seasick for the first few days; Tom and I had to figure out what would work for me in this area. We prepare lots of small portions of meals ahead of time so the captain can just pop something into the microwave while I am getting accustomed to the sea. I feel like, 'Please everyone, just leave me alone.' My body must stay lying down to adjust to the feel and motions of the boat and the power of the sea for a while before I can do much. My Lilly bucket is kept real close (used for toilet needs and vomit sessions), my bunk is made up to be comfortable with my favorite soft pillows, clean sheets, my nightie, and a water jug."

Dehydration is a problem with seasickness and to get the body back to normal you must provide drinks that replenish the electrolytes, minerals and vitamins. Because the sick person needs to regain energy quickly they need to eat. Keeping any food down can be problematical, so no spices just plain foods, little and often, which is where hard ships' biscuits come in handy. When the weather forecast looks as if we are in for a bumpy ride ahead I rely on pre-cooked meals, even if we have to eat them cold. However, mostly we set sail with a window of three or four days of good weather, just to get our sea legs and get used to being on the ocean again.

Medical Kit as per Category One

Leaving New Zealand was quite some effort. Firstly, the boat and crew were required to have a Category One Safety Certificate. An honorary sailboat inspector came and thoroughly checked our boat *Caesura* for sea worthiness, as well as checking that my Friwi and I were capable sailors and navigators. We were then issued the certificate which we had to show Customs before we could be cleared out. Only New Zealand registered boats have to pass this inspection before leaving New Zealand. Some countries have similar regulations. Part of this Cat One certificate required that we have on board medicines as per their list.

I still have a full set of dentists' tools, thermometer, bandages, needles, syringes, solutions, antibiotics, antibiotic powder and creme, eye drops, throat lozenges, anti-sting creme, sunburn lotion, high factor sunscreen, anti-histamine cream, seasick tablets, constipation, diarrhoea and pain tablets, bandages of all sizes and band aids. This all came to NZ $1600 I recall, and that was fifteen years ago. Having the *right* antibiotics for the job though was something I did not have when I needed it. I had plenty of broad spectrum antibiotics but when my Friwi got a small coral cut infected in a filthy harbour he needed a specific antibiotic. For the first twenty-four hours he was shivering cold then sweating hot, with a very high temperature, and no other outward signs so I thought it may be malaria but did not wish to treat him for it until I was sure.

Coral Cuts and Blood Poisoning

Day two made it clear it was blood poisoning. The red streak that went from his ankle up into his groin was unmistakeable. I got on the radio and called our friends who were on their way home and many miles away. Cathy is a nurse and had the correct antibiotic and intravenous injections. I radioed for any other sailboats to check if they had this particular antibiotic and a transfer was carried out mid ocean and brought to us. Cathy and Eric turned around and sailed back to us with some more antibiotics but we still had insufficient to defeat the infection. Ironic really as we had all just given our own supplies to the local hospital the week prior, and these had all been used. We got a message to the mainland for someone's brother to bring more antibiotics on the weekly plane and I learned how to give injections intravenously twice a day for several days. Thanks to a concerted effort from fellow cruisers and locals we averted what could have been fatal if we had not been able to treat my Friwi there and then. There was no international airport handy to fly him the many miles back home.

So, although I have medical supplies I have never used, I keep them all. You never know what kind of emergency you may have. A lesson learned, in the tropics we now immediately clean even the tiniest scratch with Betadine, antibiotic creme, peroxide or tea tree oil. Amanda Swan Neal who has taken hundreds of people on sailing expeditions requires passengers and crew to bring their own antibiotics with them. She herself swears by a product called Germolene, an antiseptic cream from Boots UK, which she uses for cuts, abrasions and stings. Check with your doctor before you set sail for recommendations for the correct antibiotics to treat severe food poisoning and blood poisoning from infected cuts. These are likely to be your most useful antibiotics.

Another lesson I learned was to drink more water. I had not been drinking sufficient and I got a urinary tract infection, but apart from those two health problems we have had nothing else happen in fifteen years. Long may it stay that way! Naturally we suffer bumps and bruises but with Arnica creme rubbed in well, swellings disappear rapidly. You may prefer to use homeopathic or natural medicines and there is a place for them on a boat, especially I have found, the soothing calendula creme as well as aloe vera plant juice. Most sailors have their own pet remedies to offer, and when Blue Water Women get together we swap news not only of people, places and problems but also we exchange ideas on health and fitness and most importantly, where to find things when you are new in port. I was in a marina while doing the laundry recently discussing how to keep a healthy gut flora, and now I am the recipient of new Kamboucha starter which one sailboatie shared with me. I believe bits of it are sailing many miles with other cruisers! It does not seem to matter where in the world you are, there is an immediate affinity with other sailing women, especially long-term cruisers, because you too may have experienced their problems.

Hypothermia

If you or your crew gets soaked through to the skin and then gets chilled by the wind, you need to watch out for hypothermia. This could happen when you are diving or snorkelling or simply getting drenched in rain on the boat and then sitting in your wet clothes. Shivering is a sign the body needs to increase body heat. Decreased consciousness occurs when the deep body temperature falls from the normal ninety-eight degrees to below forty degrees Fahrenheit. If you are faced with a man overboard scenario it is very important to remove wet clothes instantly and replace with warm dry ones. This applies to any time you are sitting in wet gear. You can protect your body from loss of heat most efficiently by wearing windproof and waterproof clothing and keeping your head warm.

One of the best things we did was to invest in good quality wet weather gear, expensive, but oh so worth it. I recall many wet cold watches where I gave thanks for my good jacket and trousers. One feature of my jacket that helped me endure bad weather was the huge furry lined collar which I could raise to keep the wind off the back of my head. I was glad I'd had my wet weather trousers taken up to the right length before we set sail because they were so easy to get on and off instead of having to roll up heavy, wet, unwanted fabric. The trousers are good in that they are specially made for women with a generous size Velcro opening where it matters. I tried one of those gizmos for peeing over the side and simply could not get on with it. We had hysterics with me trying to use it, and that was on calm seas. However, you may have better luck.

Contrary to what people often think, alcohol is not the right drink to warm you up when you have hypothermia. It is a stimulant which increases blood flow to the outer parts of your body not to the core where it is needed, and heat loss will increase by up to twenty percent.

Sunstroke/Heatstroke

On the beach or up on deck, whether stationary or at sea, it is all too easy to become absorbed in what you are doing and be unaware of the intensity of the heat. Physical exertion in extremely hot climates or prolonged exposure to the sun can result in the failure of the body's regulatory mechanism to keep the body from becoming excessively overheated. This results in a condition marked by fever and often unconsciousness. Prevention through covering up, wearing a hat and sunscreen is the best course of action. You do not want to end up in hospital on a drip, as I did in my youth after falling asleep on Waikiki Beach for several hours in the blazing sun. A good guideline is to sip twice as much water as you think you need and regularly replace lost body salts.

Wounds from Sea Creatures

Wounds from stings from jellyfish and other marine creatures can be excruciatingly painful and many sailors have their own pet remedies from peeing on the affected part, to putting vinegar or hot water on it. I have had The Divers Alert Network book recommended to me which is a good diving first aid manual covering hazardous and venomous marine creatures.

Suggestions for your everyday basic First Aid starter kit

- A good First Aid Manual
- Antibiotic creme or powder
- Antibiotics for specific ailments
- Antiseptic wound creme
- Antihistamine creme
- Adhesive dressings
- Seasick tablets, pain killers

- Eyedrops
- Safety pins, needles, scissors and tweezers
- Thermometer
- Sterile wound dressings
- Sunburn prevention & treatment
- Band Aids, Adhesive tape and sutures
- Bandages (including a triangular bandage)
- Diarrhoea & Constipation tablets

You can add surgical and dentistry implements and other items to suit your individual needs. Women especially will benefit from fungus infection and cystitis remedies. You can also buy pre-packaged first aid kits, though most sailors prefer to make up their own (*see* Appendix C for details of pre-packaged kits manufactured for off shore cruisers).

Cathy, our nurse friend, came over to our boat one day with a big wodge of firm sponge. "This is your head, see, I've sliced it down the middle, now I want you to use the curved needle to suture and close the wound the way I showed you," she said. I had to control any gory thoughts and just focus on getting a neat job done. I only hope I could manage to do it as well in an emergency. Do practise this if you can because it is something else which helps build confidence when you think of all those scary what-ifs.

Taking a First Aid Course certainly helped me overcome the fears my over active imagination managed to create. I felt that if the worst happened I would be able to contribute knowledgeably to the solution, and that builds up self-confidence. Having a good diagram of how to give Cardiac Pulmonary Resuscitation (CPR) could well be a life saver. The course I took was delivered by the Red Cross in a school hall. In some locations there are courses available specifically for marine safety, and some actually take place on the sea.

Cathy Gray dispensing medical care in Papua New Guinea

Fitness Afloat

Frankly I do not find it easy to keep fit on board. In the days before we had sophisticated winches, windlasses, in-boom or in-mast furling systems, engines, auto pilots or windvanes it was easy to expend energy. In fact you had to! We tend to sit a lot more than we should. Even standing uses more calories than sitting as your body constantly adjusts to the movement of the boat. Previously we did all the maintenance by hand, including sanding and anti-fouling but with the advent of machinery to do the tough jobs fitness has to be worked at. Enjoying socialising with fellow sailors is great but does have a downside. All those chips and dips do tend to add to the waistline and it takes me a lot of self-discipline to refrain, mainly because I know that I have to exercise a lot harder to stop my clothes fitting too snugly. As a recent birthday present I was given a Fitbit watch which tells me my heartbeat, calories used, steps and stairs taken, which although a bit of a gimmick, does keep me aware of where I fall short and have to work harder.

Paddle-boarding is a popular workout for the core body. I love to swim, walk and kayak wherever I can and I can do my Qi Dong exercises on board. Grit Chiu and Bev Evans swear by their daily yoga on board to keep fit. It is surprising how many yoga type exercises you can do on board; either on your bunk or in the centre of your boat where she is steadiest. A friend who has been leading yoga sessions in our marina told me she needs her regular workouts to keep strong and flexible because it gives her more confidence on the boat that she can handle any physical problem, which also helps her mental state. Many sailors have fold up bicycles to get around on. These vary in price according to the quality of components. Cheaper bikes get you wheels but also may rust more quickly in the salt air environment.

However, you will quickly find that cleaning and working on the boat can be a great way of getting some of your exercise quota. Every time you anchor in port and have to reprovision you will likely get exercise from pulling your trolley full of shopping for miles along dusty roads as well as carrying an overloaded backpack, then getting everything into the dinghy and off again and up on deck, then taken below to the galley where you have to find space for it all. Or it can be fun, finding a *cidomo* (horse drawn cart in Lombok) to take you back to the dinghy after a happy morning choosing fresh produce from a colourful market. But you still have to get it on board and put away! The same goes for refilling fuel containers of diesel and petrol—all good exercise.

31

Sailing Etiquette

Sailing is both a science and an art with ancient origins which today still has its own descriptive language along with its own standards of behavior and manners. The following words describe some of the things that tend to offend people the most. Women who belong to the South East Asia Women's Sailing group have generously helped me research this area.

Shouting, except in dire emergencies, is a no-no. Sound carries over water, over the sound of your boat engine or dinghy engine, to everyone else in the bay. Anchoring seems to bring out the beast in people and can be the subject of more arguments than any other activity. I cringe when I hear shouting between people as they anchor. This is not necessary, you simply need to create a system of clear hand gestures, or at night use a flashlight with agreed signals that you and your sailing partner can readily understand.

When anchoring it is difficult to ascertain the position of other boats' anchors or how much rode they have out. You need to know how big a circle they require to swing around in, if they are anchored or on a mooring buoy. Different boats move differently, especially monohulls and multi hulls, heavy displacement or lighter displacement boats. It is considered bad manners as well as poor safety, to anchor too close to another boat. If possible when you do your pre-anchoring survey circle and see your neighbor on their boat, it is worth asking them where their anchor lies.

Something that gets us women irate is when people forget to turn off their AIS when in the marina. If you are on a boat trying to enter a marina and using a chart plotter all one sees is a mass of lines and triangles which can obscure the marina fingers says Melinda Taylor. When in a marina please check your halyards are not loose. There's little worse when you are tired and need to sleep than to hear the flack, flack, flack, of a loose halyard against the mast. The same goes for wind generators when near other boats. When they are not in use, put a rope loop over the blades to stop them swooshing in the breeze.

In marinas be circumspect about how you hang your washing. In many places it is more considerate to hang your underwear inside or at least out of public view. Whereas it is fine to throw your vegetable peelings etc. overboard for the fishes when you are under way, this is not allowed in a marina. Neither is doing poos; many cruisers have to dive in that water to clean and maintain the hull and propeller. You have paid for toilets, so use them, unless you use your holding tank. When using tools, hose, ropes or lines on the pontoon, do as you would on your boat, keep them tidy so that people do not trip over them.

There is etiquette involved in hoisting and carrying flags and signs. For example, when your boat is anchored you should hoist a black ball on the forestay for other boats to see you are anchored.

However only a very few sailors do this nowadays. Ships do. Maritime flags are often different from the flag you fly on land. Our maritime country flag has a red background whereas the land flag has a blue background. Sailors often are unaware of the courtesy of placing the visiting country flag higher than the flag from one's own country on the starboard side of the mast at spreaders level. When you arrive in a country for the first time, you hoist the yellow quarantine flag until you have completed all entry requirements, and then you can hoist the courtesy flag.

Inconsiderate noise is the *bete noir* of most sailors. Music that blares from outdoor speakers is fine when you are at sea, but not in a marina or bay with other boats. When using electrical tools or equipment like a generator, try to use them briefly, not too early in the morning or when sailors are sitting quietly watching the sunset. We were unfortunate enough to be next to a sailboat that had its generator going for four hours each evening when they were actually off the boat!

Never climb on board a boat before you are invited to do so. The courtesy is to give a few knocks on the hull so people are aware of your presence, and they may invite you on board. Many conversations are held from dinghy level. Ask the boat owner where they would like you to put your dinghy as some owners would rather put a fender over the side for you so you do not rub and mark the hull, or perhaps they prefer simply to take your painter and secure it for you.

When you tie up your dinghy at the dinghy dock please do not wind your painter around and around the cleat. This makes it almost impossible for other people to use it. Instead, put your painter through the cleat and tie a bowline. And please, leave a long line so other dinghies can get in. All too often one sees a dinghy tied both fore and aft to the pontoon, on a very short painter, thus hogging all the space that should have been enough for a dozen dinghies!

Taking your shoes off on other people's boats is a given. If you need to use their head, just as you would in someone's home on land, ask your hosts how theirs works. They may have one with a few of its own quirks, like ours, which you need to understand. Some cruisers have a plastic bag to hold used toilet tissues so as not to cause a blockage. If you are a smoker, do not assume you have the right to smoke on someone else's boat. We have made *Stardancer* a smoke-free zone.

If you have been invited for drinks on another boat and have taken your own drinks and maybe snacks, take the empty cans or bottles home with you rather than leaving your hosts to dispose of a lot of extra garbage.

Basically, most sailing etiquette comes down to being thoughtful, behaving as you would like other people to behave towards you, and not taking situations or people for granted. Cruisers are known to be a super friendly bunch, so if you have not yet made friends don't feel isolated, go knock on a hull and start some friendships!

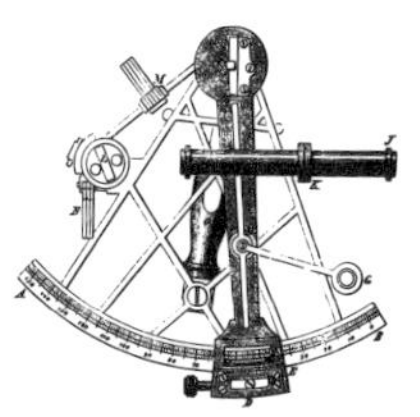

Part 4

Life at Sea

We live in a wonderful world that is full of beauty, charm and adventure. There is no end to the adventures we can have if only we seek them with our eyes open.

—Jawaharal Nehru

What is your everyday life going to be like at sea? When the sailing gets bumpy and you feel like being back on terra firma this is a time for treats and spoiling yourself. Most of our Blue Water Women feel out of sorts at some time or another. As Helen Hebblethwaite says, "Life on board isn't always easy and can be hard work, lugging heavy bags of groceries across a long hot beach, having rolly anchorages where your world just won't keep still plus long passages that leave you weary. Most of the irritants are temporary though and a calm anchorage at the end of an unpleasant trip soon settles the spirit and all is consigned to the 'remember that trip when' category of conversations. When the groceries get hauled on board and stowed away, you can put your feet up and in ten minutes all is forgotten."

View over Panasea anchorage in Papua New Guinea
with SV *Caesura* on left

Perhaps you have had an argument with your significant other, have premenstrual tension or are fed up trying to cook a meal at an incalculable angle when everything slides away from you, or you've had no good sleep for three or four days, or you are wet, bruised and miserable. Frustration, stress and tiredness all take their toll. At times like these we need more than Minties. We need spoiling. Hugs help, but spoiling is better. Even if you have to spoil yourself. Grit Chiu stacks away two pounds of dairy free chocolate for moments like these, Diana Neggo cuddles her cat Motley, Courtney Hansen always has a book on hand to read, Amanda Swan Neal has a favourite pillow, Chantal Liebet Haller contacts her Facebook friends, and I do funky embroidery. Most of us have some activity we can do to have a break from the exigencies of sailing. If you do not have a hobby or interest that is just yours, where you can disappear into another world of your own for a while, then it may be a good idea to find one.

32

Long Passages

Letting go of the notion that I had to be busy all the time was hard for me, but when I learned to take things more slowly, which you have to do on a boat anyway because everything seems to take twice as long to do, and simply focus on enjoying not having to rush, my appreciation for the smaller things intensified. I took off my watch. I stared for hours at the sails, the sky and the sea. I felt the cares of the world just drop away, stripping life bare, down to the essentials. Only then did I feel the deep joy of truly cruising. It seems to me that if you need to be busy planning and doing all day, you could well be missing what cruising is all about. To quote an old Spanish proverb, "How beautiful it is to do nothing, and then rest afterwards." I am never bored on long passages. I find I have time to pick up interests I have not touched for years; I read books I have almost given up finding time for, I am learning Italian, I embroider and I write. Or I can research the next destinations with the travel guides which I have been fortunate to find in second hand shops, a trifle out of date but good enough. Travel books and maps in English can be hard to find in many countries so it is worth taking these with you. Other products that are hard to find away from the western world are biodegradable soaps and cleaning agents, so stock up on these.

One of the most time-consuming events I find is provisioning for the passage. Love it or hate it, it has to be done. Unless you are preparing for a long passage you will find plenty of foods along the way, but for passages of over a couple of weeks you will have to plan carefully if you don't want to run out of essentials.

Fresh lobster for dinner

33

Provisioning for the Voyage

How much is enough and how much is too much? A good question! I err on the side of too much. In fact when we left Australia we took on board $3000 of food. A lot of it was actually an error on my part. I had decided not to lug all the shopping back to the boat in several trips but to use the supermarket's internet shopping and delivery service. What I did not realise when ordering was that by ticking the number one in fact I was ticking a one boxful, which contained more than one! Sometimes six! Imagine my face when I saw what was delivered to the boat and stretching way along the pontoon. Very embarrassing. It would have fed several crew as well as us. Somehow I found space for every last item and a few things were still being used three years later.

I am not the only one to make mistakes provisioning, Helen Hebblethwaite shares her provisioning gaff before she left Australia. She says, "I went to a supermarket and negotiated to buy several hundred of their plastic grocery bags so I could use them as rubbish bags. When I got to South East Asia I was astounded by the amount of plastic bags that were used and wasted and felt so silly I had worried about running out of them!"

Unwanted Pests

Whereas the odd plastic bag may be welcome aboard for putting the garbage in, do not let cardboard boxes on board because you may well have the eggs of cockroaches or larvae of ants in the folds. Now and then cockroaches fly in through the portholes and getting rid of them is no easy task. You can buy lethal sprays specifically for cockroaches and ant traps which will help get rid of ants. Some marinas are notorious for rats, in which case we ensure we close the boat up well. We also bought some Rid Rat pellets but have not had reason to use them so far. Blue Water Women suggest using bananas and chocolate to tempt rats into a rat trap. Another rat-foiler I have seen is circles of plastic on mooring lines which are designed to stop rodents climbing onto the boat. This seems like a good idea but I have not had to put it to the test yet. In some locations monkeys can be a nuisance if they get on board, getting into your food packets and generally creating mayhem. The smell of food scraps encourages them, particularly mangoes and other fruit so get rid of these as soon as you can.

Keeping Things Fresh

As a novice at provisioning for long passages I constantly referred to Lin Pardey's book on feeding the crew (*see* Appendix A for book details). I got a lot of it right but one mistake I made was when we left New Zealand and I bought king sized everything. No fridge then meant many things spoiled. We had some beautiful huge pumpkins given to us, which kept well but once you cut into them, you have to eat the lot one way or another. Cabbages with long stalks are hard to find but very worth the effort. They last a long time when wrapped in newspaper and kept in an airy place. We bought several dozen really fresh eggs which I smeared with Vaseline and kept turning every few days so no air got in, and they stayed remarkably fresh for weeks. Flour on the other hand was not a good idea in bulk. Once opened it did not take long for weevils to enter. They lay their eggs in the tiny space between the rings of the lid and the jar, even when you think you have screwed it on tightly. Milk powder too turned rancid in the tropics. Cans and dried goods keep well if you take care with the packing and check the cans for rust from time to time. For just two people I learned that buying smaller sizes was actually far more economical in the end.

No Fridge

As an avid planner I initially assigned a place for each type of item, however I found that this did not readily translate into the weekly meals I had planned, so now I have a rotation method. I keep handiest the ingredients for my planned week of meals in two large lockers closest to the galley. I move items forward into these two "everyday" lockers on a regular basis, keeping a store of dozens of cans, packets and bottles in the more awkward hard-to-reach places.

Without a fridge I relied a lot on pasta and rice and cans of tuna, salmon, chicken, turkey, ham and packets of dehydrated vegetables and dried fruits. However, we caught so many large fish, mainly Barred and Spanish mackerel with some Tuna, all over five feet in length that I was kept busy sousing them. I have Marianne on *Sostene* to thank for this wonderful way of keeping fish. I seared cubes of fish in butter in a pan, put them in glass or good plastic jars, covered them with olive oil and spices, topped up with a little white vinegar, screwed the top on well and left them for a couple of weeks. Leaving them was the hard part. She assured me they would last three months but we never found out as they were so delicious we ate them after a couple of weeks. The longer you leave them the softer they become, like butter, and can be spread on crackers. We really did not intend to catch any more big fish but then we caught the biggest fish ever at six feet tall (we measure them against Christian).

We sent out an all ships radio message to come to our boat with a salad and plate to have barbecued fish. There were seventeen people on the stern for lunch which got pretty late but was huge fun. At other times we gave away fishes to islanders we met.

Fruits that keep well are oranges and lemons and limes. No scurvy on our boat! We seemed either to have a glut of bananas or none as they tend to all ripen at the same time. Locally grown pineapples were a bit of a dried-up disappointment compared to Doles. Apples and pears last well if wrapped in newspaper and stored in a dark place. The same with potatoes, pumpkin and onions. Because fruits and vegetable give off different chemicals when they ripen, try to wrap and store them separately. Bananas especially will ripen other fruits and avocadoes very quickly. Many sailors hang nets to store fruits and vegetables allowing good air flow to prevent mould which is a great idea if you have the space.

Wherever we have sailed we have managed to regularly find some fresh food basics, fresh baby tomatoes (a pleasant surprise), as well as squash, sweet corn, sweet potatoes and Chinese greens. These days in western countries there are wonderful freeze-dried and dehydrated vegetables available as well as packets of instant mashed potato. For those who use butter, New Zealand canned butter can be found in shops in Australia and some places in South East Asia or you can order the Red Feather brand through Amazon.com. However, bottled ghee (clarified butter) is readily available most places where there is Indian food, and it keeps very well.

Meal Planning

We took plenty of treats with us; vacuum packed lamb in wine sauce to name one which was a favorite, plus a whole wheel of cheese. For fresh goodness I experimented with sprouting every kind of bean I could, but now I sprout only mung beans as they seem the most reliable and easy to find. An American sailor and long-term cruiser gave me a great piece of advice before I set sail. She told me to be sure to include our favorite sauces and pickles because these are often difficult to find outside western countries. Also, she insisted we fill every crevice with treats, like dried apricots, popcorn, nuts and chocolate. We ate all the chocolate very quickly, on the basis that it would be the quickest to spoil!

Now that I have a fridge and a freezer life has changed dramatically prior to making passage. I cook large amounts of spaghetti Bolognese and make individual portions to freeze, and copious amounts of soups packed with nutritious goodies, also frozen in portion amounts. We usually start a passage with cooked chicken, and now that I can freeze bread, I can extend leftovers with sandwiches. I have the bread sliced and wrap what I need in cling film to freeze in daily portions. When I cannot find good bread, which is too often, I use round wholemeal flatbreads sealed in packs of eight which keep amazingly well. So well that I worry what chemicals they must contain. Flatbreads can be used for wrap type lunches as well as cut into segments to go with dips. Many sailing women these days have bread makers on board but I purposely gave ours away because as a Frenchman my Friwi loves nothing better than good bread and I found no sooner had I made a loaf than it disappeared and started re appearing around his middle. Sometimes you have to be cruel to be kind.

I aim to cook more than we need for the main meal so I have at least a basis for lunch the next day. We do not eat much butter but use olive oil liberally. I have found a good mayonnaise to be a wonderful standby. With a squeeze of lime and a can of sardines you have an instant dip to take to other boats. Mayonnaise is good in cakes too. I use it for lots of things, both sweet and savory.

Blue Water Woman Jane Kilburn swears by fermented foods for keeping her family healthy and makes yoghurts, kombucha and kefir on her boat. Kefir can be made using UHT treated milk which is sold in boxes, keeps well and is available in most countries. Jane and her husband are passionate about keeping fit and healthy on board and will willingly pass on recipes (*see* Appendix A for her website details).

After so many years of cooking on the boat I know what we like to eat most and what works best. I have a seven day menu in my head when we are making passage and simply repeat it so I don't have to start thinking of "What on earth are we going to have for dinner today?" I might do chicken as a curry one week, or as coq au vin the next, but it is still chicken on a Wednesday. This leaves a little room for flexibility as simply changing the spices can provide a wholly different meal. Having a shopping list with menu ingredients truly helps when you are provisioning, making it so much easier to know what to buy and how much. This way you are not tempted to buy things you will never use. For example, I love the idea of pomegranate sauce, but as yet have not opened the bottle I bought five years ago! Now I always write a strict shopping list, because otherwise I know I forget things or get side-tracked, and once we up anchor shops and markets can be few and far between.

Once you are at sea the efforts to stock your boat with all necessities for your voyage are reduced to simply maintaining the stock levels, however those initial efforts can be quite tiring. To make shopping more fun a group of women went provisioning together with a pre-shop coffee of course. Afterwards Liz Stewart took a well-earned rest in the easy chairs outside the supermarket before facing the next few hurdles of getting it all in the car, off into the dinghy then onto the boat and put away (*see* Appendix A for reference material on Provisioning).

Christian hunting for spare parts in Indonesia

Local Foods

Arriving in port in a new country never fails to excite me because it is an opportunity to explore the local markets and find out what the locals eat. Visiting local markets is always an adventure. The sights and smells are intoxicating. Mounds of colourful spices delight the senses, vegetables and fruits you may have never used before are fun to try. I love the buzz and vibrancy of markets in every part of the world. This is the cornerstone of local life. Chickens are often sold live and as I find plucking a messy business I get the chicken plucked and chopped, although this is rarely done without splinters so be careful when you eat it. Then I collect it before leaving the market after I have bought everything else on the list. To date in various countries we have eaten water rat, snake, crabs, indescribable shell fish, tried crickets, and once, unwittingly, cat and dog. Very often experimenting with eating local foods from street stalls can be cheaper than cooking on board and a lot more fun too. We have never had food poisoning from eating street food though we have had terrible diarrhea after drinking fruit juice with ice cubes made from poor water in a five star hotel in Tahiti!

Transporting Goods

When doing a big shop we take our fold up trolley which can hold a surprising number of heavy cans and does not feel as heavy as when we carry loads on our backs. So far we have gone through six trolleys in fifteen years, mostly because they have been dragged over unmade rough roads and bumped up and down uneven steps but also because my Friwi was using them for carting heavy boat items. After the demise of the sixth trolley I put my foot down about the abuse of use, so we bought a strong fold up trolley with big wheels specifically designed to carry heavy things like batteries or diesel cans. Now we are both happy. Until I bought a special egg carrier made of plastic, we would often arrive back at the boat with at least one or two broken, but now they are well protected. Funny how something so trivial can make me happy! As many of you probably already do, I take my own bags when I go to market or the store but somehow I still end up with too much plastic.

Dealing with Garbage

It seems plastic and foil packaging is a necessary evil until all countries ban these products. Try to dispose of excess packaging before you take your provisions on board so you have less garbage. Cans I wash out and keep separately until we can find a refuse bin on shore, and food scraps feed the fish. Full garbage bags are put inside a larger black bag and tied tightly before being placed in our back yard, i.e. our dinghy that hangs on the davits. The idea of putting garbage on the stern is that if there are any bad odours, the wind will take them away. We tried putting garbage up forward near the anchor well but that was not a success. The International Maritime Organization seeks to eliminate and reduce the amount of garbage being discharged into the sea, mostly from ships, which means vessels of any type whatsoever from large to small ships, to floating platforms and pleasure craft including sailboats over twelve meters. The MARPOL agreement has instituted international guidelines for garbage discharge in many of the world's seas, but sadly not all. For more information *see* www.imo.org.

34

Fun on Board

Sailors who do chartering or make long passages, stock up on plenty of games like monopoly, scrabble, chess and card games. These games involve people of all ages and cultures, overcoming language barriers as well as being source of fun, companionship and laughter. Having plenty of games on board is especially important when you have kids on board, your own kids or your grand kids. When we had kids visit our boat from the local school on Natuna Island in the South China Sea who had no English language, Chutes and Ladders was a great hit judging by the loud squeals of laughter.

When we are on shore, we play with a set of Petanque (Boules) which requires a relatively flat space, though slightly uneven beaches make the game a bit more of an interesting challenge! I am told it helps the skill of the players if they can hold a glass of wine in one hand, French style. Locals love to join in. We taught some islanders how to play the game using coconuts. Frisbees, baseball,

Local school children on board in *Natuna,* South China Sea

rounders and beach cricket are good fun for all ages and cultures. So when you are doing your provisioning, remember to include some games on your list. Water sports can be fun too. In one anchorage, *Caesura* and four other sailboats competed in a dinghy obstacle course race where the fun started days before the race, working out engine power and handicaps for each dinghy. Race day came and we were surprised to see the beach was lined with locals come to cheer on their favorites. We learned later that they had actually taken bets on their favorite dinghy to win! Simple fun, but it gave us all a day to remember.

Many boats carry diving equipment not just to enjoy the marine life beneath the sea, but because someone will have to dive under the boat from time to time to clean the barnacles or as is sadly the case here in SE Asia, to free the propeller from plastic rubbish or fishing nets. When buying your snorkelling gear remember to buy spare goggles; we seem to either lose them or break them at an alarming rate. Also they make wonderful gifts in more remote places.

If you can play a musical instrument it is an instant entree into making friends, both with other cruisers or with locals. It doesn't matter what it is, a guitar, violin, ukulele, flute, recorder, tambourine or the comb; anything goes! In some marinas there is a regular musical night around happy hour where you can make new friends. My Friwi played guitar in the middle of the Borneo jungle. We had travelled up a narrow river to see the orangutans and the boat boys were trying to play The House of the Rising Sun, which pretty much everyone knows, so my Friwi borrowed their guitar to show them how it goes, I sang, and we made new friends. So make a note when provisioning to include musical instruments. Music transcends borders and cultural boundaries. We bought half a dozen recorders and gave them to a school in remote Papua New Guinea which has helped them start an orchestra of sorts.

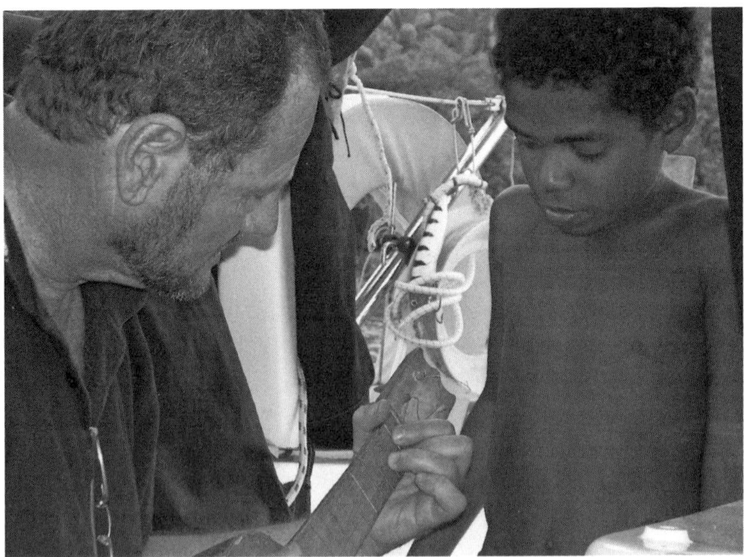

Christian on Joel's ukulele, sharing a tune

On one remote island we had been visiting a friend and been given bags of fruits and vegetables. Two young lads of about twelve years of age had been pressed into carrying them back with us, a way over on the other side of the island. As we went I taught them how to sing rounds of the one song they knew in English; we sang "Michael Row Your Boat Ashore" all the way over the hills and through the jungle to our anchorage. I was amazed they knew all the words! Ah, the power of music.

We also stocked up on balloons, pencils, crayons and exercise books which in more remote areas were hard to get and therefore very much appreciated. On Panapompom Island in Papua New Guinea we were overwhelmed by the gratitude of the school when we visited with a bundle of exercise books and posters. Not only did they perform welcoming dances for us but had a small ceremony when the gifts were locked away in a big, empty, tin trunk. The teacher said, "We were poor, but now we are rich", words we shall remember for ever. It is moments like these that make sailing experiences so special, moments when we realize how privileged we are.

35

You and Kids at Sea

You may already have kids and be thinking of going sailing with them, perhaps home schooling them for a number of years or maybe you have grand kids coming to visit and are wondering how they will get on with being on your boat and what you can do to make their time special for everyone. Or perhaps you do not have kids, yet, and are thinking of starting a family during your cruising years. Each stage of a kid's development brings its own issues regarding safety, a healthy diet, and medical, educational and socializing concerns. Four of our Blue Water Women share their experiences of having babies while cruising, bringing them up on board and sending them off to college.

All four mothers are very positive about the advantages of having their child brought up on a boat. Although my sons were adults by the time we set sail, from the many families afloat I have met and observed over the past fifteen years I can whole-heartedly say I have never encountered such close families or well-adjusted happy kids as sailing kids. I wish that we had started sailing a whole lot sooner, just so that our kids could have been on board with us.

Babies on Board

Anna Fourie is now in her forties and had son Louis seven years ago. Cate Storey is in her thirties and recently gave birth to baby Henry. Jane Kilburn is in her forties and has a daughter Milly now six years old. Frederique Fontaine is in her forties and her son Axel is now twenty and has taken his French Baccalaureate in a high school in Kuala Lumpur, Malaysia, after being home schooled on board for twelve years.

In Anna's own words she describes what it was like having a baby on her boat and bringing him up around boats. "When I started my adventure on the water, the idea of having children was the last thing on my mind. In fact the idea of being pregnant whilst living 'the dream' of sailing around in the deep blue did not seem like a compatible combination. I was career motivated and kids were not in the picture. But then we got to Brisbane and tied up on the pilings next to the Botanic gardens right in the heart of downtown. We had just sailed across the Pacific … and having been afloat for almost a year my then husband and I decided that it would be a good time to settle while on the boat and have a family.

"Three years later we welcomed our lovely son Louis into the world. Pregnancy afloat was a dream. Perhaps the continuous rocking from the ferries counteracted any nausea typical of the first trimester, because I never suffered from any signs of morning sickness."

However, Cate Storey was not so lucky. Like Anna, she too had a high-powered executive position but was depressed for almost a year after quitting her job. She says, "I attribute this to the time it took to value, and make friends with, a non-working me.

I believe it is the same journey that many women go through when they suffer post-natal depression. I am very thankful that I went through this journey before getting pregnant and welcoming Henry into the world." It is at times like these if you are feeling the post baby blues that you need good care and to be among friends and family or at least comfortable, which is when a stay on shore for a while may be a good idea.

Soon after they started out on their Pacific sailing adventures Cate and David began to talk about having a family. She says, "The world we were discovering was so beautiful it seemed only natural to introduce it to a child." When they reached Fiji she found she was pregnant but she had a difficult time with morning sickness. Cate says, "In Fiji we were meeting people who valued family above pretty much anything. When we took kava ashore and introduced ourselves we were usually invited in and offered a cup of tea, then when they found out I was pregnant I would be directed towards the guest bed. Everyone we met seemed keen to tuck me in and put me off to sleep. It was such a lovely gesture. In the west we tend to fight the messages our body gives us and there was no doubt I was exhausted in my first trimester. I was really touched by people's hospitality and kindness, with my friend Maria from Rabi Island giving me traditional Banaban pregnancy massages."

Cate says she spent a lot of time in Fiji observing how parents interacted with their children. "The children seemed to be brought up by the whole community. The older children looked after younger children and babies were passed happily between adults. During an afternoon gathering, a number of babies would be asleep under a mosquito net. When one baby cried an older child would pick the baby up, sooth it then pass the baby to one of the adults. The baby would then be passed along until it reached its mother. Once fed, the baby would then be passed back again without a single break in the conversation. From an outside perspective everything seemed easy and relaxed. I hope I have adopted a Fijian parenting style and am working on building a whole community of people who will love and advise Henry as he makes his way in the world."

Anna had a great support community, the sailing community on the piles. She says, "One of my fondest memories of being pregnant on the dock was the support and camaraderie of my fellow sailboatie neighbours. This wasn't just *my* baby; my pregnancy and this baby were already part of the community. One day, I was heavily pregnant and about to carry huge jerry cans of fresh water to the dinghy, then onto my boat (a regular task when you live aboard) but as I was about to lift the jerry cans I saw at least two dinghies heading straight towards me with great shouts of alarm. It was my sailboatie neighbours forbidding me to go any further. Then they dutifully lifted the jerry cans as well as poured the fresh water straight into my water tanks, and thereby presumably prevented me from an early labor!"

For Cate's twelve-week scan they sailed back to Savusavu where she lined up with all the other women in the antenatal clinic in the Savusavu Hospital. This trip turned out to be a highlight for Cate "Because," she says, "of the connection I felt with the other mothers-to-be and the feeling that my excitement was shared by the doctors and nurses and the thrill of knowing my baby was real." The hospital was old fashioned but functioned well. Cate says, "The nurse was dressed like a typical 1950s matron; starched white dress, white knee high socks, chunky rubber shoes, nurse's watch, and stiff white cap with a Red Cross on it. I was really well cared for."

However, Cate was very pleased that she was in Australia for the birth. She says, "We all have to decide how intrepid we want to be. We came back to Australia to avoid the cyclone season, but it also coincided with the last trimester of my pregnancy. I arrived back just in time to do my twenty-five-week scan. Not long after I came down with a raging kidney infection that could have easily put me into early labor. I was unbelievably grateful that I was in

Australia at the time. Henry's birth was protracted and problematic. I was pretty beaten up and couldn't get on or off the boat for the next few weeks. There is good medical care in most of the places you can sail to, all I recommend is that you have an obstetrician that you trust, a midwife who has a good relationship with the obstetrician and a nearby hospital that can deal with any eventuality. You never know what is going to happen when the time comes." Baby Henry recently put on his lifejacket for the first time. Soon he will be having sailing adventures in the Pacific again.

Baby Henry in his life jacket

Safety for Little Ones on Board

Having an extra person on board always means a redistribution of space as Anna found out. Keeping baby safe was a priority. Also, she wondered how this would affect their lifestyle. "I remember clearly Louis's father jokingly telling me it was either the baby or the sewing machine," says Anna. "So, with the sewing machine gone I set about making a cot for Louis, I could always borrow a sewing machine. A cot for a sailboat cannot be bought at Mothercare. The making of this cot became the centre of discussion among the sailors on the piles discussing the design, materials and how it would work. Louis's first cot consisted of a plywood base with carbon fiber rodding, housed in white linen and suspended by spectra lines onto a simple system of blocks and pulleys so the cot could glide smoothly in and out of the quarter berth. There was even a computer fan to provide baby with appropriate ventilation."

This was a great way to keep Louis comfortable and very safe. Many parents put their baby into homemade cots that are suspended from the ceiling of the cabin so the baby can enjoy the soothing, rocking motion. Cate made one for Henry, his "baby cage" as she calls it, using the lee cloths of the pilot berth and the dinette seating squabs.

When Louis entered the world there was no pram or buggy, being totally impractical on a boat, so Anna carried him everywhere on a pouch attached to her body. She says "It felt very natural and he seemed really happy with the arrangement. He had a lot of physical contact with me and his father and consequently was a very contented baby. I had maternity leave from work and this was one of my favorite times with Louis. We sailed from Brisbane around to Darwin and those months sailing with Louis were bliss. We were very lucky to spend such quality time together. I don't know many other kids who were able to spend all their time with both parents twenty-four-seven.

"When Louis became a toddler we put fine netting against the stanchions around the boat because he could move amazingly fast. The net was a definite safeguard as well as giving us a bit more peace of mind."

Caring for Baby

Anna says, "Despite the flexible lifestyle afloat associated with the cruising lifestyle, we saw the need to have a strict timetable, endorsed by Gina Ford's *Contented Little Baby Book*. This way we could time our visits ashore. I also breastfed, which was a great advantage, it meant I never had to prepare any bottles in advance. Introducing him to solids was easy, I simply made extra of the bland food we were eating and mashed it up thoroughly."

If, unlike Anna, you are not breast feeding and need to provide bottles of formula, it is wise to take this with you before you set sail because you may well not be able to buy formula in other countries. For drinking milk, however, powdered, full cream, and skimmed milk is available in most places but needs to be kept in a cool place. We buy UHT treated milk in one-litre boxes and stockpile them for countries where there is no milk except perhaps cans of condensed milk.

Now that more boats have watermakers it is easier for mothers to use cloth diapers and wash them regularly, although disposable ones are indispensable for on shore excursions. However, disposable diapers become a smelly problem at sea when they become soiled and need to be put in the garbage until you get to land. As with much of our garbage, there is no easy solution. For spills and instant clean up wherever you are, carrying a good supply of packets of wet wipes is vital, and not just for the children either.

Louis, passage making on SV *Thula Mama*

Making Friends

Anna recalls, "Louis's first word was 'dinghy'. Much of his life was spent traveling as we sailed through Indonesia. His blonde hair and big smile were our entry point into many local homes and friendships. Women and children would dash out of their homes to see us come by. Mothers and aunties came rushing up to pinch Louis's cheeks to get good luck. There were no sanitized kid's zones and Louis would play on the mud floor of the local islanders' homes with their children. He played in the dirt, on the beach and in the sea and has consequently built a robust immune system. I can count the times on one hand that I have taken him to see a doctor in his seven years. As a result of Louis's popularity across the Indonesian islands, by the time we arrived in Singapore he believed he was a celebrity!"

"I know people worry about children reared on boats not having enough interaction with other children, but in the marina Louis is known by all the boat boys, security team and fellow dock dwellers. At eight years old he knows almost everyone and uses the marina as his playground. He pops over to a friend for a soft drink, he knows who has TV where he can watch movies or football and will ring the doorbell of Singapore's largest super sailboat until his favorite stewardess will come to meet him with drinks and homemade biscuits. He has learned to ride his bike and scooter here and play football. The dock is his home. There is an instant rapport between fellow dock children so there are always friends for him. It helps that he is a gregarious outgoing kid. He also loves to invite his land-based mates because they are always in awe of his cabin and unconventional lifestyle. It is important that kids have their own cabins to decorate as they choose, to be their own personal space so they feel happy being there."

"Louis is as comfortable with kids as adults and it is my belief that his independence on the dock has made him this way. His favourite thing to draw is boats and he recently started his official Opti sailing course although he has been sailing his own Optimist unofficially since he was four."

Anna has one worry, that Louis will grow up and come home one day saying, "Mum I want to be a tax accountant." "Not a bad profession," Anna says, "but I wish for him a life of adventure out on the water. I hope that boating becomes a way of life and not just something his crazy parents did."

Jane's little girl Milly is a real tomboy and has been at home in the water and around water since she was a baby. She is an

Milly

extrovert, making friends easily with people of all ages but even so Jane is aware she needs plenty of kids her own age to play with and this affects their sailing plans. "We make decisions on where to cruise based on where other kids might be." A recent trip of three months to Sumatra was cut short to return to the marina to find kids for Milly to play with. There can be up to twenty or more kids in the marina some years, of many nationalities. The marina is Milly's playground and is a safe place with no cars so kids can happily explore. They can enjoy the beach and swimming pool, learn to ride a bike or skateboard or play in the rainforest.

Frederique Fontaine says, "Kids need to spend time with their peers. However, as kids reach their teens there are fewer that age around. Wherever possible for a rounded upbringing, we have made a habit of ensuring Axel has young people to mix with for one week every month or so. We also encourage him to play sports and as we are sportive parents we play plenty of games."

Education

Wanting a good education for your kid to give them a great start in life is only natural. Given the state of the job market it is important to get those certificates that are necessary for a young adult to follow their career course, but to have a rounded education there needs to be more than bookwork. Some kids are academic, others are not and prefer a more hands on approach to life. All a parent can do is provide what they think is the best way possible to give their kid an education that suits their nature and abilities. The word "education" implies more than job training. Enjoying the world from the perspective of a boat allows your kid to experience a wide range of interests, interacting closely with Nature and introducing them to different cultures and ways of being. The sailing way of life encourages tolerance and understanding and enables kids to become independent thinkers as well as physically adept.

Some parents opt for a mix of home schooling and land-based schools, others choose home schooling to give them more freedom when long term sailing. Perhaps you are sailing just for a short time, say, a couple of years. It is possible that if your kid is already in school on land that you can discuss a learning program with the teachers, take the necessary text books and support material on board, and send schoolwork back by email for marking. Or for long term sailing you could opt to home school for several years, as did Frederique and her husband. It can be hard work to be disciplined teachers but for family bonding and educational results they believe home schooling Axel was worth it.

Axel with Alain Fontaine

When Frederique sailed from Reunion, where Axel had been to his first school, she and her husband then became Axel's teachers. "But we are not teachers, and being twenty-four-seven together it was hard work sometimes," says Frederique, "as well as being mother, lover, navigator, banker, home maker, medical expert, crew, and cook." She started home schooling on board when Axel was seven which entailed making certain hours of the day dedicated school time. Axel has a quiet nature and took well to home schooling although Frederique says the French home schooling requirements are very strict.

At nine years old Axel sailed with his parents to Malaysia where they have spent the last few years. This has given him stability and lasting friendships. Each year Frederique asked him if he would prefer to carry on with home schooling or go back to normal school and each year he chooses to stay. She says, "If he had chosen to go to normal school we would have stopped sailing straight away and we would have returned to France." He studied on board to take exams in Kuala Lumpur for his Baccalaureate. Frederique believes he has learned much besides formal educational requirements, "He has learned diligence and self-discipline, he is happy with his own company but open to new friendships, appreciating and getting on well with people of all ages and cultures. He has learned about the environment first hand, about water conservation, not dumping garbage into the ocean, using power and looking after our wildlife. He has learned how to fix mechanical things around the boat. Like any teenager he is into the internet and Facebook and his music, though he is not interested in being a sailor!"

Jane found the early childhood Australian program was too regimented for the flexibility of a sailing life and for now she supplements Milly's land-based schooling with other learning programs that are available on line, which help Milly stay one year ahead of her age group. Now six years old, Milly goes to a small (twenty students) Chinese-run school in Langkawi where she is picking up a few words of Bahasa Malay as well as Cantonese.

From the evidence of my own eyes as well as comments gleaned from other sailors it seems that sailboatie children are usually very well socialized. They appear to be more responsible and are not shy or scared talking to others where their conversation tends to be more adult. Although home schooling can sometimes seem an additional burden, mothers agree (it seems the teaching most often, but not always, falls to the mother) it is a time for the family to become closer, and as well, by the time they teach teenagers they are often learning new things too. As late teenagers the curriculum can sometimes become too difficult for parents to teach and often this is the time when kids need to be schooled by specialist teachers and move onto land.

The benefits of cruising with kids are many as Jane says, "We have the benefit of traveling with our home, which I think as a family is a major benefit. Milly gets to sleep in her own bed every night regardless of where we are, and we can easily provide a healthy meal any time." It would appear that a mixture of on board schooling and land-based schools at intervals prepares kids best for coping with the world at large and in fact, gives them a decided advantage.

Entertaining Visiting Kids

If kids are coming onto your boat and they have not been on a boat or around boats before they will be very excited. As you would in a land-based home you need to set the boundaries straight away. When we have anyone new on board, if they are not sailors we run through the safety rules on the boat for both kids and parents at the same time, so the parents also know what the expectations are. Little ones need to be within a parent's view at all times. When we are taking kids sailing with us we insist they wear a life jacket because it is just too easy to slip and fall in the water especially with obstacles like stays, blocks and sheets on the deck when kids forget the "no running" rule. Having harnesses on the life jacket is an excellent idea, thereby limiting the possibility of drowning with little ones who can crawl very speedily out of sight at times. We also insist on the "one hand for yourself and one hand for the boat" rule, for everyone's safety and peace of mind.

Many visitors, adults and kids alike tend to get seasick with the motion, sometimes even before leaving the dock or when the boat is at anchor, so then it is best to stay above deck in the fresh air and keep an assortment of anti-seasick devices ready as well as lots of distractions. Although we may not have kids sailing with us very often we keep a good assortment of games; board games, cards, balloons, crayons and paper, dolls, trucks and Legos. Kids often pick up on their parents' feelings, so if the parents are scared, the kid will think there is something to be scared of too. We have found that if we can involve visitors old or young in some aspect of sailing, perhaps the navigation for example, this focus stops them thinking about being sick or feeling fearful.

The navigation station bristles with knobs and levers with bright red, green and yellow lights making it very attractive, a real magnet for little hands. A few years ago when we had kids on board for the day I wondered why the water had stopped with nothing coming out of the faucet, then I heard the whirring of the pump. I could not hear the pump at first over the chatter of voices but on checking I found a water pressure button had been pressed! We were lucky the pump did not burn out. Lock away anything you do not want handled including your medicines.

I keep an assortment of treats handy just in case we have unexpected young visitors, things that keep well and are healthy like homemade muesli bars, frozen fruit juice on a stick and some not so healthy items like chocolate cookies. Popcorn is a great favorite and so easy and quick to make. I detest the huge amount of sugar, artificial colouring and flavors in fizzy drinks that crowd the shelves in stores and will not buy them, so kids on our boat do not get sodas, they get fruit juice or water. If you have warning that young visitors are due it is wise to ask their parents to bring alternative foods if their kids are allergic to certain foods or on a special diet. We have had friends stay on board who have celiac disease and it is not a simple task to find anything except rice that is gluten free in some countries, which can make mealtimes a bit of a challenge.

Healthy Kids on Board

Good health starts with a series of inoculations for babies if this is your choice, with ongoing regular top ups as they grow. For convenience these first vaccinations are best done in your home country although they are available worldwide. Your doctor can give you a forward timetable for booster shots. Keeping mosquitoes away from baby's soft skin is a major prevention activity. There are gentle natural creams on the market to take with you, but wearing long garments and sleeping under mosquito netting are probably the best ways of keeping baby safe from malaria or dengue. If you are breastfeeding, your colostrum will pass on your antibodies to your baby for added resistance to disease.

Once kids are crawling they will most likely pick up bugs from the dirt but their immune systems will cope and strengthen. Something to guard against is worms that live in the sand on certain dirty beaches and enter the body through the soles of the feet. Naturally when outdoors in the heat, kids need to wear cool clothing, a hat and plenty of sunscreen. Sunglasses for kids can be a good idea in some parts of the world where due to the thin ozone layer the light is excruciatingly brilliant and can harm the eyes. Soaking kids clothing in fresh water, including putting a wet cloth on the head, can help keep them cool. Anna says, "We kept Louis cool in the tropics by sitting him in a bucket of sea water which kept him entertained for hours."

If on the other hand you are in cold climates of course the opposite is true, keep kids bundled up with warm, windproof clothing. As our heads are where we lose the majority of our heat, good heat retaining fabric hats are essential. There are many manmade fabrics on the market today that can be made into kids clothing which are very light and specially made to retain heat. Another benefit of these fabrics is that they are quicker to dry than heavy wool.

When kids mix with other kids it is common for them to get head lice so remember to take some shampoo to delouse the hair. I was shocked to find out my son had head lice at school as I associated them with dirt until the nurse told me they only jump onto clean hair. A special de lousing shampoo followed by combing out with a special comb, and that was the end of them!

The main thing when sharing the voyage with your kids is for them to enjoy it as much as you, for you as a family to share happy experiences which will create wonderful memories, memories they in turn will pass onto their own kids. Remember, the photos you take and the videos you make will be important to your kids and so need to be kept in a safe place for the future. The opportunity you give them to see the world on a boat is the best present they could ever have.

Celebration time in Papua New Guinea
with Elizabeth, Terecita, and baby Bruce

36

Women's Matters

We women often put ourselves last; after your partner, after the kids, after the crew, after the cleaning and sometimes if we are lucky we have time for ourselves. It is important that you do have time out to do what you want, because you are an important part of the voyage and need to be happily satisfied with your life on board. Perhaps your roles have changed dramatically since you left land and you are having a hard time adapting. Or perhaps you are struggling with menopause or other health issues. Or feeling lonely. Or needing time off the boat. The answer to happiness is different for every one of us. We are all so different, yet there are some issues and feelings as women that we all share.

Your Menses

I am so glad I am past this stage of life. I found this was one of the more unpleasant things to deal with on the boat. I wrapped my used tampons well and put them in a tight-fitting plastic bag until I could burn them but I was always aware of potential smelliness and could hardly wait until we got to a beach to dig a hole and have a bonfire. However, this is not always possible and you have to wait until you put your garbage in a bin on shore. Sailing through the Pacific and most of the Indonesian chain all I saw in little shops were sanitary napkin pads and it was not until we reached large towns that I could find tampons. In the islands they use rags which they boil and reuse and as I certainly did not want to do that I made sure I had a large number of tampons stowed away.

I am one of the fortunate ones who had no problems with premenstrual tension, but my Friwi probably would disagree saying he could always tell what time of the month it was. It certainly does help if you have a partner or mate who is sympathetic and understands how you feel during your period time. If you need a hot water bottle to cuddle and a lie down in bed, you need to be able to do so without feeling guilty, even if it means finding an anchorage earlier than planned or heaving-to for a time. Some women say that the relaxing motion of the boat helped them and that the sailing life helps reduce PMT symptoms. Maybe the reduction in stress also has something to do with it.

Menopause

Then along comes menopause. Before I set sail I visited my doctor for last minute pap smears and tests. I was very stressed at the time and not handling menopause that well. It was interfering in my busy life, so she put me on HRT. In hindsight, I do not think I needed it because when I was happily on the boat crossing the Pacific I was fine. After a year or so I gradually took myself off the tablets. But tablets or not, I sweated profusely, could never get cool enough and my feet and hands got very hot. Advice from

Bernadine Reis is to "Take a frozen bottle of water to bed with you." Also, drink plenty of water!

Blue Water Woman Cathy Gray had the same overheating experience as I did. Her husband put two fans in her cabin for her, one at her head and one at her feet. I used to put a towel on my pillow and wet my head before I went to sleep. During the day I would wear a wet tee shirt. Except for the odd hot flash and having my body temperature control system set too high I hardly noticed menopause really. When I came out of it the wrinkles multiplied rapidly, tissues shrunk and gravity is now definitely winning but I seem to have got full energy back. Of course, inside I am still thirty.

You may not see your doctor for quite some time, so take careful note of what medicines you are on, and when you last had your pap smear or breast screening. Just as you would if you were setting off on land travel, you will need to make sure you have sufficient quantity of your personal medications as well as check up on when you need booster shots for your vaccinations.

Sexual Health

There are condoms available everywhere though I gather in third world countries they are not always guaranteed reliable. In remote Papua New Guinea one couple was giving away condoms free at their shop to try and educate the locals because PNG now has one of the highest rates of AIDs per head of population in the world. The condoms were disappearing like hot cakes, they could not keep up with the demand. Soon they found out what they were being used for; the locals were blowing them up, drawing on them to look like fish and using them as fishing lures.

It was sad to see the island girls rush to the visiting trading boats from the mainland where they could get cigarettes in exchange for sexual favors thereby possibly spreading disease.

Cathy Gray being a nurse was asked to speak to women on health matters by a village chief. Many women and their children came from neighboring islands. What they wanted to find out about was AIDS, how to control it but also sadly, how to cure it. Cathy left behind a wonderful book with photos for the women about their own bush medicines, had it translated into their own language and then laminated the pages. Because knowledge means status, people often keep knowledge to themselves. This way they can share the knowledge with future generations.

Cruising Sex

Girlfriends have asked me, what happens to your sex life when you are on long passages, just the two of you? Surely one of you is on watch all the time? I can honestly say I have enjoyed the best sex ever as we have been sailing. There are always overlaps when on watch and on beautiful days with a steady breeze filling the sails, mid ocean and miles from anyone else there is a sense of liberty. We sail naked when no one else is around, or at most very flimsily dressed, and even at our age there is something tantalizing about sex in the open air. In Tonga I recall we found an empty island, a paradise where love, lust and sex were part of our enjoyment as we wandered and swam, at one with nature.

As Helen Hebblethwaite says, "Sometimes it can just be too hot in the tropics for sex, which can be hot and sweaty, rather than steamy!" Sailing *can* be very romantic in the tropics because, I think, that it is much easier to even think of sex in the warmer latitudes wearing fewer clothes than the colder latitudes. Undoing all my straps and ties of my wet weather gear in a cold climate is a frustration at the best of times, not a happy prelude to spontaneous sex! Simply cuddling up can be wonderful in cooler latitudes. If you have guests on board it is sensitive to leave them on the boat by themselves for a while and go out in the dinghy. Other couples play loud music to alert you. And other couples just let it all hang out and you can see the boat jiggling up and down!

For Grit Chiu, "The biggest thing to improve our life on board is making each other and therefore ourselves, sexually satisfied. Sailing with my boyfriend has been a dream come true. We have gotten to know each other so much better while in a confined space and still not tired of each other." Sex at sea can add to your happiness. It is up to you to take advantage of the freedom from routine and perhaps embrace different ways of doing things.

Friendships with Other Cultures

A major part of voyaging for me is interacting with people of other cultures. I am fascinated by the differences and the similarities to my own culture. I want to know how they live their lives, what they think about the world in general, what makes them happy or not. I want to stop and spend time with people not just "here today, gone tomorrow." In some remote islands I was fortunate to be able to give something back to the islanders who had been so welcoming. Over a ten-week period a group of cruisers got together to teach the locals how to use fiberglass while building a thirty-six-foot sailing trading boat with them out of two disused "banana" boats. This way they learned new skills, and could fix broken water tanks as well as fix their canoes. In the new sailboat they could take people to hospital, take produce to trade at the market a day's sail away and get the high school kids back to school on time. While the men were doing that we women were busy at the local school or spending time with the women of the village. Alexandra Mateer rates her experience of teaching math using beans at the little bamboo school as one of her most treasured cruising memories.

Local children coming to play in Papua New Guinea

One day ten village women, old and young, came on board Sailboat Erica for morning tea and to go through the bags of second hand bras and reading spectacles we had brought with us. As you can imagine this was a hilarious affair where the boatload of women had a great time. Creating bonds with the locals, spending evenings singing in the chief's hut, playing games together, laughing and crying together; these are among my most precious sailing memories. In Fiji where Cate Storey found that when she had to take kava to the village chief before being granted the right to explore the village and surroundings, it was always a great opportunity to meet other women, and in her case, other pregnant women. One family in particular are now baby Henry's godparents so the link with Fiji will continue and add another dimension to their lives.

Christian and I have been adopted by a family in Larantuka, Eastern Flores, Indonesia. We have spent happy times in their homes and at big picnic-type celebrations which seemed to always end in long circular dances. Our inability to follow the steps caused much laughter. The *Bupati* (Governor) of the island invited us into his colourful home to have afternoon tea which was beautifully served on bone china plates and through his English we were able to find out a lot more about the history and trade of the island. We have visited Larantuka twice, sailing in laden with second hand clothing, quilts and gifts for the children of the Rainbow Orphanage. We hope to visit again, perhaps by motorbike this time.

Donated spectacles on board SV *Erica*

Finding out that the people we meet are just like us is a big part of cruising; they too love their families, enjoy a good laugh and are keen to make friends. Like us, they have problems too and if we can assist in some way as we sail through, the world is a better place. If you just stick to making sailor friends you will miss a large part of what makes cruising special. We still enjoy contact with friends around the world whom we met when we first sailed into their country many years ago, and this eclectic mix of friendships is a major pleasure. Before you set sail visit a second-hand clothing store and fill a bag to give away or trade with and so create opportunities for creating new cross-cultural friendships. It is not all about money either. A gift of fish hooks or school books, or simply time spent talking with them is often much more appreciated than money.

Clothing

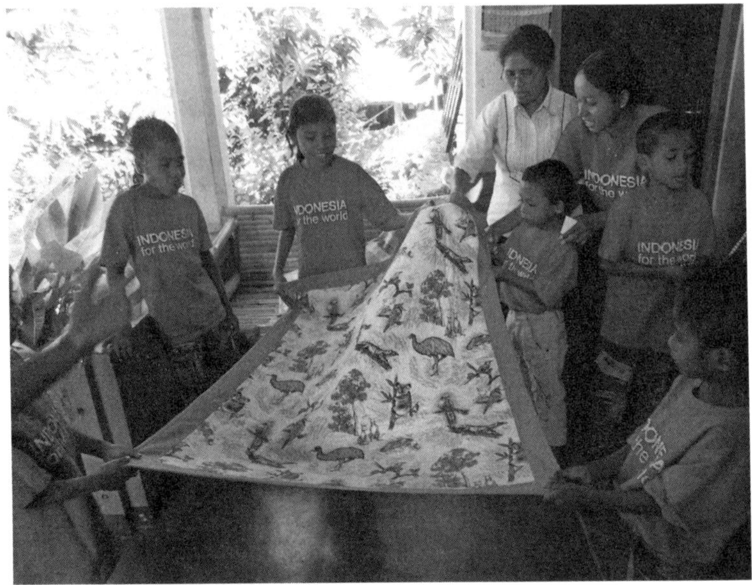

Donating quilts at Rainbow Orphanage
in Larantuka, Flores, Indonesia

We were buddy sailing through the Pacific with a stylishly dressed French couple. I was surprised to be told that every item was from a second-hand clothing store. In the Pacific there are lots of stores where they sell the clothes that churches donate, many of them with high end labels. We had a competition to see who could be "best dressed for less" which was a whole heap of fun as well as putting money into the local economy. We also were able to offload lots of clothes that no longer suited our cruising lifestyle because I have found it is only too easy to keep things just in case I might wear them. I love clothes and find it hard to part with ones in good condition but it makes sense that someone else could be enjoying them instead of them lying stored under my bed, so if I have not worn something for two years I will give it away. Often old tee shirts get used for rags as we seem to need plenty. When we set anchor in Papua New Guinea for our boat building project we brought with us a huge bag of rags we had bought for five dollars at an op shop in Australia. Next day we saw the rags, hanging on a washing line, all clean, but sewn together overnight to make a bed cover for the chief's house!

On board sailing in the tropics I like to wear loose dresses, I find they are even cooler than wearing a swim suit, though I know many sailing women wear bikinis, but my bikini wearing days are over now. I keep a couple of dresses that I can wear for special events on land, otherwise when on land I wear shorts and cool tops. Although white seems like it should be a great idea in hot weather it is not really practical. Dark colours are too hot, so the most practical colors for shorts are grey, kaki or beige. In hot climates just wearing clothes makes you hotter but I try to wear natural fabrics that breathe and cover myself where I do not want to get sun burnt, though I am probably a few decades too late!

Wherever we sail we try to dress like the locals. When on shore in most countries we wear shorts and t shirts, in Muslim countries the dress code is to cover shoulders and knees. In one Muslim country I was wearing three quarter pants, which in the crowded bus had ridden up to show my knees. As one old woman got off the bus she tapped my knees hard with her fan as she walked past. Obviously the sight of my knees was offensive. I now carry a sarong to cover any bare bits of skin, and when entering a temple as well as covering up, I remove my shoes. It is all a matter of showing respect for the country you are in.

On Board Beauty

Most women have a fear of becoming "Grotty Cruisers" and like to keep a certain standard of hygiene and presentation while on board. What I started off thinking was essential for me to be happy with myself in the ways of presentation-to-the-world has changed dramatically since I began cruising. I started applying makeup when I was about fifteen or sixteen years-old and this routine became an integral part of who I was for most of my working life. I probably have looked in the mirror at myself for thousands of hours over a working life of about fifty years and applying makeup was a hard habit to shake. I still feel better looking with mascara on, but getting it off every night became a chore. So for the past decade I have rarely used mascara because of swimming and snorkelling. Also my need for others' appreciation has dwindled. But as I have aged I notice my eyebrows disappearing and it has proved too much of a hassle to pencil them in every day so I had them tattooed with a special organic product supposed to last three years. This has proved quite liberating! I love it. Jenny Gordon-Jones and Anna Fourie have had eyeliner tattooed and the results are great. I have seen other tattoos though here in Asia which are not so great, more like solid slabs of dark ink, so it pays to find someone well recommended if you decide to go this way.

As for foundation makeup in the tropics, forget it. It just slides off the face if you perspire even a little bit, and the sailing life is tough on the skin. Moisturising your whole body is important because either the wind, sun or the salt water will dry out your skin, or the air conditioning or heat in the boat will. There are conflicting opinions regarding the safety of suntan lotions on your skin but organic ones using PABA or zinc are often safest for the delicate skin on your face. Best by far though is to cover your skin and wear a large brimmed hat. However, I for one loathe wearing hats or more clothes than I have to and have paid the price of courting the sun when I was a young woman. I look back in horror to remember we used to use olive oil and vinegar as a suntan lotion!

Happy Hair

Some of our Blue Water Women are fortunate to have partners whom they trust to do their hair on board. One sailor took her husband with her to her hair salon before they set sail specifically so he could take a video and learn how to cut her hair while they sailed, and the results are very good. When I set sail in 2005 I had a shoulder length page boy style that I could tie back out of the way, but it proved to be a problem when washing and rinsing as it took precious water. Having a lot of hair was great in cool temperatures because it kept my head warm, but in the tropics it was a nuisance. In Tonga we met sailor Hazel who had just cut a woman's long hair to short and very curly, and it looked good. Foolishly I had mine cut too. I vividly remember sitting on an upturned bucket on the beach while Hazel hacked. She was not so good at fine very straight hair and the result looked like it had been gnawed by a rat. As soon as I could get to a good hairdresser and was pleased with the cut, my Friwi took photos with the iPad to show subsequent hair dressers on our voyage, and this strategy has worked well.

However, my experiences leads me to believe longer hair tied back may be easier to look after than fiddling with shorter hair. I am at the stage of letting the grey hairs show rather than going through the bother of coloring them because I always seem to manage to spatter a few drops and stain the surfaces in the head or galley. Sailing has prompted me to become more natural in my appearance which is a long way from the fashionably made up and manicured woman I was. Now my sole vanity at keeping up appearances is to always wear toe nail polish. Somehow even with my gnarled old feet, it shows I care.

Socialising

When I first set sail I really missed my women friends. I missed the sharing and the laughter and I wondered if I would find women who were interested in the same things I am. As much as I enjoy the sailing life there are times when I need a change from always discussing routes, repairs and where to buy things with my Friwi and others. As Bev Evans advises, "There will always be boat maintenance, and the men folk talk constantly of solving each other's problems, be it fridges, to batteries. … The list is endless and I warn you it can be boring sometimes listening to them. … so shift your seat next to the women and start your own conversation."

On the other hand, there are women sailors who are fascinated by discussions on repairs, engines and routes and so on and are very knowledgeable, but if you are not one of these women and want a break from these conversations it is good to know there are others like you.

I was not prepared for the openness, sharing and support that I have found with other sailing women. There is an automatic bond that goes beyond language or nationality. It is an unconscious acknowledgement that the new friend has experienced most of the things you have on your voyage and dealt with similar issues, so there is already a lot in common.

There is always so much to be learned from other sailors' experiences. Conversations spring up spontaneously with people you have never met before, perhaps around the laundry or in the showers, or waiting at a bus stop or in a market. Anywhere, in fact. If you are in an anchorage with a couple of other boats you simply get in your dinghy, go knock on the hull of the other boats and after a conversation perhaps about where they come from or are going to, before you know it you have invited them to come visit your boat, and new friendships are formed. Whereas on land perhaps with your neighbors or workmates you have what I call functional friendships, with fellow sailors you have the kind of friend who will help you find that lost anchor, or tow you to a safe port if the engine breaks down, or actively help you with a myriad of issues on board your boat. The support of fellow sailors makes for a happy community with people generously giving their time and knowledge to help each other.

We were caught in the terrible floods in Brisbane River in 2012. Our boat was almost the last to leave the pilings because my Friwi was busy helping others either to leave or to readjust their mooring lines. Many boats had made the mistake of tying their lines fore and aft too tightly, so when the water came over the top of the piles the boats could not rise and were flooded. It is an unspoken rule that cruising sailors help each other, often without being asked and not seeking acknowledgment. We have been involved in numerous situations where we have helped others, and equally, we have been the recipients of a wealth of helpfulness from others. It makes me wonder why life on land cannot be like this.

In 2012 we joined a rally for the first time, mainly because it made getting the entry papers and sailing permits so simple. Although we did not stay on the rally route we made some good friends, friends we hope to have for a lifetime. One sad part of always moving on is that you are not necessarily going to meet these new friends again, but if you do, the reunions are a wonderful surprise. You could be sailing into a bay where you recognise one of the boats, you see it is your friends you met maybe ten or more years ago, and suddenly it is celebration time!

When there's no one around to talk to and I need a friend, I turn to my next best friend, my journal. Many sailing women write journals and blogs of their experiences. Writing a journal has several positive outcomes; firstly, as an *aid memoire* but also as a way of you dissipating upset feelings or the occasional blues.

Sharing your innermost aches and joys with someone who knows and understands you better than anyone else, yourself, is liberating. Then you can move on.

Keeping in touch with your friends these days is easy via email and Facebook. My laptop and pad are also my filing system; over the years we have collected so many cards both from sailboating and repair contacts that they take up a lot of space, so now I wait until I have a dozen or so and take a screen shot of them and file them that way. As well as a boat stamp we have had boat cards printed with our email addresses on it. We do not put phone numbers on because we change them too often but can write them on as they change from country to country.

When in port our days take on a certain schedule; early morning for exercise or market, lunch times or after for snorkeling when the sun hits the water for the best view, early evening with friends to share sunsets, then dinner and bed. Sometimes the schedule changes to accommodate skeds or participating in a "net" to catch up with news or friends on the VHF or SSB. These communications help to make you feel part of the community and are a good way to settle into an anchorage.

Landlubber Friends

Having your friends come and stay on board with you is something you look forward to. Getting the timings and arrangements to work out well though, can be a headache. We have found it works best if we say, "We will be in port x around the beginning of May for three weeks if you would like to visit," rather than react to their schedule. We have found through experience that we do not ever want to rush to get to pick up friends, or drop them off for their plane. The weather dictates what we can do and when and where we can be, not someone else's itinerary. So now we suggest they stay a day or two or more at an hotel either end of their stay, which if we encounter bad weather and cannot meet them for several days means they can enjoy their surrounds while waiting for us.

There is a big difference between having guests on board who are sailors and those who are not. Sailors understand the rules around water use; not having a freshwater shower every time they swim several times a day, putting the plug in the sink, using minimal water for rinsing dishes and general water conservation. Sailors understand the importance of putting things away and not leaving them strewn about the place in a small space. They understand about not putting wads of paper down the loo. Sailors understand the need to be quiet so as not to disturb others on board or in the dinghy near other boats, because sound carries over water. However, non-sailors know none of these things and it can be tiresome reminding guests several times during a day, finding yourself turning into a nag. Barbara Gladney says about guests, they "tend to treat us like butler and maid at a hotel, they do not understand the nuances of living aboard versus in a house. It is nice to have visitors but in some instances it has been good to see the back of them when they are gone."

Be prepared to do all the cooking and maybe you will get some help washing the dishes. You will have to do the extra provisioning, cleaning and re-provisioning. So you will need to be super-efficient in order to make time to relax and enjoy being with your guests.

With non-sailors, coastal hopping is easier than undertaking long trips because guests can go souvenir shopping and sightseeing ashore leaving you time to catch up on the boat if you are not going with them. After being just the two of us on board for so many years it is quite a disruption to have friends on board. Although we are delighted to see them we have come to believe two to three weeks maximum stay is about right before we start to become irritable, and they start to really miss the comforts of life ashore.

Comfort on Board

Your boat is your sanctuary, your safe haven. You are about to spend considerable time on her so you want her to be as comfortable as possible. It used to be that you could not use the words, "comfortable" and "boat" in the same sentence; they just were not compatible but since production boats have come onto the market, a lot more thought has been given to making them as comfortable as possible. If your boat is over ten or fifteen years old chances are that the seating has straight backs. This is to save space, but is rarely comfortable. One solution is to have lots of small, squashy cushions to put around you or you could do what Lin Pardey did on *Taleisin*, as she describes in one of her books, "We had the settees designed by a skilled furniture maker," she says, "though they look deceptively simple, by making sure the cushion heights and depth were right with a lumbar support style roll at the back rest, they are so amazingly comfortable our guests often don't want to leave."

As extra seating for unexpected guests we have two fold up stools which fit neatly into a carry bag for storage or carrying on shore. The comfort factor improves 100% by putting a cushion on top. For the cockpit I have made cushions filled with beanbag pearls so they dry quickly without going moldy or smelling. I was recently on a boat where the owner inadvertently snagged a hole in the stitching of their beanbag cushion and the polystyrene beads streamed out, dancing in the wind, with most of them being sucked over the side. Learning from this I have made the inner bag extra strong for my own cushions! A note about piped edges on squabs, although they look smart they can be quite uncomfortable to sit on for any length of time.

Another form of comfort is to be able to shower regularly or like Lin and Larry Pardey, take a bath. Lin tells Larry's joke, "Lin finds me much sexier when I am clean." They put their sitz-tub in the space where an engine would normally be, in an airy position so there is no mould build-up. Other sailors have made temporary baths on deck from canvas or tarps hooked up on four corners to give a depth of about thirty inches. These are filled with hot and cold water by the bucket and used to clean the deck when emptied. There will be a creative solution for you if you can use a bit of ingenuity and think "outside the box." A project that could be a lot of fun too.

We prefer to shower on the stern in warmer climes rather than indoors which can make the head steamy and prone to mildew. Usually the loo roll gets a shower too and ends up a soggy mess. For me though, there is nothing to compare with showering on the stern under the stars after a hard day's work or play.

Personal Privacy

To some of our Blue Water Women lack of privacy matters, to others it is not a problem. There are many opposing attitudes towards it. For Gwen Hamlin it is desirable "to have enough space to have a comfortable place to carve out your privacy. Sometimes that's a spot on deck, sometimes it's having a kayak to paddle in, and sometimes it's the corner of the saloon with a fan where you can tune everything out and do whatever interests you." She adds, "One of the hardest things for me is being able to sleep in dark and quiet while my husband wants to watch shoot 'em up movies, so ear phones and two cabins really are essential."

It can help to have doors on your boat when you really need privacy. Jane Hiett says she only just managed to keep the door to the toilet when all the others were being removed from her catamaran to make it lighter. My Friwi and I now have separate cabins on our boat, and when we want privacy we simply shut the door, whereas Jane Kilburn manages her personal privacy "by not having anything I need to hide from my husband and daughter. Open book is the only way."

Anna Fourie's attitude to privacy is if you need it, book a hotel. She says, "Recently we sailed with nine friends on board including two kids. Personal privacy was not really an option so perhaps the secret is only to sail with good friends." Expedition members on Amanda Swan Neal's boat agree to a privacy statement which reads, "I agree to be responsible for my personal belongings and hygiene. I will respect each expedition member's berth as being their own space and realize we will be living in close quarters and that cooperation and consideration are key to a successful expedition." This is just as applicable to you and your crew or guests when on board your boat.

Barbara Gladney admits personal privacy can be hard to come by and "especially when in a marina when boats are only a fender width apart. We tend to keep the blinds closed on the portholes and shades over the windows at times when we want privacy from curious neighbours. Even if it's just to relax and watch television in our saloon we like our privacy. As far as personal privacy, well you just have to work at it and at times that just isn't possible. It's one of the trade-offs for living this life. We tend to live it out loud and in front of everyone whether we want to or not at times."

A large boat cover can serve two purposes Barbara adds, "In Thailand we had a huge awning made that covers the entire boat to protect us from the heat but it also serves as a privacy cover when we pull the sides down."

How Do You Keep the Romance Alive?

In answer to this question some of our Blue Water Women replied, "What's that?" but most were willing to share their thoughts on this subject. It seems that if you do not have a partner with a romantic side before setting sail, this will not change much at sea. Jane Hiett says, "It's the same problem wherever you are when you've been married forty-plus years." Various replies were, "Being on a boat together can be romantic, but there are long periods of boredom and silence," and "we stop and have a cuddle every day and tell each other we love each other, out of the blue" or "it was important for us to have goals we could focus on together." Gwen Hamlin adds, "I think we were better [at romance] on the boat than we are on shore. Ashore we have divided up to different interests which works counter to it." I agree with the necessity of having some common goals to share, even if they seem very pragmatic because taking the steps to get there and enjoying the results together keeps you close to each other, so that romance is just an easy step away.

Several women agreed that the way to a man's heart is through his stomach and the preparation of nice meals with treats works well. Add a few candles and some lovely music and the meal becomes a romantic occasion. Also, we need to remember to thank our lover and friend, male or female, for all the things they do and let them know how much we appreciate them.

Lin Pardey told me Larry is the more romantic one of the couple and I vividly recall advice from him prior to us setting sail. Larry told me it is important to get off the boat once a month at least, dress up and make a special occasion of it, maybe by going to a show or the movies. I have tried to follow his advice but not as regularly as I would like. However, simply that total shift in lifestyle makes you look at your partner differently, and vice versa of course—he's not just that grumpy person who is forever swearing at things which break down!

Lin says, "Larry often asked me to accompany him for a special night out, often suggested a few days in a nice hotel. In fact, when we sailed into Rio de Janeiro after sailing from Africa, he wandered off on one of our bicycles, came back a few hours later and told me to pack up enough nice clothes for three or four days.

He'd rented a waterfront hotel room on Ipanema Beach (modest but lovely hotel room). It was only twenty minutes' ride from the marina where we had left the boat. But what a fun time, taking part in beach life, wandering the streets of Copacabana, enjoying music in some of the cafes." Sounds like the kind of romantic break we all would appreciate!

Many of our Blue Water Women have found regular date nights something to look forward to, often taking turns with their partner to do the organising. This makes for some creative arrangements when in certain locations around the globe.

Just us in paradise in Papua New Guinea

Keeping the romance alive can be difficult at the best of times but it is worth the effort when you are in a confined space with your partner, focused on the boat, not each other, for long periods. The majority of our Blue Water Women found visiting beautiful places, sharing sunsets and nights under the stars with their partner to be the ultimate in romantic moments, and there is no shortage of beauty when you are sailing!

Relationships on Board Versus on Shore

Our Blue Water Women were quite vocal when asked, "If sailing with a man," I know many women either sail solo or with other women, and sailing is no longer thought of as a male environment but still the majority of women sail with a male, "what did he do to ensure you were happy to sail with him?"

Helen Hebblethwaite's husband Phil has done numerous alterations to improve comfort and convenience on board including the recent addition of an electric toilet for her. Phil represents the majority of our male partners. It is these kinds of pragmatic activities which mean the most to nearly all of our women. Because the major focus is always the boat, the boat, the boat, it feels great when you are considered in the long list of things to do and repair. My Friwi has improved the lighting in the galley and installed bright LED lights over the bunks for reading and this means a lot to me.

As so often is the case, it is the little things that count the most. When I get up first in the morning I will make the cups of tea but if I am still in bed, my Friwi will bring me tea in bed. Small courtesies, small gifts of thoughtful actions, these are what make for a pleasant atmosphere.

The word Respect came up many times in replies to this question. It is essential we respect the strengths and the weaknesses of each of each other, respect each other's boundaries, that we show respect around lack of knowledge rather than using it as a put down, that we respect differences in communication styles and show respect for the different things that are important to men and to women.

Several women appreciate the way their male partners sail deferentially, for example by reefing early when by nature they would prefer to wait and see what the weather does, or putting the anchor alarm on or ensuring the boat is not heeling over too far when you are trying to cook in the galley. However, not everyone is born thoughtful, so you may have to ask for these considerations to ensure your happiness. As Jane Kilburn says, "My happiness is my responsibility."

When we set anchor and go ashore it is most likely we will each have our list of tasks to do but I truly enjoy accompanying my Friwi to hardware shops. There is something very real about them being so full of practical stuff. I used to find them full of mystery, but now I feel proud of myself knowing what most items are used for. When I am there with my Friwi I learn more about how things work and what is needed for repair, what paint is best for anti-fouling, and so on, as well as the names of items not previously in my vocabulary!

Mostly we go to do the provisioning together, however I have asked my Friwi to meet me at the checkout to help with packing the shopping because when he comes in the supermarket with me and pushes the shopping cart, somehow I seem to be forever tracking the disappearing cart when he has found something that catches his interest in another aisle. So, I do the product choosing and putting in the cart, but I really do appreciate the help with hauling groceries. When we are away from the boat it is too easy to each follow our own interests to the exclusion of the other and I have to make a mental effort to share my experiences with him more often than I would if we were on board together.

Many Blue Water Women have similar feelings regarding spending time on shore versus on the boat, but others have said their relationship on shore is just the same as on their boat. Rarely if ever though, does the relationship on board improve if your relationship on shore is not already sound.

Men, How to Ensure Your Woman Is Happy to Sail with You

Men, we respect you and your ability to do things we may not be able to do, we respect you for many things both on the boat and off it, and we acknowledge that we may think and communicate differently from you. We wish to be good sailing partners, however there are things that could be improved upon, probably on both sides, to make this wish a reality. Jenny Gordon-Jones reminds us that many women are well out of their comfort zones and are only on board because their menfolk want to go sailing, so what can men do to help ensure their partner is happy to continue to sail with them? Men, the following is for you.

It is very true, "Men are from Mars, women from Venus." We are very different regarding approaches to problems, doing the job, different in the way we think and communicate, with different things being important to us. So, Men, it takes an effort to understand what the woman in your life needs to make her happy to sail with you. The advice from our Blue Water Women will head you in the right direction.

Judy Hildebrand sums up replies regarding advice from just about all women when she says, "Do not YELL. EVER!" She adds, "If you are the experienced one, share your knowledge with your partner so you are on a more equal footing. Help her build her confidence, remember if you go overboard, she has to come and get you if no one else is aboard! Make the boat acceptable for women … meaning a clean, non-smelly bilge, a clean non-smelly YOU, put the seat DOWN. … What are you doing peeing standing up at sea anyway? Don't make her feel like a camper. Please don't be all macho and insist on too much sail so the boat is heeled over uncomfortably. … You aren't going any faster! Choose good weather windows so neither you nor the crew are beat up unnecessarily. Throw away the damn schedule! If your mate enjoys the comforts of a marina, spring for one every now and then. Do Not YELLLLLL!!!"

Too many women who have been on the receiving end of the behavior indicated above have decided sailing and a life at sea is not for them whereas it could have been otherwise. No one likes being shouted at. No one likes to hear criticism too often. No one likes know-it-alls; we all make mistakes. Help your woman to learn the essentials. Encouraging your partner to feel valued and thereby more confident in her learning in what is still mainly a male environment will ensure you enjoy a long term happy cruising partnership.

Some women are used to an all-male environment, and enjoy it. Others do not. In Alexandra Mateer's words, "It's horrible. It's the last bastion of sexism. Men learn differently; just throw them into the situation and they learn on the job (or pretend to). As a woman I like to have things explained to me beforehand, so I have a picture in my mind what I might have to do. I like to gradually build up my knowledge and feel confident about what I have learned. I hate being screamed at, at the last minute, when danger arrives. ... I think sometimes, when the men are scared, or lack confidence in themselves, or don't know what they are doing, or have made a mistake; they take it out on the woman. Having said that, there are moments when the courage, strength, ingenuity and mechanical skills of those same men are what keep you alive and afloat in the middle of nature's wrath!!!"

Whilst on the subject of mechanical skills and repairs etc, Men, the following may not apply to you, you may be a No Mess Charlie, but I hear complaints from many women on the subject of mess and muddle. When undertaking a repair you are probably focusing on getting the job done rapidly, and may not be thinking of protecting the paintwork or whatever else is in the area surrounding your repair but, in order to keep your woman happy do spend a few minutes in preparation by putting down cloth or paper to protect the surrounding vicinity. Even if you personally think it is not necessary. Getting paint or oil on her precious things will be guaranteed to upset your partner. To her your boat is a cherished home, a place where she can feel at home and works hard so you will treat it as a home too, to her it is not a workshop. This applies to the cockpit too. Perhaps you can do that long and tedious repair job on land? Naturally there are times when the whole boat just has to be a workshop but hopefully not for too long. Women will nag you if you leave your tools around and don't tidy up after yourself, leaving stuff out because you are coming back to it, maybe tomorrow, or longer. So, if you want to keep your woman happy discuss your plan of repairs with her so she knows she will have to put up with mess and muddle for a certain time only. Maybe you can encourage your woman to help you with repairs and maintenance, and so get the job done in less time? We know you can do it by yourself much quicker but many of us enjoy learning how to fix things and feel good about ourselves when we can master something new.

Kaci Cronkhite adds, "Be sure the women on your boat know how to navigate and how to use the radio to call for help or connect with others. Women are, generally speaking, keenly aware of how our lives affect others—children, aging parents, you and the crew. If she knows where she is and how she can communicate, it will exponentially improve her experience and overall safety and success of the voyage. From my experience on my circumnavigation, I'd also add that women should know how to drive the dinghy and to row. Like having our own cars on land, the dinghy allows women to have their own schedule and a vital sense of freedom from the boat." So, gentlemen, help your partner to help herself and enjoy her newfound confidence and independence.

"Include your woman in ALL things" says Lilly Service, "even if she does not seem interested in something like refrigeration repairs." She adds, "My husband Tom says that if he cannot explain a situation, a problem or planned action to me so that I can understand it, then we BOTH need to keep working on it until we do. I am guilty of at times just nodding my head to avoid the frustration that can build from not being understood." These things take patience and goodwill, because it is important that your woman really does understand. Sometimes the explanation can be too long and technical, so bear that in mind when you are explaining something. As Lyn Johnstone puts it, "Don't patronise, and be kind. Recognize their [your partner's] skills, praise them verbally and help them learn if there is something that will help them enjoy it more."

Men, you may well have the majority of the knowledge and experience but as Jane Hiett says, "Don't be bossy. Don't try to be too ambitious early on. Make sure your partner gets confident and doesn't scare off early. Do some other non-sailing things like inland travel, trips home occasionally etc so it doesn't get too same-ish."

Have you thought what's in the sailing experience for your woman? Gwen Hamlin suggests, "Think carefully about what's in this trip for your partner? Respect that. Enhance that. Don't be the kind of guy that will do everything for her, help her to be competent. It will help her to avoid feeling scared. And for God's sake don't force her into anything!"

"Communications are the key to good partnerships on shore and afloat". Sound advice from Lin Pardey. So, Men, can you take time in *advance* of an action, if practical, to explain it to your partner before you actually have to do that action, rather than assume she will understand last minute? There are many differences between men and women in the way they prefer to communicate but given time and goodwill, you and your partner or crew will work out how best to communicate with each other. Lin Pardey suggests in one of her books that one way to learning how to communicate afloat with your partner is to "start with some confidence-building sailing experiences, adding some adjustments to make your boat easier to handle for her and you will increase your partner's enjoyment and sense of self sufficiency." She adds "Work at proving you want to keep your lover and your efforts could pay dividends far beyond your cruising years."

One last little piece of advice from Victoria Power, "Make her feel like *she* is the journey and your boat the mode of transport."

And men, if you need any further advice on how to ensure your woman wants to continue sailing with you, read Nick O'Kelly's book *Get Her On Board* or Lin Pardey's *Sixteen Ways to Keep Your Lover.*

37

The End of the Dream—Swallowing the Anchor

Depending on your age you will either have fairly definite ideas on what you will do when you end your cruising days or else you will not have thought of it at all.

When we left our homeland and set sail we were so focused on the present that we did not really think much about the future other than to have a vague idea that we would return to New Zealand to our township to live. We realise now that this is not possible because after fifteen years of enjoying full time sailing life we have changed. We would not fit in with society in our hometown because it has become gentrified and ultra-chic and that is not who we are any more. Also, we do not wish to become ensnared in consumer society which is hard to resist when you are living in the middle of it. Our values are out on the ocean with the freedoms it brings. I cannot see a future without access to the sea, but I know we have to be prudent and face the fact that the day will come when we will have to move ashore but until then we will keep on sailing as long as we are enjoying it and are fit enough. When it comes time to think about an alternative from sailing; the leads will line up!

Panasea Lagoon Beach in Papua New Guinea

About half of our Blue Water Women have a base on land already which may ease the transition. Judy Hildebrand says, "I currently live on land with a home base. It's always hard when I return from a long stint at sea but I have many land friends, so I ease into it. I also live on a mountain with no neighbours. It would be hell if I returned to city life! It doesn't take long before I am itching to feel a solid deck under me and the thrill of rolling along in the trades going to some exotic port."

After eight years sailing Barbara Gladney and Frank are trying to adjust to more land-based living. They sold their house in

Colorado when they left and would stay with friends and family when they came back for three to four months but grew tired of not having a place to hang their hats. She says, "We come home in the off season and as much as I enjoy being with family and seeing land-based friends, they just don't *get us.*" Recently they bought a house in Texas and are hoping for a good balance between sailing on their boat based in the Caribbean and living in their new home.

Alexandra Mateer prefers living on land in a fairly isolated spot on a mountainside because she says, "We are still in nature, so it's not like moving to a city. There is a lot of similarity between living in wild isolated bush places and being on the ocean." Many sailing women think they will adapt well to on shore living because they are basically adaptable people and tend to be positive about whatever life dishes out. Some people have a planned strategy as to how they will exit from a life at sea to one on land but others have little choice and circumstances make decisions for them, often due to illness. If Larry were not ill, he and Lin would still be cruising, but in her post-cruising life Lin Pardey is still very much involved with sailing through her writing and publishing and aims to get out in her fifteen-foot keelboat as much as possible, which seems to be a happy life balance.

Liz Stewart can see a positive aspect in living on land again after many years sailing. She says, "I think I will adjust well to being able to make a decision and within minutes, put a plan into action rather than [dealing with] the restrictions a boat can bring. I look forward to being more spontaneous in life. On land you can lock the door and leave without a second thought. Boats are not like that."

Other sailing women have got off the boat, lived on land for a while, but then started sailing again in a different way, coastal hopping but not crossing oceans. Gwen Hamlin explains, "When we started cruising together Don was fiftyish, I four years younger.

We were relatively young. There were a lot of people we met who were just starting after retirement and we thought they seemed old. Now here we are! In our mid-sixties and going again! I doubt we will cross oceans again though. It has taken me six years to carve out some sort of life ashore. I'd been gone a long time and did not return to an area I had lived in before. It was hard. No one really wants to hear about your experiences. Most people have little incentive to include you in their well-established network."

To help with the difficulties of starting all over again Gwen says, "Finding a group pursuing a shared activity works the best. A writer's group for me has brought some really strong friendships. Don made friends via motorcycles, but not as good as my group." Fitting in with friends and family again can be difficult. Lilly Service asks, "Will my friends and family be ready for a new improved worldly woman like me? All indications are, probably not. I'm getting so much more educated about the world we live in. I don't want to be the same as I was—after all, isn't that the point of traveling? We may live off the grid somewhere beautiful; we are pretty sure we will not end up where we started, upper middleclass suburbia." This is the marvellous thing about the sailing life, you do change, but the flip side is that people may feel uncomfortable with the new you. Also, it becomes harder to choose where to live and how to live after the amazing life you have been living at sea.

Mary Anne Unrau and husband have recently set sail again, bound for Townsville Australia from Victoria Canada. She says, "We plan to keep on until old age throws us on land. Then live in an old age home which will accept us and my grand piano. I could play for singalongs! And if I am old enough I'll probably enjoy having my meals cooked and bed made for me!"

Kaci Cronkhite will continue to do day and week sailing on her boat Pax, as well as crew on other people's boats through the Pacific from British Columbia and Alaska. She already has one foot on land to be closer to her mother, nieces and nephews but also as she is still fit and healthy, to get out sailing too. For those women who already have a base on land somewhere the transition back to land seems to be easier than those full time Blue Water Women who are wedded to the sea.

For many women, only health issues would stop them sailing, so they just get a different type of boat or maybe simply charter boats instead. Lisa McVey is back in "dirt world" as she calls it but she is planning on buying another boat to cruise on, but doing it differently by sailing for just six to seven months at a time and taking a break from the boat this time. This gives her a chance not to miss out on doing other land-based things. After thirty years sailing full time with little time ashore Jane Hiett now wants to "spend more time seeing family, doing cultural things, for example going to the theatre, music, galleries and traveling inland. I have had enough of the rough stuff which John is happy to do and I will join him here and there around the world. My ideal would be six months sailing and six months ashore doing other stuff." She adds, "It seems that when you are approaching seventy your thoughts of the future are sharpened by seeing friends and family fading away or dropping by the wayside. When we were young we thought we were immortal; we can no longer pretend that is the case. We decided that if there were things we wanted to do, we had better get on with it, so we decided to try a different way of organising our lives as neither of us wanted to stop the other doing what they really wanted."

After sailing it is important to have other goals to help adjust to the changes; one sailor is thinking of crossing Russia by foot, others of our Blue Water Women are thinking of getting a mobile home and exploring countries by land, or a canal boat to explore countries by water. Or maybe you will be content to have a house off the grid and spend more time with your grandchildren. Not everyone accli matises well to land-based living and can initially suffer depression until they find another goal. Diana Neggo said, "I have had some bad experiences with trying to live back at home for extended periods. I became depressed and miserable. The trick for me is to have some kind of project, whether it be renovating or building a house, or becoming engrossed in other things I love to do like art and yoga". Since writing this Diana and Rob have bought acreage in Western Australia with fruit orchards and enough projects to keep them both busy for many years to come. My Friwi and I have short term goals, still based around the boat and travel for now, until the time comes when we simply can't anymore!

If you have a positive attitude and enjoy the adventure of the unknown, which you must if you are a Blue Water Woman, you will make the most of whatever the future holds for you. Helen Hebblethwaite and Phil are on their way back home to sell the boat and renovate their house after twenty years of sailing. She says, "I don't think you can have an adventure like this and ever be quite the same again, so I think we will adjust to land-based living with some wonderful memories, lots of great photographs and an eye out for what the weather is doing for old time's sake. I am looking forward to meeting new people in our new home and starting a whole new adventure."

Whatever age we are at we need to have adventures, to seek out new experiences to feel truly *alive!* If we dare to take the steps to a different way of living, we can lead a more fulfilling life and make the most of our time on this wonderful planet.

Mary Anne Unrau sums up the thoughts of our Blue Water Women, "If you are young, don't wait for the perfect boat, just go! First learn (and practise) all you can, ... read, read and read. If you are older, just go! If you have children (and you cannot take them with you) make sure you have set them on their way. Apart from them, do not wait for every single elderly relative to dic. Don't wait to continue your all-important job … no matter what you think, you are not indispensable."

If you have the chance to make that leap from landlubber to a life at sea, to have adventures of a lifetime; don't hesitate! Feel Excited And Raring-to-go!

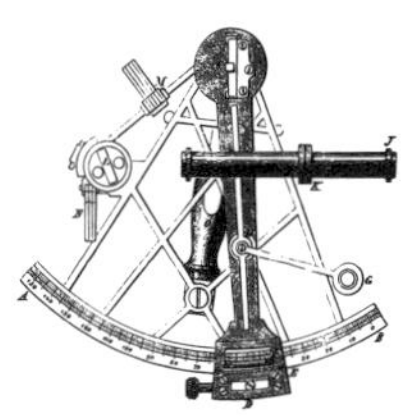

Part 5

You and a Career at Sea

You cannot discover new oceans unless you have
the courage to leave shore.

—Andre Gide

How do you combine a life at sea with earning a livelihood? If you are about to take up a career or make a change in your career path then you are one of the lucky ones. There are now many choices open to you, as Captain Pat Mundus says, "There are tons of choices out there nowadays for women who want to go to sea: maritime vocational high schools, sailboating employment, crew-finder websites and of course clubs with names like Women Sailors etc." We shall be looking at some of these options in this part of the book so you can start to plan your steps towards your goal.

38

Careers at Sea

Squid boats at night

For those of you who still have your career life ahead of you or arc contemplating a change of career, our Blue Water Women who are currently enjoying a working life at sea or have had a successful work life at sea, share their advice and career path with you. Motivations for living and working around boats and the sea can be many but for Courtney Jean Hansen she simply wanted to be as far away from the "Woolworths" mentality as possible. Courtney lived in Mackay which is the gateway to many tourist islands and dive sites along the Great Barrier Reef in Queensland Australia. She was taking a gap year between high school and university and had a dread of ending up working indoors, trapped behind a counter doing a mundane job. This dread prompted her to walk the local docks asking if anyone had work going for a hostess or deckhand, and the M.V. *Elizabeth E II* answered her and asked for an interview.

Courtney on deck of her boat in Australia

Courtney had grown up close to the sea and had spent weekends and holidays on the water with the family but she had almost no experience at sea itself. However, her high school offered a course on Marine Studies where she obtained her recreational boat license, marine radio license, SCUBA diving certificates as well as experiencing many other marine activities. The course also offered the practical experience of crewing on the tall ship *South Passage*, so Courtney with her proactive bright personality was an attractive potential employee for the *M.V. Elizabeth E II.* She was seventeen years old when she stepped aboard and she had her eighteenth birthday at sea. She says, "I was totally green. I brought with me a willingness to learn, an insatiable desire to be the best at what I was doing, and a strong work ethic instilled in me by my parents."

The Tourism industry took Courtney all over the world, and she enjoyed working in this relaxed atmosphere; however there were a few anxious moments. Courtney recalls, "I do remember being terrified the first day I was given command of a twenty-four-meter power cat that took 200 people out to the reef; the overwhelming responsibility was almost stifling for a twenty-four-year-old. Also, the day I was accepted into the cadet program at SeaSwift, leaving the comfort of Tourism to transition into the commercial sector, I was handed command of a 1000-ton landing barge; and I felt terrified all over again."

Moving out of one's comfort zone is not comfortable but is usually rewarding, and so it was for Courtney. Soon she realized she did have the knowledge and skills to transfer to the commercial sector; in fact she came to enjoy people's amazement that she was the captain of the vessel and she is now Master for the coastal shipping line, SeaSwift. Courtney adds, "The career path upwards is not without its anxieties." Like many of us, she was scared of the unknown but she took a deep breath and simply got on with the job, as author Susan Jeffers advises in her book "Feel the fear, and do it anyway."

Another trait that many of us women share is that we often doubt ourselves as being good enough. Especially in man's world. Courtney's advice is to stand by your own convictions; it is too easy to let self-doubt take over. She advocates having a good mentor which helps with your self-esteem and confidence, because it can be lonely at the top. She tells us her feelings on her current position,

"Every day is a challenge. It is lonely at the top especially being the only woman on the job. Where I once feared what the crew would think of me, wondering who was looking over my shoulder ready to pounce at my first mistake, having a malfunction or breakdown, not having an answer for a question from the crew, being in an emergency situation and making the wrong decision and so on, I think that as I spend more time out here and become more comfortable in my role of command, these are not so much fears, but incentives to make me want to learn more, become better, and prove them all wrong." That fighting spirit, that willpower to rise to the challenge is the mark of a successful leader and Courtney has proved that in her role as Master of her ship.

Being a woman in a male dominated domain is still not easy in certain areas of the maritime industry. Courtney says there is still age and gender negativity which may be changing in international shipping but domestically it is still a male domain. This requires "Broad shoulders and a thick skin" she says, as well as being a bit of a balancing act, "you have to fit in with jokes and can't be too upset at some of the comments, but at the same time you need to keep your femininity." About women in command roles Courtney says, "It has been my experience that the Tourism industry is more accepting towards women in roles of command because the industry (already) has a lot of women in it performing all sorts of roles within an operation. Typically the workforce is younger and the clientele require workers to be more empathic in nature. In the commercial sector there are few or no women in the workforce. The employees are often middle aged or older and have spent a life at sea with no women and to have a woman in command is confronting and a notion that has not been part of their work environment for the previous thirty years or so."

Keeping relationships on a good footing is not always easy at times with your own family, but it can be even harder when you have many, mostly male, crew to look after. The key ingredient

Courtney says is Respect. She says, "I endeavor every time that a new crew member walks on the vessel, to make my own observations on the person. I never take heed of the rumors I have heard about the person until I work with them. I try and give the utmost respect to every member of crew and expect in return that this is reciprocated. Don't get me wrong, there have been times when it has not been given or earned. However, this is the process of learning and growing as a person and as a leader. As a young woman in a totally male dominated workforce I have made several enemies but I have also made some incredible friends and have the utmost privilege of working with some of the highest calibre men on the planet; men who would do anything I asked of them, men who I trust and respect with the highest admiration and men who I believe, feel the same about me." She adds, "Having the respect and support of those around you can make or break you in this industry."

Looking ahead at how to reach the next rung in the career ladder or branching out into a similar but different profession is a continuing assessment in such a career. Courtney is widening her options by looking at vocational training in the marine biology area.

When I first spoke to Courtney she was excited at the prospect of sailing to Manihiki Island in the northern Cook Islands for about six months to oversee a project of salvaging equipment from the ocean floor for a pearl farm that was closing down. The objective was to remove abandoned material from the ocean floor in an attempt to improve water quality and production for current pearl farmers. She has since told me they removed 240 tons of pearl shell and biomatter, 8,500 floats and over 200km of rope from the lagoon!

Courtney is now aged twenty-seven and encouraging other young women to take to a career at sea. Recently SeaSwift has taken on another two young women into their cadet program and Courtney sees it as her mentoring role to be an example to these women to show them how you can work harmoniously in a male dominated industry.

She works on a twenty-eight-days-on, twenty-eight-days-off roster which can play havoc with her private life but luckily she has a very supportive partner who understands the rigors of the industry because he is a Master on a 3000-ton cargo ship for the same company. There are downsides to her career as there are with most careers. Her friends have to be accepting of the limited time they have with her, and it takes more effort to keep friendships when it is only part-time. In spite of the challenging nature of her position, a lack of personal privacy except in her cabin and a spasmodic land-based life, Courtney hopes she will always be involved with a career at sea. She says, "It is a career that I sort of fell into but nevertheless has been rewarding and challenging and hopefully will continue for years to come."

You may well be interested in emulating Courtney and if so she has a few words of advice to give women considering a life at sea, "I think anyone wishing to embark on a career at sea needs to be a pretty independent person. If you are someone who needs to constantly be surrounded by friends or family, the sea is not a place for you. When I am at sea, I am AT sea. I have very little contact with the outside world and am focused on the job at hand. If your mind is at home, the time at sea goes infinitely slower. I think it is important to be comfortable in your own skin because you will come across some formidable characters and you have to be confident in your abilities. I think finally, that you have to be willing to learn; Mother Nature is a wily mistress and daily challenges arise with the weather, the vessel, crew, relationships and more. You need to be able to adapt to situations, acknowledge your mistakes and learn from the Mariners who have preceded you."

Pat Mundus onboard

Pat Mundus was an early female mariner crusader in the very much male dominated world of commercial shipping. She started sailing in Montauk NY, surrounded by fishermen who didn't "get it," then worked on sailboats doing deliveries to and from the Caribbean and USA east coast in the 1970s. By chance in a bar in Bermuda (shouldn't every good story start like that?) she met a guy who told her that Merchant academies were starting to admit women. As Pat did not want to be just sailboat crew all her life she attended New York's Fort Schuyler Maritime Academy (now the State University of New York Maritime College) from 1977 to 1981 and graduated with a giant license, a Bachelor of Science in marine transportation, and worked as a ship's officer for seventeen years.

In those days Pat was one of twelve females in her class, with four in the class above her and two in the class above that; a total of eighteen females in a majority of 600 men. The general attitude among the men she says was that the women were there to either take jobs from them or they were looking for a husband. At the beginning there were no women's uniforms, so they had to have men's uniforms altered to fit, no women's bathrooms either but that all changed. Pat says she was on the mat, in front of the Admiral with the women's complaints and within six months there were huge improvements. This was ground breaking for those days, but the acceptance of women on ships was still a struggle. A struggle for both sides Pat says, "It was a two-way thing, the men had to accept changes, as well as the women had to learn to live in a male dominated workplace."

Pat started her active career in 1979 as an Intern Cadet Observer and in 1981 it became her paid position. Firstly she worked on tankers, which were smaller ships designed to go through the Panama Canal. The company owned twenty-five ships and leased another twenty-five, which were exclusively manned by World War II veterans. To pass free time on board they either made things or played cards but the situation is very different nowadays she says. Her next position was on a much larger crude oil tanker, 166-foot beam, 987-foot long, and drawing sixty-four feet when loaded. On her first two days on board, apart from standing watch and other duties she made it her business to get a flashlight and follow the route of every pipe on the ship, and to get to know every valve while all the time making diagrams in her pocket note book.

Pat makes the point that officers on board had to "work the cargo" not leave it for a night crew to do. Typically they would load in the Middle East and she tells of one particular incident in Saudi Arabia where being a woman was a problem, one that may not be so different today. They were loading 100,000 barrels an hour and it came to the stage when the refinery had to urgently slow down. However the Saudi men would not take orders from a woman. "They would simply quit and go squat against a wall and ignore me" Pat says. She tried everything to get the attention of the guy in the refinery to slow down the flow, in the end she gave two long, very loud siren hoots which of course brought everyone rushing on deck. Finally the refinery guy acknowledged the request, but often Pat had to get one of her sailors to act as Mate and relay her messages because women were not listened to.

Pat Mundus's oil tanker on the Panama Canal

When she was on board Pat had to be stoic and strong but when she was on land with friends and family she was expected to be a young lady. This meant living in a personal duality which was uncomfortable and which Pat surmises may be a reason why even today there are few long term career women at sea. Nothing has changed for hundreds of years Pat says when it comes to needing support for having a career where you are at sea for long spells. To make this career possible she says there needs to be a strong support group at home. She is very grateful to her husband of thirty-two years who was her wonderful support for the seventeen years she was at sea.

Pat currently holds a 1600-ton captain's license and an unlimited Chief Mate's license, covering any ocean, any tonnage. However, she has retired from ship life and now runs her own custom designed fifty-foot ketch for chartering each summer and mentors young women captains and encourages young summer interns to crew on her boat, because as she says, "Role models are essential." Pat Mundus has worked hard all her life to eliminate gender-specific labelling, coming from the hard knocks school of early workplace feminism. Her advice is for women to spend their time and energy on learning, practising and getting experience. "This way," she says, "they will be respected on the merits of their competency, not their looks or their marriage certificate. In this way, they will wilfully avoid any feelings of being short changed or having to play second fiddle to a man or husband." Strong words which I whole heartedly endorse.

If you do not fancy taking exams and working your way up a career ladder there are other ways of working at sea and making a living. You may prefer to have your own business acting as a recruitment agency in the marine industry like Eleanor Gassman.

Growing a business, a recruitment agency like Salty Jobs owned by Eleanor, requires sound knowledge of the marine industry. At age twenty-seven Eleanor has built a respected reputation through her ten or more years' involvement with sailing boats and those who sail them. Her experience of sailing together with her other love, her daily work in the digital industry were the foundation for her to combine both her passions and start a job-finding agency for the marine industry. This is a web based, global community.

Eleanor says, "My background of owning, racing and doing up three classic boats together with providing sail training for teenagers gave me an ideal knowledge base to start my business." Eleanor is a communicator and marketer. She recently invested in a stand at the Southampton Boat Show where she had hundreds of enquiries, mainly from marine engineers and dinghy instructors looking for work. She notes, "It was surprising how many people had little knowledge of the wide variety of jobs available and were keen to explore them."

From the employer's perspective Eleanor says, "Employers prefer to look for experience over qualifications except in sea going roles where it is essential to have the correct certificates. The AEC engineering certificate is in strong demand." Eleanor sees a great future for online interactive recruitment communities, though she says, "The marine industry can be slow when it comes to digital innovation."

Amanda Swan Neal started her seafaring career by sitting in a small sail loft in Auckland New Zealand. She decided on sailmaking as a way of possibly helping her father out because he would always comment on the cost of the sails. She worked on production dinghy sails then transferred to a larger loft where she worked on custom sails where she enjoyed a real sense of accomplishment. Amanda says, "As part of the job I was expected to go sailboat racing and Auckland offered a great racing scene, three nights a week plus weekends, resulting in a busy social calendar that I also juggled with tall ship sail training." Amanda was totally immersed in the sailing world and found she excelled at both sailmaking and training aspects.

After completion of her four years' apprenticeship for a sailmaker, Amanda moved to Sydney to work on America's Cup sails, but she found she did not fit in with the competitive attitude of the guys on the sail making floor. Hearing of Tracy Edward's *Maiden* campaign to enter the 1989 Whitbread Around-the-World Race with an all-female crew, she decided to switch jobs to becoming a rigger which improved her chances of crew selection. Being pro-active, Amanda went to a rigging outfit in Sydney to show her the ropes and the mechanical aspects of rigging before being selected as rigger. She says, "Racing round the world was certainly a highlight of my racing career. I continued working as a sailmaker and rigger while sailboat racing internationally until 1994 when I met my now husband John Neal."

Amanda feels privileged to have had a rewarding career in both sailmaking and rigging. When she first inquired about sailmaking she did not realize there were hardly any women in the trade, and as for women riggers, she knew of none. Without knowing it, Amanda has paved the way for other females to enter and be accepted into these trades. Her advice to young women starting out in the marine industries today is to "gain training and experience in a wide range of marine related skills and follow your passions."

Her marriage to John was the catalyst to another way of working at sea. They started Mahina Expeditions on *Mahina Tiare III*, where her training skills and seamanship as well as her Ocean Yachtmasters and Commercial Launch Master certificates are utilized in taking groups of would-be sailors to wonderful destinations whilst learning how to sail. They do this for seven months of the year and for the other five months they attend major boats shows giving seminars and presentations (*See* Appendix A for contact details).

Starting a business such as this may not offer you a great return for outlay invested in the short term, but over time where trust is accrued and word of mouth referrals build, this can be a way to keep enjoying a life at sea. Many of our Blue Water Women have taken on casual chartering of their boat to help with adding to the sailing kitty. You need to be very patient, accepting of others' behavior, a good cook and host and of course, bend over backwards to please your guests. As well, of course as being a great captain of your boat. It certainly is not for everyone.

Gwen Hamlin got her captain's license and in 1990 she bought her own sailboat and then began offering week-long dive and sailing charters in the British Virgin Islands. She and partner Don did this for ten years before going cruising together. Holly Scott and her partner Jo have a business mahalosailing.com which keeps them both very busy providing sailing training expeditions in different locations around the world and organizing land travel at destinations too.

Penny Whiting MBE is recognised in New Zealand for having been the first woman to devote her life to the maritime industry through fifty years of owning and running her sailing school in Auckland. I learned my sailing basics from her. To be successful for so long, training over 33,000 adults since she started in 1966 means Penny is quite a special woman. She has a lifetime's interest and activity on boats all over the world. She is extremely competent and has done all her own repairs and maintenance on her sailboat she built, *Endless Summer.* As an inspiration for other women to create a career at sea there are few more shining examples. However, perhaps the stresses of running a business are not for you. You may prefer to be simply a trainer for a sailing school, employed by someone else or training in a more lowkey approach on your own boat. However, the financial returns of the latter will probably be less. Or perhaps you would rather just sail on other people's sailboats for most of the year? You can if you are highly competent and qualified. You can then deliver sailboats all over the world.

I know of many sailors who deliver sailboats globally with no certificates and not a lifetime's experience either. But to make this a fulltime income takes a certain kind of person, one who will create an excellent reputation to gain word of mouth referrals.

Judy Hildebrand is such a person. With a love of travel above all else it was a cruise in the Caribbean that lit Judy's fire and made her determined to sail around the world. She quit her job, sold her horse, and moved to Hawaii to boat sit. She met and talked to other sailors which taught her a lot but she needed to practise. Judy was in the right place to ask around and the boat she found to crew on was S.V. Cimarron, a forty-three-foot wooden beauty as she says, "It was short on comfort but long on adventure, going to Port Townsend, WA, USA." She signed on but finally had enough of cooking and sat her US Coast Guard Master's License exam and passed with flying colours and a license to skipper a 100-ton boat. She was nervous about her first delivery but as she says "I sucked it up, held my breath and jumped in. We made it from Annapolis, MD in USA to St Thomas in the US Virgin Islands with almost everything functioning, and I was off and running as a Delivery Skipper!"

Judy's entree to skippering was not without anxieties. Back then she was concerned about being a female captain and how she would fit in as a newbie, but she was lucky enough to have a female first skipper who became her mentor and long-time friend. She adds, "I always felt that as a woman skipper I was given less leeway to screw up than men so have perhaps been more conservative but that has served me well and for the most part, kept me out of trouble!" She says, "I enjoy introducing others to sailing and this awesome lifestyle, as well as helping other women gain confidence so that they too can do this."

Working as skippers or crew on charter boats is another way of having a sea based career. With more regionally based charter companies the work is tied to the sailing seasons, however some of the larger companies operate year-round which necessitates sailing sailboats to another part of the globe. Even if you are not a skipper you can work as crew, cook or hostess for chartering companies who take on staff seasonally. Many of the Base Managers and Senior Managers for a large sailboat charter company such as Sunsail started their careers as skippers or worked on *Flotilla* where they recruit lead crews that consist of Skipper, Engineer and Host. Skippers can also work across their sailing schools teaching through to Yachtmaster Certificates, as well as take part in regattas and sailing events around the world. In this kind of chartering there is plenty of change. You get to meet new people every few days or so and can either stay in one region or travel the world.

There was a time when joining your country's navy was the only option for a woman wanting a life at sea, and rising through the ranks was tough for a woman. However, these days there is plenty to offer women and encourage them to take their place either in the navy of your country of citizenship or in the merchant navy (also known as merchant marine) where access is not based on citizenship. So what are the differences between the navy and merchant navy? The merchant navy is purely a commercial form of sea career and is governed by both private and governmental shipping companies. It often referred to as the fourth arm of the navy when their commercial ships and workforce are required by the navy to help in times of defence.

The merchant navy allows you flexibility and less demanding qualifications for entry requirements; entry level can be straight from high school or with graduate level qualifications. If you have skills in the technical department, or that pertain to a certain deck zone or servicing area you can easily have entry to the merchant navy. A national navy considers itself more elite; a career in the navy involves high respect, skills and pride. Jobs start at lieutenant level which requires an excellent standard of education and certification. A commissioned officer must have a four year degree and have gone through officer training with requirements being slightly different for each nation.

One of the biggest incentives to enter the merchant navy is the high payment scales which are set by the International Maritime Organization and the International Labor Organization. Another incentive is the tax benefits; a merchant marine professional has to spend a minimum of six months on duty aboard a vessel, following which the professional will be exempt from paying tax for the financial year. Extended vacations of a few months are a good compensation for professionals working long months at sea. Women's positions in the merchant navy are many, from marine crew to engineering officers but there are fewer women in the higher ranks. Commercial shipping companies Maersk, BP, Shell and Thorne all accept female candidates. In Japan the major commercial oceangoing company NYK has been accepting woman officers since 2004 and has recently promoted Tomiko Konishi to the position of captain. She is the first female captain in their one hundred and thirty-two year history.

Incentives to join the US Navy include generous vacation time, outstanding health-care benefits plus opportunities for advancement and for travel. Pay scales are based on the individual's ranking position and total work experience. If you would prefer part-time service you may be interested in joining the Navy Reserve which can provide paid training to help you advance. The Navy offers high quality officer training programs for enlisted recruits as well as post graduate training programs giving sailors the knowhow to work with the world's most high-tech equipment and technology. Training covers subjects such as special operations in warfare, defusing bombs, rescue and salvage operations. There are training programs for nuclear propulsion engineers, submarine electronics, pilots and robotics technicians if you are keen on science and technology. Or if you are more maritime oriented there are training programs for leadership and advancement within maritime studies including navigation and administration.

Working very closely with the Navy is the Military Sealift Command (MSC). The MSC provide and carry supplies of fuel, oil, ammunition, food and other needs for naval ships that are either at war or patrolling the waters. As third mate, for example, you could be the ship's navigator responsible for the workings of the bridge equipment, setting the sailing plan, commanding watch teams, managing traffic, radio communications and the crew. A woman named Caroline Sturgeon, a civil servant, has done exactly this and visited six of the world's seven continents. While commanding her vessel she was protected by cruisers and destroyers who in many cases were at war or preparing for war. She graduated from the New York Maritime Academy in 1999 and started at MSC working four months on and one month off. She says that the best thing about a job like hers is that anyone can start at high school level and work their way up getting experience as well as continuing their education by attending maritime school and passing the courses (See Appendix A for jobs at sea).

Working on a mega sailboat, luxury or super sailboat (all over seventy-eight-foot long) and visiting beautiful destinations sounds like a fabulous work environment. Work on these magnificent and costly boats has become sought after by many young and not so young people. Employment can take the form of either being sailboating skippers and crew, or cooks, hostesses and waiters on the hospitality side. Some sailboats have their own beauticians, hairdressers, nurses and nannies also. Although this form of work sounds ideal, there are in fact several drawbacks. Because of its allure, competition is fierce. There are companies now that offer Super Sailboat Scholarships which pay training costs for two young people a year, worth Euro 3000 each. Contracts are normally between three to nine months. I have friends whose beautiful daughters have had short term careers as hostesses on mega sailboats and although they enjoyed the camaraderie and seeing exotic ports, they worked very long hours and were on call day and night. Ultimately the work and the long periods kicking their heels waiting in port for the owners became repetitious, and because this work had little opportunity for advancement they left for something more challenging.

However, one middle aged couple I met who had been working on beautiful sailboats for many years had acquired a great reputation among sailboat owners and become quite sought after. She is a professional chef and he is a top-class valet. They managed to save a lot of money over several years at sea, working six to nine months of each year. It would seem that to make the most of it, as with most things, you need to know what you want out of the experience and train up before you go into it.

Very few people manage to sail full time and support themselves solely through their writing. Lin Pardey and husband Larry are a legend and two of the few sailors who manage to make a living full time at sea this way. Writing can take the form of blogs, articles and books which later may become videos and DVDs. Doing this successfully takes sound sailing experience, a lot of dedication and knowledge of the requirements of editors and publishers. For your writing to be accepted and stand out from the competition you must have a unique angle or at least do the "better mousetrap" thing and improve on an existing idea. You need also to accompany your writing with interesting high-quality photographs. It is so simple for everyone these days to produce great photographs using a latest technologically advanced camera that this makes it even more difficult to stand out from the crowd.

It is possible to create a niche for yourself if you write with flair and either inform or amuse or both. Lin Pardey says, "Writing is not for everyone; it takes discipline and can be a lonely business. It is far easier and more immediately satisfying to get involved with the day-to-day pleasures and chores of a cruising life than to set aside time for an endeavor that might or might not pay off". I heartily agree. In my case I used the time when my Friwi was away motorbike adventuring to grab the opportunity to have the boat to myself and write. It was great; I was able to spread out my papers and keep the printer and the laptop on the dining table twenty-four-seven. Some days the self-discipline faltered though and I found myself heading for the pool or a local café! It can be hard to keep focused when everyone else is off socializing or generally having a good time.

In her book *The Capable Cruiser*, Lin explains at length the pros and cons of being a writer and getting your work accepted and published. Coming up with a different angle or that unique experience to tempt an editor or publisher becomes harder each year as more and more people take to the sea and turn their hand to writing. That is not to say you won't be successful, but it is not something you can count on to bring in the bread, along with a little butter.

I have deliberately not mentioned financial remuneration for writing, sail-making, skippering or chartering and so on because there are just too many variables. However, you are in charge of the course of your life and if the sea is to be part of it, you have a plethora of options available. Explore some of the websites I have suggested in the resource section, and of course there are many more! Make your decision, plan the steps and go for it! Good luck and as the well-known maritime phrase goes, I wish you "*Fair winds and following seas.*"

I miss that wonderful excitement and stomach churning elation of heading out to sea. I miss that yearning for the overwhelming wonder of vastness. A time to take stock, to be humbled, to grow my inner self in quiet solitude, without the humdrum of cluttered existence that living in civilization's confinement and worldliness necessitates. Being out at sea is truly living in the now—no yesterdays and what might have been, no tomorrows with what still might be: just the now and whatever the elements have to offer. Go as soon as you are able; the adventures of a lifetime are waiting for you.

—Jeanne Pickers , S.V. *Katrine*

Evening in Tonga

Acknowledgements

Blue Water Women would not have grown from a twinkle in the eye to birth if it were not for my friend and inspiration Lin Pardey. Thank you, Lin, for encouraging me and helping me through the ups and downs of getting my book published.

Huge thanks go to the forty or so women sailing all over the world that were interviewed. I appreciate you trusting me with your thoughts and feelings which were given with such openness and honesty. This book could never have happened without you. On those days when writing was going slowly, your supportive emails were much appreciated. Special thanks go to those who gave their time to expand on certain experiences: Anna Fourie, Beth Cooper, Cate Storey, Frederique Fontaine, Jane Kilburn, Judy Rodenhuis, and Helen Hebblethwaite.

Several sailing friends helped me with technical bits and proof reading. Thank you; Jeanne Pickers, Alison Hardy, Linda Morgenstern, and Eric and Cathy Gray. And of course, Christian, my husband and my Friwi, who was alongside me on the book writing journey. For two years, he has had to put up with a wife whose mind was most often on her book. I thank you Christian for being a great sounding board, patiently answering the mind-numbing amount of questions I fired your way.

Last but by no means least, thanks go to my editor Dani McCormick and publisher Tom Doherty of Blue River Press. They eased the way for me as we worked long distance, often while *Stardancer* was at sea, to make *Blue Water Women* a book to inspire others to make the leap to a life at sea.

Appendix A

Resources

The resource categories reflect those covered in the book. Listed below are some starting points for you to continue and research on your own. Once you start looking on the internet with these prompts you will find treasure troves of other information at your fingertips.

Bookshelf

Children's Books

A Cat Adrift. Maria Coffey

Brilliant Boats. Tony Mitton and Ant Parker

Child of the Sea: A Memoir of a Sailing Childhood. Doina Cornell

How I became a Pirate. Melinda Long and David Shannon

Island of Blue Dolphins. Scott O'Dell

Merlin's Voyage. Emmanuelle Buecher-Hall

Swallows and Amazons. Arthur J Ransome

Family Cruising

Boat Girl: A Memoir of Youth, Love, and Fiberglass. Melanie Neale

Contented Little Baby Book. Gina Ford

Convergence: A Voyage through French Polynesia. Sally-Christine Rodgers

Cruising with Children. Gwenda Cornell

Lesson Plans Ahoy (Third Edition): Hands-on Learning for Sailing Children and Home Schooling Sailors. Nadine Slavinski

Voyaging with Kids—A Guide to Family Life Afloat. Behan Gifford, Sara Dawn Johnson, and Michael Robertson

Starting Out

Ashley's Book of Knots. Clifford Warren Ashley

Insider's Guide to Choosing and Buying a Sailboat. Duncan Kent

Knot Guide HD app

Leap of Faith. Ed Robinson

Learn to Sail. Tim Hore

Reeds Knot Handbook. Jim Whippy

Sailing for Dummies. J.J. Isler and Peter Isler

Sailing Fundamentals. Gary Jobson

The Annapolis Book of Seamanship. John Rousmaniere

The Complete Sailing Manual. Steve Sleight

The Complete Sailor: Learning the Art of Sailing. David Seidman and Kelly Mulford

The Cost Conscious Cruiser. Lin and Larry Pardey

The Craft of Sail. Jan Adkins

The Cruising Women's Advisor. Diana Jesse

The Morrow Guide to Knots. Mario Bigon

Inspirational Books

200,000 Miles—A Life of Adventure. Jimmy Cornell

9 Years on the 7 Seas. Anne E. Brevig

A World of My Own. Robin Knox-Johnston

Adrift. Seventy-six days lost at sea. Steven Callahan

An Island to Oneself. Tom Neale

As Long as It's Fun. Herb McCormick

At One with the Sea. Alone Around the World. Naomi James

Big Magic. Elizabeth Gilbert

Changing Course. Debra Ann Cantrell

Close to the Wind. Pete Goss

Cruising in Seraffyn. Lin and Larry Pardey

Deep Water and Shoal. William Albert Robinson

Desperate Voyage. John Caldwell

Dove. Robin Lee Graham

Feel the Fear and Do it Anyway. Susan Jeffers

Finding Pax. Caci Kronkhite

Gin's Tonic; Ocean Voyage, Inner Journey. Virginia MacRobert

High Endeavours: The Extraordinary Life and Adventures of Miles and Beryl Smeeton. Miles Smeeton and Beryl Smeeton

Kon-Tiki: Across the Pacific in a Raft. Thor Heyerdahl

Log of the Mahina. John Neal

Men Are from Mars; Women Are from Venus. John Gray

Saga of a Wayward Sailor. Tristan Jones

Sailing Alone Around the World. Captain Joshua Slocum

Sailing Promise: Around the World on a Catamaran. Alayne Main

Sea Change. Peter Nichols

South Sea Vagabonds. John Wray

The Lonely Sea and the Sky. Sir Francis Chichester

The Long Way. Bernard Moitessier

Travellers on the Trade Wind. Marcia Pirie

True Spirit. Jessica Watson

You Can't Blow Home Again. Herb Payson

General How-To Boating Books

12 Volt Bible for Boats. Miner Brotherton

12 Volt Doctor's Practical Handbook. Edgar Beyn

Boatowner's Illustrated Electrical Handbook. Charlie Wing

Boatowner's Mechanical & Electrical Manual. Nigel Calder

Cornell's Ocean Atlas. Jimmy Cornell

Cruising—Starting from Scratch. Terry Sparks

Get Ready to Cruise. Lin & Larry Pardey

How Boat Things Work. Charlie Wing

How to read a Nautical Chart. Nigel Calder

Marine Diesel Engines. David Calder

The Cruiser's AA. Jackie Parry and Noel Parry

The Pacific Crossing Guide. Kitty Van Hagen

The Voyager's Handbook. Beth Leonard

World Cruising Routes. Jimmy Cornell

World Voyage Planner. Jimmy Cornell

Marine Weather

Coastal and Offshore Weather. Chris Parker

Eric Sloane's Weather Book. Eric Sloane

Marine Weather Forecasting. Frank J. Brumbaugh

MexWX Mexico Weather for Boaters. Captain Pat Rains

Modern Marine Weather. David Burch

Modern Weather for Sailors: A Marine Meteorology Primer. John Jourdane

Northwest Marine Weather. Jeff Renner

Storm Tactics. Lin and Larry Pardey

The Sailor's Book of the Weather. Dr. Simon Keeling

The Sailor's Weather Guide. Jeff Markell

Sailing References

Chapman Piloting. Elbert S. Maloney

Farwell's Rules of the Nautical Road. Craig H. Allen

Guide to Maritime Security and the ISPS Code. International Maritime Organization

International Code of Signals. International Maritime Organization

MARPOL. International Maritime Organization

Particularly Sensitive Sea Areas. International Maritime Organization

Reeds Skippers Handbook. Malcolm Pearson

Ship's Routeing. International Maritime Organization

The American Practical Navigator. Nathanial Bowditch

USCG Navigation Rules and Regulation Handbook

Boat Registration

Boat Registrations in USA:

www.boats.com/boat-sellers-guide/boat-registrations-by-state-in-usa

Sailboat Registration Basics

www.sa.gov.au

www.yachtsinternational.com/owners-lounge/yacht-registration-basics

Boat Rituals

www.migitana.com

www.nauticapedia.ca

www.unitedmarine.net

www.veteransunited.com/network/the-navys-line-crossing-ceremony-revealed

Renaming Your Boat

www.boats.com/how-to/how-to-rename-a-boat

www.boatsafe.com/nauticalknowhow/rename.htm

www.boatnames.com.au/boat-naming-renaming-ceremony.htm

www.youtube.com/watch?v=GpFL9A5Etpc

Boat Sales and Leasing

www.4yacht.com

www.apolloduck.com

www.apolloduck.eu/listings.phtml?cid=2

www.boatexportusa.com/usa-boats-for-sale

www.boatingmag.com/boats/top-ten-tips-selling-your-boat

www.boatinternational.com/yachts-for-sale

www.boats.com/boat-leasing

www.boats.com/boat-sellers-guide/how-to-sell-your-boat

www.boats.com/boat-sellers-guide/
where-to-sell-your-boat-online

www.charterworld.com

www.cruisingworld.com/charter/
charter-companies-owning-charter-sailboat

www.escapehere.com/inspiration/
the-best-12-places-in-the-world-to-charter-a-yacht

www.investopedia.com/articles/personal-finance/091415/
leasing-yacht-stepbystep-guide.asp

www.leemarine.com

www.sdsailboats.com/our-works/sailboat-leasing

www.seaspraymarine.net

www.yachthub.com

Careers at Sea

www.careersatsea.org

www.celebritycareersatsea.com

www.royalcareersatsea.com/jobs/search

www.saltyjobs.co/jobs

www.seacareer.com

www.sealiftcommand.com

www.warsashacademy.co.uk/careers/careers.aspx

www.yacrew.com

Crewing Jobs

www.crewseekers.net

www.cruisejobfinder.com

www.findacrew.net

www.oceancrewlink.com

Cooking and Cleaning

Storing Food Without Refrigeration. Carolyn Shearlock

Omni Ovens

www.base-camp.co.uk

www.omniasweden.com/en/home

www.theboatgalley.com/omnia-stove-top-baking-oven

Solar Ovens

www.insteading.com/blog/solar-cooker

www.solarovens.org

How to Clean Sunbrella Fabrics

www.sunbrella.com/en-us/how-to-clean

Cookbooks

Cruising Cuisine. Kay Pastorius

Essential Galley Companion. Amanda Swan-Neal

Galley Guru. Lisa Hayden-Miller

The Boat Galley Cookbook. Carolyn Shearlock and Jan Irons

The Meatless Galley Cookbook. Anne Carlson

The One-Pan Galley Gourmet: Simple Cooking on Boats. Don Jacobson and John Roberts

Provisioning

The Care and Feeding of the Sailing Crew. Lin Pardey

www.cruisingworld.com/sample-provisioning-list

www.theboatgalley.com/tag/provisioning

www.youtube.com/watch?v=i5GnR3tnvSU

Communication & Electronics

SSB and HF Radio

Communication Made Simple for Cruisers. Terry Sparks

Icom IC-M802 Made Simple for Cruisers. Terry Sparks

IcomIC-M802 Starting from Scratch. Terry Sparks

www.sailboat-cruising.com/SSB-marine-radio.html

www.seavoice-training.co.uk/events/rya-online-vhf-radio-course

www.icomuk.co.uk/An-introduction-to-Marine-SSB-Radio

www.youtube.com/watch?v=uPoFDiH_wJo

www.youtube.com/watch?v=taXBKDVIoRs

www.boat-ed.com

www.rya.org.uk/newsevents/e-newsletters/up-to-speed/Pages/maydays-and-pan-pan.aspx

www.navcen.uscg.gov/?pageName=mtBoater

www.safeboatingcouncil.org/assets/gmdss.pdf

www.uscaptainstraining.com/marine-radio-operator-permit

www.sailonline.com/seamanship/navigation-a-weather/vhf-use-the-basics

http://www.marinerescuensw.com.au/boating-safety/marineradios

www.boatus.com/magazine/2015/december/vhf-radio-protocol.asp

www.oceannavigator.com/March-April-2017/Demystifying-SSB-radio

SSB Radio

www.cruiserswiki.org/wiki/SSB_Radio

www.docksideradio.com/Simplex%20Channels.htm

www.navcen.uscg.gov/?pageName=mtVhf

www.nws.noaa.gov/os/marine/rfax.pdf

Ham Radio

www.arrl.org/getting-licensed

www.hamradiolicenseexam.com

Phone and Satellite Tracking

www.bwsailing.com/bw/electronics/satellite-phones-at-sea

www.globalmarinenet.com/marine-satellite-communications

www.globalmarinenet.com/top-5-satellite-phones-for-emergency-responders

www.iridium.com/network/globalnetwork

www.predictwind.com/iridium-go

www.sailingtotem.com/2014/01/satellite-phone-or-ssb.html

www.westmarine.com/WestAdvisor/Long-Distance-Communication

www.yachtingworld.com/gear-reviews/atlantic-gear-survey-long-range-communications-sea-83429

Satellite Phones

www.globalstar.com/en/index.php?cid=8400

www.satphones.eu

EPIRB

www.epirb.com

www.marineinsight.com/marine-safety/what-is-epirb-emergency-position-indicating-radio-beacon/

www.youtube.com/watch?v=oC8SY4WOT7Y

Marine Electronics

www.boatingmag.com/2018-marine-electronics-guide

www.concordelectronics.com

www.cruisingworld.com/new-electronics-for-2018

www.imo.org/en/ourwork/safety/navigation/pages/ais.aspx

www.marineelectronics.eu

www.navcen.uscg.gov

www.navico.com

www.raymarine.com

www.sailmagazine.com/diy/electronics

www.simrad-yachting.com

www.telecomabc.com/a/ais.html

www.westmarine.com/marine-electronics

Email

www.pcworld.idg.com.au/article/89178/pocketmail

www.sailmail.com/about

www.winlink.org/WinlinkExpress

Mail Forwarders and Receivers

Australia: www.landbase.com.au

United Kingdom: www.myukmailbox.com

United States of America: www.usglobalmail.com

www.ssca.org/content.aspx?page_id=22&club_id=710182&module_id=284393

www.wanderersmailservices.com

Cruising Forums

www.cruisersforum.com

www.noonsite.com

www.ybw.com/forums

Flags

www.beaufortonline.com/nautical-flag-guide/

www.marineinsight.com/guidelines/nautical-flag-etiquettes/

Embassies

www.embassy.goabroad.com

www.usembassy.gov/

Emergency

Ultimate Guide to U.S. Special Forces Skills, Tactics, and Techniques. Jay McCullogh

www.ccg-gcc.gc.ca/eng/CCG/SAR_Gmdss

www.international-maritime-rescue.org

www.marad.dot.gov/ports/maritime-emergency-preparedness-and-response

www.sailnet.com/forums/seamanship-navigation

Finances

www.2checkout.com

www.oanda.com

www.paypal.com

www.paytrust.quicken.com

Health

International Travel, Health, and Vaccinations

www.who.int/ith/en

www.who.int/ith/updates/20110427/en

Exercise on Board

www.allatsea.net

www.offshoresailing.com

www.sailingtotem.com

www.thewaywardhome.com

www.wellnesspirates.com

Medical

Comprehensive Guide to Marine Medicine. Eric Weiss MD & Michael Jacobs MD

Doctor on Board. D. J. Hauert

First Aid Afloat. Sandra Roberts

First Aid at Sea. Justins and Berry

Marine Medical Guide. Robert S. Richards & Matthew L. Peers

Medical AMA Family Medical Guide. American Medical Association

On-Board Medical Emergency Handbook: First Aid at Sea. Spike Briggs & Campbell Mackenzie

The Onboard Medical Handbook. Paul G. Gill

The Ship's Captain Medical Guide, app and e-book. Maritime and Coastguard Agency, UK

Where there is no Doctor. Jane Maxwell

www.bluewatersupplies.com

www.cpr-savers.com

www.gov.uk/government/publications/the-ship-captains-medical-guide

www.healthfinder.gov/FindServices/Organizations/Organization.aspx?code=HR2207

www.imaworldhealth.org

www.mymedic.us

www.ncbi.nlm.nih.gov

www.offshoresailing.com/how-to-overcome-seasickness

www.pbo.co.uk/seamanship/coping-with-seasickness-43182

Marine First Aid Courses

Australia

www.eastsail.com.au

www.marine-aid.com.au

www.marinetraining.com.au

www.southerncrossyachting.com.au

New Zealand

www.boatingeducation.org.nz

www.woodgrouptraining.com

United Kingdom

www.ddrc.org

www.medipro.co.uk

www.rya.org.uk

United States of America

www.oceannavigator.com

www.us.falck.com/en/us_emergency

www.wildmed.com

Dangerous Marine Creatures

Dangerous Marine Animals: That Bite, Sting, Shock, or are Non-edible. Bruce W. Halstead

Dangerous Marine Creatures. Carl Edmonds

www.healthline.com/health/marine-animal-stings-or-bites

www.ncbi.nlm.nih.gov

Kids on Board

Kids' Safety

www.boatingsafetymag.com/boatingsafety/teaching-kids-basics-safe-boating

www.boatsmartexam.com/boating-with-kids-know-these-top-safety-tips

www.boatus.com/magazine/2015/april/boating-with-children.asp

www.discoverboating.ca/beginner/safety.aspx

www.sailingmagazine.net/article-1423-cruising-with-kids.html

www.yachtingmagazine.com/family-living-aboard

Sailing Kids' Education

www.boatnotes.de/what-about-education

www.sailingbritican.com/young-boat-kids-whats-the-scoop-with-putting-them-int

Sailing with Children

Voyaging with Kids—A Guide to Family Life Afloat. Behan Gifford, Sara Dawn Johnson, and Michael Robertson

www.yachtingworld.com/practical-cruising/family-cruising

Learning to Sail

Sailing Schools for Women

Australia

www.aegeansailingschool.com/sailing/

ladies-only-sailing-courses/

www.southerncrossyachting.com.au/ladies-sailing-courses/

New Zealand

www.pennywhiting.com

www.sailingaway.co.nz/

United Kingdom

www.girlsforsail.com/

www.hamble.co.uk/ladies-only

United States of America

www.sistersundersail.com/sus2012/WomensSailingProgram.php

www.uscg.mil

www.ussailing.org/

Women's Sailing Associations

www.annapolissailing.com

www.blackrocksailingschool.com/womens-only-courses

www.boss-sail.co.uk/ladies-sailing-courses

www.girlsforsail.com

www.joyridecharters.com

www.ladyshipsailing.com

www.learntosailnz.com

www.mahalosailing.com

www.mahina.com

www.narragansettsailingschool.com

www.offshoresailing.com/women-only-sailing-programs

www.rya.org.uk/courses-training/courses/Pages/hub.aspx

www.sailingbreezes.com

www.sailingforwomen.com

www.seasenseboating.com

www.sunsail.com/sailing-schools/specialist-courses/ladies-only-week

www.ussailing.org/

www.womenonthewaterlis.com

www.womensailing.org

www.womenundersail.com

Marine Insurances

www.agcs.allianz.com/services/marine/yachts

www.allianz.com

www.caribbins.com/ciml

www.commutercruiser.com/prepare-for-a-boatinsurance-survey

www.globalmarineinsurance.com

www.pantaenius.com/en-

www.topsailinsurance.com

www.yachtlineinsurance.com

Marine Surveys

GRP Blisters

www.boatus.com/magazine/2013/June/

hull-rx-when-and-how-to-repair-gelcoat-blisters.asp

www.hotvac.com

www.yachtsurvey.com/BuyingBlisterBoat.htm

Marine Surveyors USA

www.femas.info/registered-surveyors-list.php?country=2

www.marinesurveyor.com/usa.html

www.namsglobal.org

National Vessel Documentation Center

www.boatingworld.com/asktheattorney/shedding-some-light-on-the-maritime-title-search-proces

www.dco.uscg.mil

www.marinetitle.com/library/vessel-abstract-summary.htm

www.vesseldocumentation.us

Mind Mapping

www.mindmapping.com

www.youtube.com/watch?v=3qim3GndRAgwww.tonybuzan.com

Power

Hydro, Solar, Wind

www.yachtingworld.com/gear-reviews/wind-water-and-solar-power-65797

Renewable Energy Sources

www.cruiserswiki.org/wiki/Power_Generation

www.cruisingworld.com/gear/green-power-passage

www.emarineinc.com/Wind-Generator-vs-Solar-Panels-Which-is-Better-For-Your-Boat

www.sailorsforthesea.org

www.yachtingworld.com/sailboats-and-gear/generating-power-on-board-64034

Batteries

www.boatingmag.com/how-to-choose-right-boat-battery

www.practical-sailor.com/blog/Gel-Versus-AGM-Batteries-for-Boats-11351-1.html

www.victronenergy.com/blog/2015/03/30/batteries-lithium-ion-vs-agm

www.westmarine.com/WestAdvisor/Selecting-a-Marine-Storage-Battery

Voltage

www.aglobalworld.com/international-voltage/country-voltage.php

www.worldstandards.eu/electricity

Steering Systems

www.boatingmag.com/perils-autopilots

www.cruisingworld.com/autopilots-spare-helmsman

www.hydrovane.com

www.lewmar.com/steering

www.raymarine.com/autopilot

www.vetus.com/en/steering-systems.html

www.westmarine.com/marine-autopilots

Quarantine

Yellow Flag

Flag Etiquette. Barbara Theisen

www.catamaranguru.com/education/seamanship/flag-etiquette

www.sailingbreezes.com/sailing_breezes_current/articles/bs03/flags.htm

www.ssboatsaustralia.com/services/customs-and-quarantine

Pets

www.cruiserswiki.org/wiki/Pets_Aboard

www.yachtingworld.com/features/pets-on-board-how-to-go-long-distance-cruising-with-your-dog-or-cat-68437

Rallies

www.yachtingworld.com/features/our-comprehensive-guide-to-bluewater-sailing-rallies-around-the-world-67863

www.worldcruising.com/world_arc/event.aspx

Safety

Life rafts

www.bwsailing.com/cc/a-guide-to-life-rafts-their-equipment-storage-and-deployment

www.lrse.com/pages/life-raft-101-what-is-a-life-raft

www.lrse.com/pages/life-rafts-101-life-raft-types

www.mailspeedmarine.com/on-the-water/featured/choosing-the-best-life-raft

www.switlik.com/blog/life-rafts-101-a-buyers-guide-for-responsible-offshore-anglers

www.westmarine.com/WestAdvisor/Selecting-a-Life-Raft

www.winslowliferaft.com/deployment-tutorial

www.yachtingworld.com/features/focus-on-liferafts-618

Grab Bag

www.alphatozulu.com/articles/grab_bag.html

www.pbo.co.uk/gear/what-to-pack-in-a-grab-bag-19301

www.safetyatsea.co.nz/Product-Catalogue/Grab-Bag-Essentials?industry=marine

www.yachtingworld.com/features/what-should-you-keep-in-your-grab-bag-or-panic-bag-on-a-long-voyage-67498

Man Overboard

www.boatus.com/magazine/2012/october/assets/pdf/MOB_USCG_Boat_Crew_Seamanship_Chapter_16.pdf

www.coastguardmarlborough.org.nz/download/training-modules/Man%20Overboard%20Proceedures.pdf

www.cruisingclub.org/2017/safety-sea-seminars-cca-stc-mtam-others

www.marineinsight.com/marine-safety/3-important-man-overboard-recovery-methods-used-at-seas

www.psychosnail.com/sailing/sailinglessonmanoverboard

www.rya.org.uk/knowledge-advice/cruising-tips/boat-handling-sail/Pages/man-overboard.aspx

www.ussailing.org/news/man-overboard-recovery-procedure

Travel Warnings

www.sailboatingworld.com/practical-cruising/world-cruising-still-safe-elaine-bunting-talks-long-term-cruisers-80972

www.travel.gc.ca/destinations/germany

www.travel.gc.ca/travelling/advisories

www.travel.state.gov/content/travel/en/traveladvisories/traveladvisories.html

Heaving To

www.asa.com/news/2017/03/24/heaving-to-steps

www.yachtingworld.com/heavy-weather-sailing/get-heaving-strong-winds-83704

Visas

Australia: www.australia.gov.au/information-and-services/immigration-and-visas

Canada: www.canada.ca/en/immigration-refugees-citizenship/services/visit-canada.html

New Zealand: www.immigration.govt.nz/new-zealand-visas/options/visit

United Kingdom: www.gov.uk/apply-uk-visa

United States of America: www.travel.state.gov/content/travel/en/us-visas.html

Weather

Forecasts by Radio, Email, Ham, and SSB radio

MarineTraffic app

PredictWind app

Wind Meter app

WindyT app

Forecasts by radio, email, ham, and SSB radio

www.buoyweather.com

www.hurricanezone.net

www.itic.ioc-unesco.org

www.metbob.com

www.metservice.com/marine/recreational-marine/auckland

www.nhc.noaa.gov/aboutintro.shtml

www.passageweather.com

www.prh.noaa.gov/cphc

www.stormcarib.com

www.tsunami.gov

www.voyage.gc.com

www.worldweather.wmo.int/en/home.html

www.wunderground.com

www.yachtingworld.com/features/offshore-weather-planning-65545

Weather Fax, National Weather Service Radiofax

www.nws.noaa.gov/os/marine/radiofax.htm

Weather Fax Plugin

www.opencpn.org/OpenCPN/plugins/weatherfax.html

Bad Weather Boat Handling

www.boatsafe.com/nauticalknowhow/heavy.htm

www.docksidereports.com/rough_water_seamanship_3.htm

www.offshoresailing.com/weathering-unexpected-bad-weather

www.yachtingmonthly.com/sailing-skills/heavy-weather-sailing-31647

www.yachtingworld.com/heavy-weather-sailing/get-heaving-strong-winds-83704

Advanced Heavy Weather Boat Handling

Storm Tactics. Lin & Larry Pardey

www.youtube.com/watch?v=CGElP1m9wiY

www.youtube.com/watch?v=eRb92xlq140

www.youtube.com/watch?v=WUb6iOoWor4

Appendix C

Stardancer Maintenance List

Note: entire books have been written about each of the categories below, so please treat this as a memory jogger, not a how-to.

Generally, problems occur using bad material or poor workmanship, as well as areas of motion, vibration, tension, compression, and friction. Wear develops, things become loose or break, so these areas need the most regular checking.

BELOW DECK

Engine

Check:

- if all the gauges work properly, check for wire corrosion and poor connections

- the throttle cables and connections are reliable
- gear box and engine oil levels. Replace oil filter at every (or every second) oil change, replace diesel filters and water/ diesel filter/separator regularly
- clearwater cooling level is correct. Check anti-freeze in cold areas
- raw water cooling system flow. Clean strainer frequently. Check raw water pump, its impeller, and the condition and connections of the hoses
- ensure seacocks close and open with no effort
- belts' tension and wear. Always have the necessary spare belts
- stern gland efficiency—if it needs grease, tightening, etc
- engine mountings and their fastening parts. Time, vibration, oil, diesel and other causes could weaken some of their components, e.g. rubber parts. Check if bolts and nuts need tightening
- grounding systems – check if the motor has its own protective anode(s) for the internal raw water cooling system and replace when needed
- if cooling exchanger system needs cleaning. For old motors, the manifold may need a good clean up
- propeller shaft alignment is correct and the connection to engine gearbox is sound
- exhaust system for possible leaks. Any doubts, fix or replace sources of possible problems. We do not want fumes and hot (or cold!) raw water flooding our cherished boat while we are motoring!
- the engine compartment and its bilge are clean; free of oil, grease, water, debris and loose parts

Diesel Tank(s)

Check:

- tank(s) and fittings for possible weaknesses. Check if it needs to be grounded
- the deck fitting is waterproof and its hose of the required quality and well installed
- the vent system is efficient

Water Tank(s)

- same as for Diesel tank

Steerage System

Check:

- the quadrant, cables, chain and connections. Check sheaves, sprocket, bearings

Batteries

Check:

- if the batteries are correctly installed and very secure. No loose batteries!
- If their compartments have good ventilation, especially with open lead acid batteries (commonly called 'wet batteries') as they produce flammable gas. If charged too quickly they can produce a lot of gas! When checking any type of batteries, remove any metal bits and tools which could inadvertently touch the terminals, thereby creating shorts and sparks

- health of wet batteries with a battery testing hydrometer to test the specific gravity
- alternator(s) efficiency
- the conditions and connections of wiring and cabling to eliminate electric resistance and electric leaks, in order to have optimum charging power. Check belts
- smart charging system adjustment for the type of batteries in use and check the wiring system and its connections
- main switches of the batteries. Check if the quality is still good and if they have clean, good connections

Electric Wiring (AC and DC systems)

Note: We consider that a good quality digital multi-meter is an indispensable tool to have on board. We have a top-quality one plus two small spares.

Loose connections or corroded wire can cause excessive heat generation due to increased electric resistance, and that could cause a fire!

Check:

- entire boat for tidy, well insulated and secured electric wiring and cabling installations
- eliminate all possible electric leaks. Electricity leaks can cause stray current which may affect immersed metal parts of fibreglass and wooden boat. They will particularly affect the hulls of aluminum and steel boats, and their underwater metal equipment such as the propeller and propeller shaft. When installing new equipment or replacing old wires use tinned wire of the correct gauge and check connection systems are good. Ensure you

have the correct circuit-breakers and fuses to protect your electric and electronic equipment

- DC (12 or 24 volts) ground equipment wires and connections
- if the on-board AC (120 or 240 volts) wiring, equipment, protection and ground systems are correct and safe for marina use. A CAUTION for US boats having AC 120 V wiring systems, equipment and tools. Most marinas outside the US operate only on 240 volts. Before leaving the US create a system converting the 240 V to 120 V. You do not want to fry your 120 V tools and the on-board 120 V equipment. The caution is also for non-US boats using 240 V on board wiring, equipment and tools. If you sail to the USA you will need to convert the marinas 120 V to 240 V. So, be aware of the voltage and amperage difference!

Underwater Hull Area

Note: Electricity leaks can create stray currents. Dissimilar metals when immersed in a conductive liquid, e.g. water, create galvanic corrosion. To protect immersed metal fittings we fix zinc anodes in strategic underwater areas. The anodes, being a metal less noble than the underwater metal parts, will corrode first and will thereby protect those nobler metal parts. As long as the anodes are working properly, the other metal underwater parts (cathodes) are protected. On aluminum and steel hulls, anodes will also be fixed strategically to under water areas to protect the hull and its underwater fittings and equipment.

Check:

- at your annual haulout, check the state of the hull/ keel joint, the rudder (s) and bearings, the propeller and shaft for pitting, propeller shaft bearings for play and replace anodes

- water outlet and inlet seacocks. If metal, check for corrosion. Check they are closing and opening smoothly
- in-hull hoses are in good order and they are fitted properly to the seacocks. Check they have 2 S/S reliable hose clamps
- the fibreglass hull for developing blisters. This could be osmosis or it could be created by solvents becoming trapped during the construction. Identify the cause and assess how extensive the problem is, then look for options

Toilet Care

Check:

- for calcium build up in the outlet hose
- the valve on the vented loop
- impeller, motor, wiring and connections on electric system. Have spares!
- seacocks work well, and that hoses, connections and hose clamps are in good order

ABOVE DECK

Sails. Rigging, Running and Fixed Parts

Check:

- sails for chafing points, unraveling stitching, potential need for patching

- for wear and tear on sheets, cleats, bearings, blocks and sheaves connections, and indications of fatigue on rigging, rigging terminals, turnbuckles and chain plates
- condition of winches

Anchor Winch/windlass, Chain and Anchor

Check:

- windlass circuit breaker, the quality of the electric cables and their connections. This is very important because for most of boats it is the piece of equipment requiring the highest amperage
- if oil level needs a top up
- condition of chain and that the shackles connecting the chain to the anchor are secured
- ensure chain's other end is strongly secured to the boat!

Safety

Gas

Check:

- ensure the gas bottle(s) locker's drainage is not blocked and the bottle(s) firmly secured
- condition of bottle(s), fittings, regulator and hoses. We turn off the gas at the bottles when we leave the boat for more than a couple of days

- connections at the stove. Gas is heavier than air. Escaping gas could collect in the bilge, with possible explosive consequences!

Safety Features

Check:

- update yourself on how to use your flares and all safety gear in case of emergency
- expiry date of flares, fire extinguishers and other safety gear
- lifelines and connections
- if the life-raft is due for inspection and repacking
- the lines and lights of the Danbuoy and lifebuoys. Ensure they are ready to be used efficiently
- all the bilge pumps for efficiency and check accessibility of their strainer for cleaning
- all navigation lights for potential malfunction. Ensure you carry spare bulbs

In time, you will create your own Maintenance Checklist. This one created by Christian is only his starter list and was tailored to suit *Stardancer*, our 47.2-foot, 23-year-old monohull. On purpose, I have not made a list with a suggested frequency beside each item because frequency depends on so many factors like age, design, and the construction of your boat, type of equipment, etc.

Our go-to reference book is a much-battered copy of Nigel Calder's *Boatowner's Mechanical & Electrical Manual.*

Contributors

Alexandra Mateer

Ex SV *Shaolin*
USA and Australia

Alex Mateer has worked in education for most of her life in many types of schools. Home is now the tiny village of Glen Davis in Central West, New South Wales, Australia where she lives with her husband Rick on their small organic farm. For many years, they lived on Rick's boat *Roxanne* sailing to Papua New Guinea and coastal cruising along the east coast of Queensland in the early 2000s. Later, they became owner/operators of a charter business Shaolin Low Isles Cruises, and then became the Low Isles caretakers, where they lived for several years. Alex is now looking forward to more sailing, this time with her son, who owns a catamaran based in Fiji.

Amanda Swan Neal

SV *Mahina Tiare III*
USA, New Zealand, and Australia

Amanda grew up in New Zealand and sailed to North America as a teenager in a boat she helped her family build. Upon returning down under, she became a sailmaker and rigger, completing the 1989 Whitbread Around the World Race aboard *Maiden*, the first all-women Whitbread boat. Since 1994, she has been co-leader on sailing training expeditions with her husband John Neal aboard their Hallberg-Rassy 46, *Mahina Tiare*. Amanda's 308,000 sea miles include two Sydney-Hobart races, seven Cape Horn roundings, tall ships sail training, and women's race coaching. Amanda is author of *The Essential Galley Companion* and holds a New Zealand commercial launch master's license.

Anna Fourie

SV *Ma Ja Belle*
United Kingdom and Singapore

Anna grew up in the seventies in the United Kingdom. Before her sailing adventures began, she had a career in Human Resources, starting as a recruitment consultant in London. She was later to use these skills to earn sailing kitty funds around the world as she sailed with ex-husband David, leaving the UK in 2002 as a complete novice. However, she learned a lot on their trans-Atlantic passage to the Caribbean on 30-foot catamaran *SY Ruach*. They travelled from the west coast of the USA to French Polynesia, then through the Pacific to Australia on a 38-foot Sparkman Stevens. Then they voyaged from Australia to Singapore on their 48-foot Radford.

Anna currently works for Microsoft as Lead University Recruiter in Singapore, living aboard her boat with her son Louis. Anna captains her own boat, a 41-foot Beneteau Oceanis *SY Ma Ja Belle*, and enjoys exploring Indonesian waters in her spare time.

Barbara Gladney

SV *Destiny*
USA

Barbara grew up in Longview and Houston, Texas. Her family did not own a boat, but she loved the water and took advantage of every invitation to go boating of any kind, whether it was to waterski, fish, or sail. In her late forties, she met her husband Frank and moved to Colorado where he taught her to sail on his 26-foot custom designed yacht. When Frank retired in early 2008, they purchased *Destiny*, a 485 IPY in San Diego. They sold their home and moved aboard, sailing from San Diego down the coast of Mexico. They made the jump across and cruised the Pacific through Indonesia. They have now enjoyed a season in Italy and Spain, with plans to set sail into the Caribbean to eventually bring *Destiny* to Texas.

Barbara Sherry

Tallships crew
Australia

A New Zealander by birth, Barbara has spent many years on the Queensland coast of Australia. Coming from a farming family, Barbara had no sailing experience until ten years ago when she started weekly social racing in Australia. She also volunteered at Queensland Marine Rescue as a radio operator and regularly volunteers as crew on South Passage, a tall ship with programs for disadvantaged youth. With First Aid, Navigation, and Diesel Mechanic accreditations under her belt, she became professional crew and regularly crews for friends in the Mediterranean and South East Asia. She also cares for her daughter and is a working mother and grandmother.

Beth Cooper

SV *Sarah Jean II*
Canada

Beth has been sailing since a child, starting on dinghies at the family cottage in Ontario. She is also actively involved with the Bluewater Cruising Association, serving on the Vancouver Watch, and co-presents with husband Norm at educational seminars. Beth has trained with the Canadian Yachting Association (CYA) and Sail Canada, with offshore instruction through Mahina Expeditions. Beth contributes to *Currents*, the magazine of the Bluewater Cruising Association, and has been published in *Bluewater Sailing Magazine*. She has Wilderness First Aid and CPR certification and is also an Advanced PADI scuba diver and licensed ham radio operator. When not sailing, Beth continues to work part time with her husband on OceanForestVoyaging.com and as an occupational therapist.

Bernadine Reis

SV *Scott Free II*
Canada

Bernadine is fifty-eight years young with her home in Victoria, Vancouver Island, British Columbia, Canada. She worked as a Laboratory Technician in a hospital for thirty years. When her husband Alan retired in 2012, he thought he would like to buy a boat, learn to sail, and travel somewhere. He had a couple of friends who took them out sailing on their boats. They bought a boat, sight unseen, on the hard in Langkawi—no brokers, surveyors, etc.—put the boat in the water, and started learning to sail. Two years later, they vaguely, sort of, know what they are doing. Up to Thailand, down to Singapore, up to the Perhentian Islands, and back to Langkawi with many adventures and misadventures.

They now have their boat up for sale and will have more adventures on the small holding back home that they have recently bought.

Beverley Evans

SV *Muscat*
Australia

Bev is fifty-four years old and went from being yoga teacher and fish and chip shop owner in Queensland to sailing to South East Asia from Australia through the Indonesian chain with her partner. She had learned to sail on a sailing catamaran she lived on for two years before setting sail on their steel, engine-powered catamaran and becoming a Blue Water Woman. Bev loves life on the boat where she can still practise her yoga and assist with maintenance when she can. They are now back in Australia with plans to sail the inland waterways of USA and Europe.

Cate Storey

SV *Snufkin*
Australia

Cate's career has been in high-profile International Aid. She was working as a volunteer for the UN in Bangladesh when she met David, an avid sailor. Two years later, they settled into life together on board David's boat on the Brisbane River. Starting with no sailing knowledge, Cate has since sailed to New Caledonia, Vanuatu, the Solomon Islands, Wallis, and the Marshall Islands. For Cate, the joy of sailing comes from the people she meets. Cate became pregnant in Fiji and is now a proud mother to baby Henry and a temporary landlubber. She is currently gardening their yard to become self-sufficient in vegetables and eggs. But sailing beckons, and they will shortly set off on new adventures with Henry.

Cathy Gray

SV *Erica*
New Zealand

Cathy was born with her twin to a farming family in New Zealand in 1956. When she was fifteen years-old, Cathy met her life-partner Eric. They both wanted to travel, and Cathy wanted to be a nurse like her mother. She and Eric later married and had two children. They love the sea and had several boats before designing and building their yacht *Erica* for ocean crossing. After seven years, they were ready to launch her at the end of 2001 and left New Zealand in 2006. She has since taken them safely around the world for over eleven years. To fund their trip, Cathy flew to remote parts of Australia to work as a nurse. They are now based back in New Zealand in a marina with no intentions to move onto land but are enjoying family life for a change.

Cathy L. Simon

SV *Celebrate*
USA

Cathy was a vice president of a bank in San Francisco before she became a world sailor. Cathy and her husband have been sailing for almost forty years with over 100,000 sea miles together. World circumnavigators, Cathy and her husband finished their 26,000-mile circumnavigation in 2015, having visited five continents, several countries, and crossed three major oceans and many seas. Sailing highlights include passages to Alaska, through the Panama Canal, in Caribbean, and up the East Coast of the United States to Nova Scotia. Originally from the Pacific Northwest of the United States, Cathy is a member of many sailing organizations. Currently, she and Norm are taking an expedition sail to Alaska.

Chantal Lebet Haller

Ex SV *Micromegas II*
Switzerland

Chantal was born in the Jura Mountains of Switzerland, and skied nearly every day as a child until she moved to Geneva. She studied at the Ecole Hôtelière de Lausanne and worked in the hospitality industry before working in financial trading for a bank. Chantal found it was a big change to leave work and sail around the world for seven years with Fredy, her husband. After crossing the Atlantic, they sold their GibSea 37.2 and bought a Lagoon 41-foot catamaran. Highlights were sailing into New York harbor, then enjoying the islands of the Pacific. They have since bought a smaller boat to sail the Mediterranean a few months of the year and are enjoying spending more time with family.

Colleen Wilson

SV *Mokisha*
USA

Colleen grew up in the military, moving every few years. She is also a Pisces which, when put together with the lust for traveling and water—voila!—you get cruising! She and husband Tom left California in 2002 and are currently enjoying the diving in the Philippines. Finding the best diving sites to visit determines their sailing routes. They love to experience different cultures, and their travels have been richly rewarding. After sixteen years, they are in no hurry to speed up. Trips back home and girls' days out keep sailing fun. In 2007, they crossed the Pacific Ocean to French Polynesia in twenty-one days. They have cruised Indonesia, Thailand, the Andaman Islands, Malaysia, Borneo, and the Philippines. Raja Ampat, Palau, and Hong Kong are on the list before moving west.

Courtney Jean Hansen

MV *Malu Chief*, SeaSwift Line.
Australia

Courtney was born in 1988 in central Queensland, Australia and was a water lover from a young age. Her passion for the ocean has taken her around the world in a variety of different capacities from research assistant to dive instructor to vessel master. In 2014, at age twenty-six, Courtney became the first female Captain for Australia's largest privately-owned shipping company. In 2015, she went on to win the Llyods List Young Mariner of the Year award for Australia. Courtney is also involved with training in the maritime industry. She has recently been on a salvage operation with the black pearl farmers of the Manahiki, Cook Islands. She and her partner, employed by the same company, have become proficient at juggling time off to be with each other.

Diana Neggo

SV *The Doctor*
Australia

Born in Perth, Australia, Diana's love of sailing began with weekends spent on her father's clinker-built boat. After university, she became an art teacher. She and husband Rob were looking for some excitement, so they bought their first 26-foot boat together. Rob was a willing learner and soon was almost as passionate about sailing as Diana. They joined the East Fremantle Yacht Club and raced on the Swan River and cruised to Rottnest Island just off the coast. They did a three years' circumnavigation of Australia and wrote about it in their book, *Tell Tales*. When Diana retired in 2010, she project managed the refit of their 45-foot Atkinson sloop *The Doctor*. Since then, she has captained the boat through Indonesia to East Asia, lived on an island in Thailand, and is now ready for their next adventure, small farming in Australia.

Eleanor Gassman

SaltyJobs.com
United Kingdom

Eleanor is twenty-eight years old and has been around boats for the past ten years. Inspired to sail through volunteering opportunities with sail training charities around the UK, she gained sponsorship to do her RYA Yacht Master certificate. She has owned and skippered three of her own boats, from a 25-foot gaffer to a 53-foot ex-MFV. Alongside her love of boats and sailing, Eleanor has always been an entrepreneur at heart, and had a career in digital marketing and social media strategy for international agencies and brands. Combining both of her passions for working around boats and the digital industry, she has launched SaltyJobs, an online community encouraging others to follow their dreams.

Frederique Fontaine

SV *Ouma*
France

Frederique was working in administration for the French army in Réunion when she and husband Alain decided to set sail with their seven years-old son from Réunion to Langkawi Malaysia.

They began their 10 years sailing in a 10m steel boat but later bought their present boat, a steel ketch, Ouma, a Brandlemayr 52'. Sailing was a huge change from working in the army, however it was not the sea Frederique had doubts about but having to be a mother and a teacher to Axel, who is now at Lycee. With her bright and positive personality Frederique, and her husband, recently became employed full time as yacht brokers based at Rebak Island Marina, Langkawi. Precious free time is spent playing guitar and exploring Malaysia by motorbike.

Grit Chiu

SV *Escape*
Canada

Born in Dresden, East Germany, Grit's parents escaped communism for the family to live in Vancouver, Canada in 1977. Grit is a registered nurse working in Vancouver and has two adult sons. She has also lived in California, Ottawa, and Europe. Grit met her sailing partner in 2012, and that is when her life changed completely, and her adventure began. Their circumnavigation started from Vancouver in September 2012. Now the boat is in Southeast Asia after having sailed 11,000 miles. Grit is comfortable in her own skin, loves nature and the outdoors, and no longer needs the constant distraction and media stimulation of city life. She is looking forward to the next leg of her journey.

Gwen Hamlin

SV *Tackless Too*
USA

Gwen is a journalist who has applied her skills to the maritime world of blogging, co-founding the website WomenandCruising.com, and writing articles for journals. She has notably written seventy-seven articles in the "Admiral's Angle" in the sailing magazine *Latitudes & Attitudes*. Gwen started her sailing life when she did a dive course, fell in love with diving, and went to live in the Virgin Islands for thirteen years to operate a dive-sail charter business. She left with husband Don in 1999 to cruise full-time for ten years on *Tackless II*, a CSY 44-foot cutter-rigged sloop. They now sail on their catamaran, *Tackless Too* and continue to give advice on buying, refitting, and setting sail on their website, www.thetwocaptains.com.

Helen Hebblethwaite

SV *Meridian of Hobart*
Australia

Formerly working as an administrator in Australia, Helen and her husband Phil left Hobart, Tasmania in 2006 for "seven years to sail the seven seas" aboard *Meridian*, their 40-foot monohull. They have experienced the adventure of visiting foreign ports, exploring beautiful cruising grounds, traveling overland, the drama of an offshore mast loss and working and living in boatyards in SE Asia.

Ten years, thirteen seas, and 15,000 miles of adventure later, they are back in Tasmania. For Helen, the people they've met along the way have made cruising a very special experience. In 2017, they completed their voyage and are now renovating their home and looking forward to adventures of the land kind.

Holly Scott

SV *Mahalo*
USA

Holly calls Seal Beach California home when she is not at sea. Being at sea is her preferred place, running Mahalo Sailing Adventures with her partner Jo Russell. Holly has been on the water since she was three years old and has been sailing for about fifty-nine years now. After college at Western State Colorado University, she started her working life in the maritime industry and worked for West Marine. Holly is an accomplished professional in a wide variety of marine occupations including delivering, renovating, buying, and selling boats. She has a 100 tonne Master's License and is owner-operator of two businesses, Charlie's Charts and Mahalo Sailing, where she not only takes people to exotic sailing destinations, but arranges land excursions also.

Jane Hiett

SV *Barnacle C*
United Kingdom

Jane, an ex-psychologist, and husband John spent almost 365 days a year together for over thirty years sailing around the world and having wonderful adventures. They set sail on a Rival 32-foot, later buying a do-up project, a 44-foot catamaran on which they have sailed for the past ten years. At almost seventy years-old, the time came when Jane wanted a change. These days, she is based in the UK where she can catch up on missed cultural activities and family, as well as do more land traveling. Jane also flies to spend time with John at wonderful locations as he sails around the world again, so each of them is doing what they want in life.

Jane Kilburn

SV *Ananda*
United Kingdom

Over thirteen years ago, Jane was rescued from her corporate shackles by husband Tricky who suggested they move to New Zealand, buy a boat, and sail the world. As a suit-wearing accountant, she took the plunge along with the first step in changing her life. They sailed the Pacific on SV *Lionheart* for four years. On returning to land life, they jumped headlong into helping start up a business, buying a house, selling the boat, and having a child. But after five years, Jane got itchy feet. They eventually bought SV *Ananda*, a 43-foot Catamaran in Southeast Asia a few years ago. Daughter Milly enjoys being partly home schooled, partly land schooled while Tricky and Jane have started Wellness Pirates, an on-line health business for yachties.

Jeanne Pickers

SV *Katrine*
South Africa and Malaysia

A nursing sister by profession, and a farmers' wife, Jeanne and husband Don built their 40ft catamaran on their farm in South Africa and when life there became untenable they decided that the sea would be a safer place to live. They left, never having sailed before, with just the possessions they could fit on her and US$2000. After 18 years of adventure, living on *Katrine*, sailing half way around the world, building up a charcuterie business, (whilst still living on board) they have now retired on land to run Peacehaven bed and breakfast on the island of Langkawi, Malaysia.

Jenny Gordon-Jones

SV *Faraway*
Australia

Jenny was born in Wanganui, New Zealand to the son of a sheep farmer, however Jenny's working life has been mainly in Queensland, Australia as a school psychologist. In her late twenties, she joined an Adams 36-foot as crew and spent a year cruising to Fiji, Vanuatu, and New Caledonia. It was the happiest year of her life at that point and a life changing experience. Since then, she has crewed in the Mediterranean and to Papua New Guinea. In 2009, she had the opportunity to buy an ex-charter boat, a Bavaria 44, in Croatia in partnership. Jenny is now her own skipper and sails extensively throughout the Mediterranean each summer season. In the off season, you can find her in her motor home exploring Australia.

Judy Hildebrand

Skipper/various
USA

Judy grew up in a small Pennsylvania town far from the ocean with parents who neither swam nor sailed. Today she is an accomplished captain with a USCG 100 ton Master's license and over 100,000 blue water miles. Sailing for Judy started in Hawaii followed by two years as a charter chef in the Caribbean, commercial fishing in Alaska, and many years in Florida as a delivery and charter captain. Her present home is perched on the side of Lookout Mountain near Chattanooga, Tennessee where she also pursues her other passion of hang gliding. Judy was a three-time member of the US Women's World Hang Gliding Team. These days, she spends a lot of time wandering the seven seas as a delivery skipper with some charters thrown in for good balance!

Judy Rodenhuis

Ex SV *Meridian of Sydney*
Australia

Judy started teaching in 1961 and retired in 1999 to go cruising on *Meridian of Sydney*. She had loved every moment on her teaching career, teaching students up to sixth grade, but her joy was teaching those who had learning or emotional problems. Judy was assistant principal of her school before she retired. Life on the boat was a huge change. She and her husband Paul sailed the coast of Queensland down across Bass Strait to Tasmania, which, true to its reputation, was an interesting passage! Highlights of fifteen years' cruising in the Pacific and Asia were Vanuatu, Borneo, Taiwan, and Japan. The end of sailing for them was marked in 2014 due to health issues, so they sold their boat and became landlubbers after their many adventures at sea. They are very happy to be near family now, but ever-grateful for the friends they made and the memories they have of their cruising life.

Kaci Cronkhite

SV *Pax*
USA

Kaci Cronkhite began life on a cattle ranch in Oklahoma. Horses and wind, not boats, were her inspiration. At twenty-one, she saw the ocean. At thirty-one, she went sailing and fell in love with life at sea. By the time she was forty, she'd sailed 65,000 ocean miles as professional crew, including four Pacific voyages and a west-about circumnavigation of the world. In 2001, she became director of Port Townsend's Wooden Boat Festival and later bought Pax, a 1936 Danish Spidsgatter. In 2016, she published *Finding Pax*, her quest to find the boat's lost history in three countries. Kaci's life is in happy balance between her publishing ventures and her love of sailing.

Laila Kall

SV *Comedie*
Sweden

Born 1951 in Gothenburg, Sweden, Laila has worked for thirty-five years as a human resources manager. Laila speaks several languages. After gaining her Offshore Yachtmaster Diploma, Laila and her husband Claes-Olof Kall left Sweden, their son and daughter, and families in 2007 in their Hallberg-Rassy 42 F *Comedie*. They completed their circumnavigation in 2014 and have since been sailing half the year in the Mediterranean, spending the other half at home in Sweden.

Laila and her husband share most of the work onboard with Laila's main responsibilities being navigation and night watches, while Claes-Olof takes care of the technicalities on board.

Lilly Service

SV *Tiger Lilly*
USA

Lilly is a multi-faceted person: pioneer professional female athlete, sports model, independent small business owner, and proud Mom to her son Ryan. As a young woman, athletics were her forte: as a preeminent cyclist, she was an expert road racer and mountain biker. She was the team captain and MVP of a national championship woman's water polo team and a charter member of the initial United States Triathlete Team. Lilly has owned several successful small businesses in the service sector, focusing on residential and commercial carpet cleaning and flood restoration. Lilly and her husband Tom live aboard their CSY44 *Tiger Lilly* and are out discovering the world together. Their blog is: http://www.sailblogs.com/member/tigerlilly.

Lin Pardey

SV *Felicity*
USA and New Zealand

Lin has voyaged more than 200,000 miles on boats ranging from 24-feet to more than sixty. Her seminars, twelve books, and five videos have encouraged thousands of potential voyagers to set sail. After forty-seven years of voyaging, she settled in at her home base in New Zealand to care for her husband Larry through his decline due to Parkinson's disease and dementia. With Larry now in full time care, she has once again set sail towards Australia as crew on David Haigh's 40-foot Van de Stadt, *Sahula*. Between return visits to see Larry, she looks forward to sharing more cruising.

Linda Morgenstern

SV *Serafin*
USA

Linda grew up in New England USA and earned a Master of Business Administration degree. She has always had an insatiable appetite for adventure and, after moving to Seattle, she was 'bit by the sailing bug' and acquired this unshakable idea to sail the world. Despite having zero experience, within two years she purchased her first and current sailboat, a Liberty 458. Three years later in 1999, at the age of thirty-nine, she retired from her finance profession at Microsoft. Today, Linda continues world cruising, being the captain of her boat, and is currently in Southeast Asia on *Serafin*.

Lisa McVey

Ex SV *Seahorse*
USA

Lisa grew up in Sedona, Arizona and moved to Kingman, Arizona in the nineties where she and her husband bought their first boat, a San Juan 23. They learned to sail on Lake Mead. Chartering larger boats in the Northwest and Caribbean, they honed their sailing skills for their big trip. They lived and cruised on a Tayana 37 from 2001 to 2004 in Mexico, Central America, and the Caribbean. They continue to sail on the lakes in Arizona and hope to retire in about five years and buy another boat to cruise in Mexico.

Liz Stewart

Ex SV *Rumrunner II*
Australia

Liz grew up in inner-city Melbourne, Australia where her parents owned a small motor boat which gave her a keen interest in the water and boating that would last a life time. Liz owned a busy hairdressing salon in Sydney, which she gladly gave up to pursue a sailing life with her husband. She dived in headfirst to learn to sail and to race. They bought a Cole 43 Australian design that was intended to be used for racing. After making some modifications, it became an extremely fast and fun cruising yacht for exploring Southeast Asia for four years. Liz is now back in Australia and currently enjoying cruising in the comfort of a 63-foot power boat.

Lyn Johnstone

SV *Vittoria*
New Zealand

Lyn was born in New Zealand and considers it home. At seventeen, Lyn and husband Dave bought their first boat together, and fifty-three years later, they still sail together. They have always had boats, finally buying their 35-foot blue-water cruising sloop, *Vittoria*. Since then, they have sailed many times to different Pacific Islands, including extensive cruising in beautiful French Polynesia. They also sailed to Australia, cruising the East Coast and Tasmania. For the last five years, they have spent New Zealand winters sailing their 30-foot Moody in the Mediterranean, returning to sail on *Vittoria* for New Zealand summers. You could say sailing has been a life-long addiction!

Mary Anne Unrau

SV *Traversay III*
USA and Canada

Born in Colfax, Washington, Mary Anne Unrau grew up in Edmonton, Canada. Loving both young children and music, she started teaching in the public schools in Ottawa and Toronto, where later she and Larry Roberts married. Mary Anne went on to have a career in music, teaching piano privately and at the University of Ottawa. On a sailing trip to Hawaii in 1993 on *Traversay II*, they decided to have piano and scuba-equipped *Traversay III* built for them. Mary Anne and Larry have sailed over 100,000 miles, crossed every meridian, and reached the extremes of latitude 65 south and 80 North. Recently, they sailed a fifty-five day trip to Australia and on to New Zealand. Their home port is Victoria, British Columbia.

Merinda Kyle

SV *Guiding Star II*
Australia

Merinda grew up loving the water. She lived her early life in Mosman, a harborside suburb of Sydney, Australia, with the beach as her playground. Merinda's brother raced sailing dinghies, but being too young, she could only watch with envy. She married, had children, and then moved to another watery place, Bayview on Pittwater. She dreamed of being out on the water and read many sailing adventure stories. Then, at age forty, she met a man who had the same dreams and set sail on their Adams 45-foot to have adventures. At age fifty, they set sail from Sydney and have since sailed up the east coast of Australia, through Indonesia, to Malaysia and Thailand.

Pat Mundus

SV *Surprise*
USA

Pat Mundus was born in 1957 to a fishing family in Montauk, New York. She honed her big boat sailing skills on deliveries and Caribbean charter boats. Sensing early pangs of feminism, in 1977 she enrolled in New York Maritime at Fort Schuyler, graduating in the earliest wave of female merchant marine officers in 1981. Pat spent seventeen years as an oil tanker deck officer, owning and sailing her own boats during her off-time. Now retired, she restored and cruises her 57-foot ketch *Surprise*, winters in the western Caribbean, and runs a small charter yacht brokerage in the summers. Pat currently holds a 1600 ton Master's License and an unlimited Chief Mate's license. She enjoys mentoring young women and contributes articles to *Classic Boat*, *WoodenBoat* and *Soundings* magazines while underway. Pat resides in Greenport, New York.

Penny Whiting, M.B.E.

SV *Endless Summer*
New Zealand

Penny started sailing with her father and has been sailing all her life. She helped her father build several boats before the age of fifteen when she crewed with him in the Whangarei to Noumea yacht race. Penny started the Penny Whiting Sailing School in 1966 and sailed to the Pacific and Alaska before building the boat she has today, *Endless Summer*. Penny married Doc Williams and had two children, Carl and Erin. Over fifty-one years, Penny has taught approximately 33,000 students from all around the world and has been awarded the Member of the Order of the British Empire for her services to New Zealand. Today Penny is enjoying teaching her five grand children about the sea and boats.

Victoria Power

Crew/various
United Kingdom

Victoria was born in England in 1965 but calls Spain home when she is not sailing. She learned to sail on her father's 18-foot *Silhouette*. In the UK, she was a kitchen designer while bringing up her two boys outside Cambridge. She moved them to Spain to give them experience of living in the Mediterranean. After the boys left home, Victoria was free to follow her passion, the ocean. She took a PADI diving course, got her power boat license, and joined the Costa Blanca Yachting Association. She signed on a crew finder website and started crewing around the world, focusing on exotic places where she could enjoy her passion for diving. Victoria has made her dream come true and now crews almost full time, occasionally coming back to *terra firma* at her cottage in Spain.

About the Author

After many miles in small sailboats travelling up and down the east coast of New Zealand, Gina de Vere and her husband Christian bought their first cruising boat in 2005, a steel 40-foot monohull, to take them on adventures through the Pacific to Australia. They went on to Papua New Guinea, where they created boat-building projects and lived with the islanders. After sailing through Indonesia to Malaysia, they sold their beloved steelie and bought Stardancer, a lighter beamier boat in Australia, a Gib Sea 47-foot monohull. This meant they happily sailed through Indonesia again, enjoying more adventures in the South China Sea. They are currently based between Malaysia and Thailand.

Born in New Zealand, Gina has been sailing around the world fulltime for the past fifteen years. However, sailing was a huge change from the career Gina had enjoyed as university lecturer in marketing, innovation, and entrepreneurship, and as CEO of her company Masters Consulting. She continues her work as life coach. Gina's newest adventure is as a published author. She has written several articles about their adventures for sailing magazines in Germany, USA, Australia, and New Zealand. Gina's aim in life is to inspire and support women, in particular, to find the courage to make that 'leap' to a more adventurous, fulfilling life. Future plans include sailing to Sumatra and the Indian Andeman islands, back to Thailand, and then across the South China Sea to Borneo, the Philippines, and Sulawesi.